C ... :

'In this witty, ... ts through the illusions and r...

Ben Rogers, *Financial Times*

'Budiansky is an excellent science writer' Andrew Brown, *Guardian*

'This book gives many fascinating examples of how we misunderstand dog thought processes and ways of mending our mistakes'
Peter Lewis, *The Oldie*

'A book well worth reading . . . it explodes many of the myths about the dog and I feel sure would help many people to understand – and enjoy – their dog better' *Dog World*

'A serious book indeed: the text shows great depth of study and anyone who wishes to know what is going on in the mind of their dog will find this book a fascinating and important work . . . Perhaps a few eyebrows may be raised' *Dog Training Weekly*

'Extraordinarily entertaining' *New York Times Book Review*

Stephen Budiansky is a scientist, journalist, and author of eight books about animals and nature. A former Washington Editor of the scientific journal *Nature*, he is a correspondent for the *Atlantic Monthly*.

By Stephen Budiansky

The Character of Cats
The Truth About Dogs
Battle of Wits
The World According to Horses
If a Lion Could Talk
The Nature of Horses
Nature's Keepers
The Covenant of the Wild

The Truth About Dogs

An enquiry into the ancestry, social conventions, mental habits and moral fibre of *Canis familiaris*

STEPHEN BUDIANSKY

PHOENIX

A PHOENIX PAPERBACK

First published in Great Britain in 2001
by Weidenfeld & Nicolson
This paperback edition published in 2002
by Phoenix,
an imprint of Orion Books Ltd,
Orion House, 5 Upper St Martin's Lane,
London WC2H 9EA

First published in the United States in 2000
by Viking Penguin

Fifth impression 2005

A portion of this work first appeared in *Atlantic Monthly*.

A CIP catalogue record for this book
is available from the British Library.

Printed and bound in Great Britain by
Clays Ltd, St Ives plc

www.orionbooks.co.uk

For Martha

CONTENTS

CHAPTER 1

The Irredeemable Weirdness of the Dog: An Introduction

If some advertiser or political consultant could figure out just what it is in human nature that makes us so ready to believe that dogs are loyal, trustworthy, selfless, loving, courageous, noble, and obedient, he could retire to his own island in the Caribbean in about a week with what he'd make peddling that secret.

Dogs belong to that elite group of con artists at the very pinnacle of their profession, the ones who pick our pockets clean and leave us smiling about it. Dogs take from the rich, they take from the poor, and they keep it all. They lie on top of the air-conditioning vent in the summer, they curl up in front of the fireplace in winter, they commit outrages upon our property too varied and unspeakable to name. They decide when we may go to bed at night and when we must rise in the morning, where we may go on vacation and for how long, whom we may invite over to dinner, and how we should decorate our living rooms. They steal the very bread from our plates. (I am thinking here of a certain collie I used to have whose specialty actually was toast.) If we had a roommate who behaved like this, we'd be calling a lawyer, or the police.

I don't generally consider myself a pushover, and it's been

years and years since I believed that any dog of mine was as faithful as, well, a bird dog, never mind as kind as Santa Claus. But not long ago, as a result of a sequence of events that I cannot fully reconstruct, much less comprehend, I found myself believing it perfectly normal behavior on my part to carry a sixty-five-pound collie dog up the stairs to my bedroom every night, and back down the stairs every morning. This went on for months. I had no choice in the matter.

Flip open any veterinary journal these days and your eye is almost certain to land on a case report of a dog that has completely taken over a household, cowing its nominal owners into submission and obedience to a routine that the dog himself has dictated:

> An 18-month-old male Irish Setter was owned by a young childless couple. The husband was often threatened by the dog and had been bitten several times. The dog would growl whenever the husband entered the room. This usually occurred if the wife and dog were in the room before the husband entered. The dog would willingly go for walks with the husband, but only the wife could be in the kitchen when the dog was eating. The dog was most likely to attack the man when he tried to enter the bedroom if the wife was already there.

Dogs that have their owners tiptoeing around them as they lie in their favorite spots on the living room floor, owners who are terrified to move the dog's food bowl or clip a leash to the dog's collar, dogs that refuse to allow their owner to pass through a door before them, dogs that forbid boyfriends or husbands to hug, kiss, or dance with their female owners, dogs that menace their owners into petting them on command, walking them on command, feeding them on command—

these are staple characters in the reports that pour in from veterinary clinics. But this is nothing new. *Cave canem*, the Latin phrase that Roman householders liked to inscribe in their mosaic floors two thousand years ago, means "Beware of the dog." I think it was a not entirely facetious suggestion that this might have meant beware of the dog *not* in the sense of "don't get bitten," but in the sense of "Please be careful not to trip over him because he's not going to get up and move out of your way."

Almost as common as the clinical accounts of dogs who have seized effective operational control of their households are the accounts in veterinary journals of dogs who engage in eccentric and obsessive behaviors that, were they exhibited in humans, would lead to swift institutionalization—or justifiable homicide by anyone forced to share living quarters with the patient. Yet in dogs these behaviors are suffered and endured year after year after year: chasing imaginary objects, running in circles, consuming excrement, barking incessantly. One five-year-old Shetland sheepdog was reported to have spent two years compiling an ever-growing list of things to bark at, which eventually included:

Large truck passing
Pots and pans banging
Hair dryer turned on
Person walking quickly
Dog's water bowl being filled
Toilet flushing
Owner brushing her teeth
Door of dishwasher being opened
Person sneezing
Leaves blowing in wind

Frequent reports of dogs that chew up shoes, books, newspapers, bedsheets, currency, laundry, sofas, rugs, tables, wallboard, wood trim, doors, stairs, and window screens appear in the scientific literature. Perhaps even more impressive than the things we put up with are the things we are successfully conned into. Dogs feign illnesses with an inventiveness that rivals that of any human exhibitor of Munchausen syndrome. Having learned what makes their owners lavish attention, petting, and special food treats upon them, dogs exhibit lurid symptoms that have no organic basis; documented cases of fabricated ailments in dogs include coughing, profuse nasal discharge, diarrhea, vomiting, anorexia, ear problems, lameness, muscle twitching, and paralysis. Dogs are sharpshooters. We are saps.

As I write these words, I have the distinct sensation that off in the distance I can hear a faint whirring noise, the sound of a thousand computers coming to life as incensed dog owners from across the land prepare to compose outraged letters of remonstrance against these slanders. So let me hasten to add: I am joking. Mostly.

I love dogs, and more than that I am fascinated by them, and by the interaction of our two species. Dogs are extraordinarily beautiful animals, and they are extraordinarily interesting animals, too. Just as an amateur student of animal behavior, if absolutely nothing else, I personally find that the rewards of living with dogs far outweigh the costs. Yet as an amateur student of animal behavior I also am keenly aware that my personal calculus of benefits and costs is not one that makes much biological sense; I am keenly aware, too, that most if not all of the conventional explanations of where dogs come from, how they ended up in our homes, and why they do what they do just have to be wrong.

There has been a great surge lately of scientific and not-so-scientific publications claiming to show the medical benefits of canine companionship in lowering our blood pressure and cheering up old folks in nursing homes. I would be the last person to deny the very real joy and pleasure that dogs bring. But neither joy nor pleasure, nor even low blood pressure, is an evolutionary force that carries very much weight. For this much-vaunted "human–companion animal bond" to have been a force of evolutionary significance—for it to be the biological glue that holds our species together, as the authors of such papers claim—it would have had to confer some tangible, adaptive value to humankind that translates into net increased survival. The key word here is *net*, and if one objectively adds up the biological benefits of dogs and sets that against the biological costs, it does not compute. The relentless force of evolution has no room for sentiment, much less retrospective sentiment, and the fact is that tens of thousands of years ago, before there were cities or even villages, before there were farms, before there was writing, before people could afford the meanest luxury, before people fretted about stress, before humans were indeed scarcely human, dogs latched on to human society, survived, and flourished.

Dogs, in short, are a brilliant evolutionary success almost without parallel in the animal world, and they owe that success to their uncanny ability to worm themselves into our homes, and to our relentlessly anthropomorphic psyches that let them do it. Throughout much of Africa and Asia to this day, millions upon millions of dogs roam freely through villages and even cities; they are generally despised, shunned, justifiably feared as dangerous and disease-ridden, occasionally eaten; yet they flourish in spite of it all. However consciously and rationally humans may dislike or distrust these free-ranging dogs, however much humans may determinedly try to relegate them to the mental category occupied by rats, lice, and pigeons, still, when man comes face to face with dog, the will to inflict serious bodily harm mysteriously melts away. Dogs, in an evolutionary sense, know this. They cringe, they whine, they look soulfully into our eyes, and we say, "Aww, the heck with it," drop the rock, and go our way.

The wild ancestor of the dog, the wolf, is practically extinct. There are probably no more than 100,000 wolves left in the entire world today. The world's dog population easily exceeds that by a factor of a thousand. For all the myths and tales of the dog's service to man, only the smallest fraction of dogs that live off human society today earn their keep. No one has done an actual study of this, but there is reason to be very suspicious even of the most common rationalization of dogs' utility to man, as guardians of property or intruder alarms; for every tale of a dog successfully frightening off burglars, there are thousands of dogs who bark incessantly at every goddamned thing that moves, and then sleep blissfully through a crime in progress. For all the myths about how some caveman or cavewoman adopted a wolf cub from the wild and found him a valuable guardian and hunting companion, the behavioral and archaeological evidence now strongly points to a conclusion that even thousands of years ago the overwhelming majority of dogs were biological freeloaders. The things that a small number of modern-day dogs do that clearly pay—assisting the blind and disabled, herding livestock, providing recreational sport for hunters and racing enthusiasts—were late developments in the dog's checkered career. Every great crime family turns out a few solid citizens eventually.

If biologists weren't victim to the same blindness that afflicts us all, they probably wouldn't hesitate to classify dogs as social parasites. This is the class of manipulative creatures exemplified by the cuckoo, which lays its eggs in the nest of some unsuspecting dupe of a bird of another species; the poor befuddled parents see this big mouth crying out for food and stuff it full of worms at the expense of their own offspring. Every time they turn their backs, the cuckoo hatchling shoves another of its foster parents' flesh and blood overboard.

Calling dogs parasites is fighting words, but what can I say? Dogs have got us exactly were they want us, and we, idiotic grins fixed to our faces, go along with it all. If we can manage to don our unsentimental evolutionary spectacles, dogs loom large as a huge net biological burden upon mankind, competing for food, diverting vast economic assets in the form of labor and capital, spreading disease, causing serious injury. Dogs may not quite reach the perfection of the cuckoo in their parasitism on human society—they have not quite displaced human children, at least not in most households, at least not yet—but it is striking that dogs in the United States bite a million people a year seriously enough to require medical attention, most of them children; dogs actually manage to kill twelve people a year, again mostly children. Insurance companies pay out a quarter of a billion dollars a year in claims arising from dog bites, with total costs to society estimated at more than a billion dollars.

A billion dollars, though, is canine chump change when it comes to diverting the wealth of one's best friends. Most dogs weigh less than most people (though the trend toward larger and larger dogs, especially in cities, is growing dramatically), but they consume about twice as much food per pound of body weight; factoring all of this together, it works out that the 55 million canine residents of the United States eat about as much as the entire human population of the greater Los Angeles metropolitan area, at a cost of more than $5 billion a year. Veterinary services currently add about $7 billion a year to the economic tab. The market for canine health care is, however, growing rapidly thanks to the twin forces of high-technology and "alternative" veterinary medicine on the one hand, and the apparently limitless guilt of owners on the other. The *New York Times* reports that dog owners are lining up for veterinary acupuncture sessions at $75 per half hour and described the case of a young couple in Greenwich Village who had worked their way through $3,500 for hydrotherapy treatments for their twelve-year-old Shih Tzu, recovering from disk surgery. Canine behavioral therapy is a booming business, as are canine cancer surgery and chemotherapy, canine CT scans, and canine ophthalmology.

No one has calculated the economic cost represented by the time people spend picking up the 2 million tons of dog feces deposited annually on American streets, parks, and yards, but it must be considerable. Two million tons is a difficult figure to comprehend. By way of comparison, the United States each year produces 3 million tons of aluminum and 4 million tons of cotton. The 4 billion gallons of dog urine generated each year in the United States, on the other hand, could fill all the wine bottles from a full year's output of the vineyards of France, Italy, Spain, and the United States combined, if, as Groucho Marx once said in a slightly different context, that's your idea of a good time.

Dogs, and their copious effusions, are significant vectors

and reservoirs for more than sixty-five diseases that can be passed to humans, many of them too revolting or hair-raising to be mentioned in a book that may be read by small children or those of a sensitive nature. A few of the more mentionable ones are rabies, tuberculosis, Rocky Mountain spotted fever, and histoplasmosis. Dogs threaten not only humans but wild species; epidemics of canine parvovirus that have decimated struggling wolf populations have repeatedly been traced to domestic dogs.

Deep down, we know there's something very strange going on here, and are disconcerted by it. "Dog" is an old and nearly universal term of contempt in human language. Look up *canis* in a Latin dictionary and you will find that the ancient Romans used it to mean "parasite, hanger-on." In the Hebrew bible the word for dog, *kelev*, appears far more often in a derogatory figurative sense than in a literal one; *kelev* was for the ancient Hebrews the particular term of choice for describing male temple prostitutes and false prophets. Freud thought the only possible explanation for man's taking such an attitude toward his "most faithful friend" was that this particular friend liked to stick his nose in really nasty places, and that that upset us. Of course Freud thought everything had to do with sex and excrement. Sometimes contempt is just contempt.

Did I mention that I love dogs? In spite of what I have just said in my role as brutally objective observer, I do love dogs. And I think the secret of loving them—of *not* feeling contempt, even repressed and subconscious and guilt-ridden and Freudian contempt—is to see them honestly and frankly for what they are. This is where science helps, a lot. Yes, dogs are manipulative parasites. But they are also beautiful and fascinating, and even more, they are windows on a series of beautiful and fascinating, and wild and strange, worlds: a world of animal minds and animal senses, aswirl with perceptions and awarenesses and emotions that are ever so familiar yet ever so alien; a world of deep and elemental forces and motives, the very engines of evolution that have forged the entire raw story of life on earth; a world of distant human pasts, of hunters and campfires on the tundra, of Roman legions and war and migration; and a microscopic world within, of molecules that miraculously encode the nature of us all. It is increasingly common to cast science as a spoilsport, reducing the poetry of the world to an equation, love to a hormone molecule, sunsets to diffraction phenomena; and there will be some, I am sure, who would rather not know what science has to say about dogs. But I have never believed that science takes the magic out of things; even when it destroys sometimes treasured myths, science always has something better to offer by way of compensation. When I look into my dog's eyes, I see worlds and eons that I can touch nowhere else in my modern life, and to me that is worth several tons of tripe about "unconditional love."

The other thing that dog science has going for it is that it is good for dogs. Dogs that are treated as furry little people who ought to love and be grateful to us for the muffins they are baked and the little birthday hats they are forced to wear are not happy dogs, for they invariably suffer the consequences of our unrealistic expectations. The number of complexes dogs develop as a direct result of their anthropomorphic owners ought to give pause to everyone who thinks we are somehow "denying" dogs their due by insisting on a rigorous and unsentimentally scientific view of their intelligence, understanding, and behavior. Owners who think their dogs are conscious of their guilt when they poop on the oriental rug, owners who try to reassure and comfort and reason their dogs through their fears, owners who desperately want their dogs to desperately adore them—these are the owners of dogs that more often than not are maladjusted and miserable. Punishing a dog for defecating even seconds after the fact is futile, for dogs do not make such connections over time and space; but dogs will earnestly search for some connection between events in their immediate world and the immediate consequences, and a dog who is punished whenever his owner returns to find poop on the rug will very quickly learn to fear his owner's return, period. A dog that is rewarded with petting and soothing words when he trembles during a thunderstorm will quickly learn to tremble all the more, and on more and more occasions, in pursuit of such rewards. A dog whose owners want love at all costs quickly learns to be a domineering bully—such is the nature of the wolf-dog social structure. It can be worse: his owners can actually achieve their ambition, and the dog can become neurotically dependent on them and go into hysterics at every parting.

Seeing dogs as they are, with doglike understanding, doglike motives, doglike perceptions, and doglike instincts, is to see them with a respect for their true natures and true capacities, to see them as they are rather than as we, with our remarkably self-centered and limited imaginations, would imagine them to be. Grasping what makes dogs tick is a way to avoid a lot of misunderstanding, hurt feelings, and unnecessary strife in our ever so peculiar relationship with them.

The very peculiarity of this relationship of ours with dogs, though, is one hell of an evolutionary tale, and that is part of the consolation science offers us as recompense for robbing us of fairy tales. That dogs exist, and flourish, and thrive in our company when perfectly sensible biological reasons exist for them to have been exterminated every last one, is a biological story of astonishing evolutionary cleverness; it is a story that is also terribly revealing about ourselves, and I am grateful for the self-knowledge that the company of dogs provides us. For dogs (or evolution, I should really say) have discovered the chink in our armor.

Parasites can never launch a direct assault, as most all organisms have active defenses to fend them off. Parasites instead are evolutionarily guileful, and the most successful ones are Trojan horses that play on the foibles or features of their host—best of all, on foibles or features that are indispensable for the host's survival under every other circumstance. We humans are possessed with a surprisingly suspicious and calculating mind that is always plotting stratagems and imagining the stratagems of others. Dogs evade this formidable defense by playing to our equally formidable weaknesses. Give a goose a rock the shape of an egg, and it will sit on it, tend it, turn it several times a day, guard it to the death. Give many a pregnant female mammal a stuffed toy, even one that bears only the vaguest resemblance to an infant of its species, and the female will carry it around like a real baby and try to get it to nurse. Give a human a puppy, and something remarkably similar, and almost as inane, happens.

Animal behaviorists used to refer to such phenomena as "innate releasing mechanisms." The behaviorist view is rather out of fashion now, but they were clearly onto something here—certain behaviors are just so visceral and so obviously purposeful that they must be hardwired deep in our minds. We see a snake, we jump. Show a cat a mouse, it attacks. Show us something small and helpless with big eyes and a round head, and we feel an innate inhibition against harming it. When you consider how strong the predatory and territorial instinct is in many species, ours included, it makes strong evolutionary sense that there would be some very powerful instinct such as this to protect the young of one's own species from harm. Of course parental feeling in humans is vastly more complex than this; in humans, as indeed in many species, it involves considerable learning and environmental influence. But it is hard to deny that we feel a very fundamental, innate, unlearned, and in that sense quite irrational attraction toward cute little things, especially helpless cute little things. Dogs take advantage of this no end. They play us like accordions.

Part of the enjoyment and fascination we find in studying nature comes from learning the remarkable and clever ways species have adapted to exploit their individual niches. Dogs and wolves are remarkably exploitive species, in an especially intriguing way, not in a physical or predatory sense but rather in a quite sophisticated, social sense. That said, dogs and wolves are also, and truly, a remarkably cooperative species. People who are uncomfortable with the amorality of nature and natural selection tend to ignore or reinterpret dogs' exploitiveness while extolling their cooperativeness. My contention is that we should neither condemn the one nor praise the other; we should admire, and be intrigued by, and marvel at, both. We might as well. We didn't choose dogs, after all. They chose us, and we're stuck with them.

Zoologists have never been particularly inclined to view domestic animals as real animals. They have long regarded domestic species as "degenerate," artificial products of man's tinkering, lacking the full set of wild-type behaviors exhibited by real animals.

We are all of course guilty of taking for granted whatever is familiar and close to home. It certainly is more impressive to study grizzly bears on the Alaskan tundra or elephants on the African plains than it is to study chickens down the road or dogs in the backyard. And so scientists know infinitely more about the genome of even the mouse and the fruit fly than they know about the genome of the dog; they know infinitely more about the social ecology of even the newt—and for that matter of the wolf—than of the dog.

It has taken a very long time, but scientists at last are beginning to notice what has been right under their noses. They remind me of some character in a Jane Austen or Anthony Trollope novel who pursues love and beauty all over the place only to discover in the last few pages that the perfect wife for him is his cousin, who has been living in his house since he was four years old. (Duh.) The fact is that if that overworked but ever-useful personage, the man from Mars, were to arrive for a quick biological survey of our planet, nothing would strike him as more astonishing than the existence of billions of domestic animals, the remarkable diversity in physical appearance within each of these domestic species, the novelty of their behaviors, and their shrewd adaptation to the ecological niches that human life has created. In some ways, dogs are degenerate, watered-down wolves, but in some ways they are wholly novel creatures who do things wolves would never dream of doing. Far from being degenerates, dogs exhibit behaviors that are complex, original, and creative.

Recently our terrestrial scientists have begun to recognize that their colleague from Mars is onto something, and dogs have started to come in for some serious scrutiny from branches of science that never paid them their due in the past. That is good luck for those of us who love dogs, and it is good luck for those of us who love the knack science has for casting the seemingly familiar in a shocking new light. Genetics, archaeology, biomechanics, cognitive science, neuroanatomy—all are shaking up the old stories about dogs.

Looking over the paean to science I have just written, I worry I might be giving a slightly misleading impression on one point. I do not believe science is the be-all and end-all, and there is an element of our admiration for and enjoyment of dogs that transcends any scientific explanation. For one thing, dogs are often simply beautiful. Attempts at "scientifically" explaining beauty and love are usually rather glib and ridiculous, and I am not for a second trying to suggest that by focusing on hard scientific facts I am providing anything approaching a complete description of what is going on between dogs and people. There is another truth that I would not deny for a second, namely that those rare humans who have a real gift for training and working with dogs owe that gift to experience, intuition, and a certain kind of empathetic reasoning that has almost nothing to do with science. There are many things science can never touch. But science *can* take us places that our own experiences cannot, and can show us things we never could imagine if left to our own devices, and that is ever more so in an age when we drift ever further from personal experience with the natural world. And it is in that spirit that I wish to explore what we actually and truly know from the scientific investigation of *Canis*, not really so *familiaris*.

CHAPTER 2

Proto-Dog

HUMANS AND WOLVES have shared much the same ecological niche for more than half a million years. To speak of "humans" half a million years ago, though, is almost to stretch the point. The first hominids that appeared in Europe and Asia 600,000 years ago had long, sloping foreheads, heavy brow ridges, no chins, and brains half the size of modern man's. They had mastered fire, and they knew how to make small stone tools, but that's pretty much all they had going for them. They were not impressively good hunters; the bones of elk, wild horses, and wild cattle from their campsites were apparently scavenged from kills made by other, more skillful carnivores. It would be another several hundred thousand years before humans would begin living in tents and huts and burying their dead, 500,000 years before they would acquire chins, perhaps as much as 570,000 years until they could speak, certainly that long until they would begin making ornamentation and producing artwork, 587,000 years until they would figure out how to manufacture pottery, 589,000 until they would begin farming, 595,000 until they would learn to write and to build cities, and 599,900 until they would invent dog food.

It is still not uncommon for biologists (and it is de rigueur for animal rightsniks) to characterize domestication as "slavery," the conscious subjugation of another group of beings by man, the bending of them to his will, for his ends. But a number of biologists in recent years have sharply questioned the assumptions that lie behind this view. The domestication of both plants and animals necessitated genetic changes that humans of any age would have been hard-pressed to anticipate, or consciously seek out. Conscious human intent is demonstrably neither a necessary nor a sufficient condition for domestication to occur; there are perfect analogues of domestication throughout nature between species (such as ants and aphids) neither of which is conscious or human. By the same token, out of more than 4,000 species of mammals and 10,000 of birds that have inhabited the earth for the last 100,000 years, only about a dozen have ever entered into a domestic relationship with man. The ancient Egyptians, as we know from depictions of their failed experiments that they ingenuously carved in stone, tried unsuccessfully to domesticate antelopes, ibex, gazelles, and hyenas, none of them improbable candidates on their face. Wolves, aurochs, jungle fowl, wild rabbits, and wild horses did become domesticated; coyotes, bison, grouse, squirrels, and zebras did not. It is hard to escape the conclusion that success had as much to do with them as with us. The anthropologist David Rindos has shown that even many crop plants are more likely to have "domesticated" themselves, infiltrating their seeds into the rubbish piles of hunter-gatherers' campsites, than to have been deliberately sought out by man. The "paradigm of consciousness," the belief that man is the author of his own history, is a hard one to shake. Domestic animals shake it, and none more so than the dog. The dog's intimate association with man stretches back to a time when humans were not doing much of any conscious thinking or planning for themselves, even on a good day.

MOVING IN WITH MAN

The earliest fossil evidence of an animal that is unquestionably a dog dates from about 14,000 years ago. Skeletons from this period found at several sites in the Near East exhibit a shortened jaw and crowded teeth that definitely set them apart from the local wolves. This was before the rise of agriculture and permanent settlements, before any other plant or animal had entered into a domestic relationship with man, though not much before: by about 11,500 years ago the agricultural revolution had begun in earnest in the Near East, with the cultivation of wheat and barley, and by 9,500 years ago goats and sheep were being herded in great flocks. The subsequent establishment of permanent villages and farms coincided with an explosion of the dog population and a spread of the species throughout the world at an astonishing pace. By 7,000 years ago, a blink of an eye in the history of life on this planet, dog skeletons appear in great numbers amid the archaeological detritus of peoples in places as far-flung as China, South America, and Britain. A remarkable burial site found at Ein Mallaha in northern Israel, dating from about 12,000 years ago, contained the skeleton of an elderly man in semifetal position, his left hand resting on the skull of a four- or five-month-old puppy.

The Standard Myth of the origin of the dog is that man thought a wolf puppy might make a useful guardian or hunter (or, in some versions, that woman found him cute), and took him in. As nicely as this tale may conform to the paradigm of consciousness, it suffers from one glaring defect: a wolf is not a dog. Even when socialized with humans from puppyhood, wolves retain a high, and dangerous, degree of unpredictability. While it is true, as wolf lovers often assert, that extremely few if any reliable accounts exist of other than rabid wolves attacking and injuring humans in the wild, that is mainly because wolves in the wild are wary and generally maintain a substantial distance from humans. But wolves that are raised in captivity lose some of their fear of approaching humans—and with proximity comes trouble. Erik Zimen, a German biologist who carried out extensive behavioral studies of wolves, both in captivity and the wild, found that the captive wolves who had the closest relationships with humans were by far the most dangerous and unpredictable. Anfa, a year-old female wolf who had been completely socialized to people since infancy, greeted familiar humans much as any happy family pet would, with wagging tail and licks on the face. But on at least four occasions, without any warning she launched terrifying attacks at people whom she had just greeted. The victims included both unassuming strangers and people whom she saw frequently and had had perfectly friendly relations with. Two of her male human victims were bitten quite hard through their trousers directly on the penis, which must have been a rather vivid experience.

Both wolves and wolf-dog hybrids kept as pets have attacked young children without warning, apparently when the child's running, crying, or stumbling triggered a predatory response. Predatory attacks always come without warning, for to be an effective hunter in the wild, a predator must of course be stealthy. That even socialized wolves can display such extremely dangerous, and extremely instinctive, behaviors makes it highly unlikely that wolves could ever have made workable pets, even to a bunch of hairy guys with clubs.

For some time, a few biologists have suggested that perhaps the domestication of the dog was preceded by a much longer period of loose association, in which some wolf populations became "preadapted" to human society. Scavenging campsites, following human hunters (or perhaps vice versa: human scavengers following wolf hunters), perhaps even occasionally sneaking in to share the warmth of a fire, those wolf subpopulations that were less fearful and more subservient in their approach toward man would have gained an edge in the Darwinian struggle for survival. Wolf skeletons have been found in association with human remains as far back as 400,000 years ago; these were not burials, but they show that wolves and humans were sharing the same territories and must have been in frequent contact.

Much more recently, genetic evidence using DNA probes has established not only that wolves and man were sharing geographic and ecological niches for many tens of thousands of years, but that these proto-dogs may well have become genetically isolated from wild wolves very early on, far earlier than the archaeological date of 14,000 years ago would suggest. Long before they began to change physically in a way that would leave solid evidence in the forms of fossilized bone, wolves became dogs nevertheless.

The search for this more recent evidence has taken advantage of a genetic chronometer inherent in an extremely peculiar structure within the cells of animals. The mitochondrion is a sort of cell within the cell; it is the cellular powerhouse that converts sugars to energy with the aid of oxygen, and it has its own DNA that guides its cellular machinery and reproduction. Most distinctively, it reproduces asexually, and every mitochondrion in the cells of an animal carries DNA that derives 100 percent from the mitochondrion of that animal's mother. If you look at the regular garden-variety DNA of an individual—the DNA in the nucleus of a cell—and compare it to the DNA of either parent, it will exhibit huge differences. A small amount of that difference will be the result of random mutations, but most will be the result of the remixing of the genetic material that is donated 50–50 by the two parents. But any changes in mitochondrial DNA from mother to offspring can only be the result of mutation. Mutations, in which one chemical rung on the DNA helix is substituted for another, occur at a fairly predictable rate. Biologist Robert Wayne and his colleagues compared the average mitochondrial DNA sequences from blood samples of 140 domestic dogs to the corresponding sequences from 162 wolves and calculated that they differed from one another by about 1 percent. By comparison, wolves and coyotes, which are known from good fossil evidence to have diverged from a common ancestor 1 million years ago, differ by 7.5 percent. Using the wolf–coyote data as a yardstick to calibrate the mutation time scale, the direct implication is that wolves and dogs underwent a genetic split 1,000,000 ÷ 7.5 = 135,000 years ago.

Wayne's data also clearly show that wolves, and only wolves, are the direct progenitor of the dog. No less authorities than Charles Darwin and Konrad Lorenz believed that both jackals and wolves had to have been mixed up in the dog's ancestry, so diverse are the physical types and behaviors seen across the span of dog breeds. All members of the genus *Canis*, which includes dogs, wolves, coyotes, and four species of jackals, can interbreed and produce fertile offspring, so the idea is not at all implausible. Yet the mitochondrial DNA data

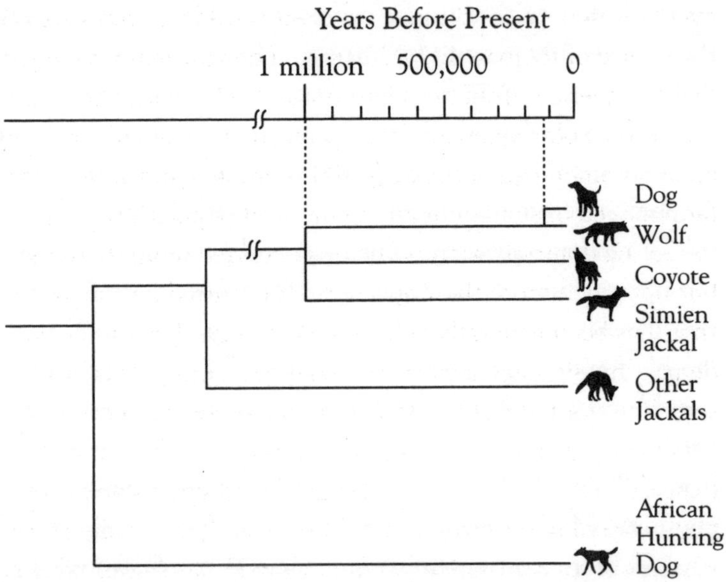

A canine family tree based on DNA similarities suggests that dogs branched off from wolves more than 100,000 years ago.

offer no comfort to great men. None of the dog DNA sequences differed by more than twelve mutations from any wolf sequence (and one particular sequence in fact occurred unchanged in both wolves and dogs), while all of the dog sequences differed from the closest jackal sequence by twenty mutations. Wayne's database included dogs of sixty-seven breeds from every geographic region of the world, so it would seem the case is pretty well closed.

Twenty-six different dog DNA sequences turned up in this analysis, and they clustered into four distinct groupings based on similarity with one another. This implies that while there was more than one "founding" event in which dogs split off from wolves (or subsequently interbred with them), such events were not continuous, or even terribly common, over the course of the past 135,000 years. The vast majority of the DNA sequences from dogs fell into a single cluster that contained no wolf sequences at all, pointing to a single common ancestor among all of the dogs in this group—and an ancestor far removed in time from any living wolf population.

So the domestication of the dog occurred more than once, but not much more than once; and it occurred far longer ago than has been generally believed. Although they did not undergo any significant physical changes during this period, somehow, for more than 100,000 years, these proto-dogs were genetically isolated from their wild forebears. There is no evidence that this isolation was geographic; humans and proto-dogs were almost certainly living in exactly the same places where wolves continued to roam. Wayne has suggested that these proto-dogs were, however, socially isolated: they were integrated enough into human society that they no longer interbred with wolves.

Those who object to this claim for an ancient origin of the dog argue that early hominids simply could not have had enough on the ball to keep their dogs separate from wolves. That was quite possibly so. But the pack instinct of both dogs and wolves tends to form a significant social barrier to intermingling. Researchers in Italy studying feral dogs—that is, domestic dogs that are now free-living on their own—found that when dogs occupied a valuable site such as a garbage dump, they tended to shut out the local wolves from their territory. Even fairly small behavioral differences, territorial habits, and feeding patterns that could have emerged quite early on between wolves and proto-dogs would have reinforced the barriers between packs. Genetic studies of modern canids show no evidence of significant interbreeding between dogs and wolves or between the various wild members of the genus where their ranges overlap.

Moreover, human occupation of an area tends to cause local wolf packs to be displaced from their territories, become unstable, and break up; it also interferes with the ability of young wolves to form new packs. So the emergence of a population of proto-dogs in association with humans would have been a double whammy that would have tended to push wolves away.

That for more than 100,000 years proto-dog did not change in physical appearance in any detectable manner in itself points to an absence of man's guiding hand. These were animals that chose to hang around humans, and in so doing to isolate themselves from their wild counterparts, by their own volition. They were not hirelings, or slaves, or even invited guests; they were party crashers who just wouldn't leave.

DOGS AS SCAVENGERS

A model for how wolves might have been first integrated into human society, with little or no effort or intention on the part of the humans in question, has been proposed by the biologist Raymond Coppinger, who has made a lifelong study of dogs and dog behavior. Coppinger has raised and raced sled dogs; acquired, bred, and provided to ranchers and farmers hundreds of livestock-guarding dogs; and traveled the world over observing the ecology and behavior of dogs in their habitats, natural and unnatural. He notes that in villages throughout South America, Africa, and Asia, there exist even today substantial populations of free-ranging scavenger dogs that, from an ecological standpoint, are extremely well adapted to their niche. These "village dogs" are typically small, about twenty pounds; they do not kill or molest livestock; they will run a short distance away if directly threatened but otherwise show no particular fear of people; and they live almost exclusively on the copious supplies of garbage and excrement that villages generate. The dogs sometimes beg for food from people, and people sometimes give them some, but for the most part the dogs forage for themselves. The dogs are not "owned" by anyone, do not enter houses, and are definitely not pets.

On the contrary, the villagers whom Coppinger interviewed almost universally expressed an aversion to the dogs. In a village in Zanzibar, he found many people who were disgusted at the very idea of touching a dog; although a few people expressed the idea that dogs might be useful as sentinels or as killers of vermin, he notes,

> the people generally do not like dogs. They feel that dogs have diseases and have parasitic organisms living in their mouths and nasal passageways. The wet noses of dogs are indications of these infectious agents and should not be touched. They are also repulsed by the thought that dogs eat human corpses; it is a common notion that stones are heaped on a grave so dogs cannot get to the body. . . . Dogs were regarded the way we regard rats: an animal ubiquitously present, a potential vector of disease, a scavenger, and occasionally a thief, whose population needs to be culled from time to time.

Humans, their habitations, and their behavior are of course part of what defines this niche that village dogs so successfully occupy. But not only is there no intent on the part of the villagers to "tame" these animals; there is no intent on their part even to have them around. Yet there they are, and tame they are. They are not at all wolflike; they have lost their wolflike predatory behavior, and they have lost their wolflike fear and shyness. They also serve no useful purpose whatsoever as far as the villagers are concerned.

This is not the model of the dog that most of us have, but it is ubiquitous. Until American cities began cracking down on stray dogs, many major metropolises supported populations of tens of thousands of free-ranging dogs that in many ways were indistinguishable from Coppinger's category of village dogs. In many villages, as in many cities, owned dogs and free-ranging dogs coexist. Often one canine population occupies dumps outside town; another occupies the town itself; and another, which may overlap with the free-ranging town dogs, is owned or at least managed by people. The unmanaged, free-ranging population is subject to many selective pressures, some the product of human consciousness, but many not. Dogs that kill livestock would not be tolerated the way scavengers are, and that presents a strong selective force for a loss of wolflike predatory behaviors. By the same token, much of the food that is available in the village niche is scavengeable, while essentially none is huntable; that, too, would work against the retention of the full suite of predatory behaviors. Dogs that are too fearful of people would not even be able to approach a village. Dogs that do not effectively deflect human aggression would be at a disadvantage; dogs that are skillful beggars and can wheedle and look appealing and helpless would be at definite advantage. Dogs that are too large would have a lower chance of surviving the competition for limited resources.

The natural selective forces that keep such scavenger dogs relatively tame are strikingly apparent in surveys of dog bites in recent years, which have shown that unowned dogs, subject to no deliberate breeding or conscious human selection, are far less dangerous than the owned pet dogs whose reproduction is almost entirely under human direction and control. Strays are much less likely to attack people, and much less likely to inflict serious injuries when they do: a survey of 1,754 bite cases in Dallas, Texas, found that pets were three times more likely than strays to deliver bites to the head, face, or neck. Some of this, to be sure, is because owned dogs are larger and thus have bigger teeth and more powerful jaws, and because people are more likely to stick their heads, faces, and necks close to pets. Still, it is striking that the available data is so one-sided: all seventy-one fatal dog attacks that occurred in the United States from 1966 to 1980 were the work of pet dogs, as were all twelve fatalities that occurred in 1986.

The forces that today perpetuate the village-dog niche could well have been operating tens of thousands of years ago. Although permanent settlements did not appear until the rise of agriculture, the Neanderthals who emerged in Europe and western Asia between 200,000 and 100,000 years ago frequently reused the same campsites and accumulated considerable garbage heaps at these places. The deep piles of debris that archaeologists have found from human camps of this period include large numbers of bones of small and medium-size prey animals: proto-dog's proto-dumps.

Human dumps have certainly been an attractive feature of human life from the dog's point of view. But so have humans, even generally hostile humans. As Coppinger found, village dogs are today despised, sometimes eaten, occasionally culled, yet they still evoke odd bursts of sympathy. They beg for food, and such is their ability to activate something deep in our psychological makeup that they sometimes succeed, even with humans who harbor an otherwise intense aversion to them.

When threatened, the dogs cower and cringe, and it takes a hard heart not to soften. Alan Beck, in his classic 1973 study of free-ranging dogs in Baltimore, found that many poor inner-city residents—who bore the brunt of the dogs' disruptive and often disgusting habits, such as barking incessantly, knocking over garbage cans, defecating on the streets and in the parks, and occasionally biting—nonetheless frequently took the side of the dogs against city authority in the form of the dog catcher. The residents readily projected their distrust of the police and the white establishment in general onto the dogs, and saw them as fellow victims when someone with a badge showed up to haul them away.

Such instinctive empathy for nonhumans, or sometimes even for inanimate objects, is a well-established human phenomenon. We are, as the British animal behaviorist John S. Kennedy so aptly called us, "compulsive anthropomorphizers." We read human social signals into everything around us. We are especially on the lookout for motives such as loyalty, betrayal, and reciprocity—so much so that we readily attribute these motives to people, animals, the weather, volcanoes, internal combustion engines, gravity, and many other things, objects, and forces of nature. Undeniably, such motives are things useful to be on the lookout for when one is a group-dwelling animal whose greatest threat to survival is not being eaten by a wild animal but being stabbed in the back by one's fellow group dweller. The human cognitive ability to ascribe motives to others is the basis of a lot of what makes us human: it allows us to imagine what others are thinking, to make the remarkable intuitive leap from our own minds and thoughts to the minds and thoughts of others; it may even be the basis of our capacity for creative thinking altogether, of having thoughts about thoughts apart from immediate experience. But it truly is compulsive. We can't help seeing a humanlike purpose in the things around us. Thanks to the wolf social structure, dogs were prewired in many ways to exploit this foible of ours to a tee. The subsequent natural selective forces that operated in the scavenger-dog niche fine-tuned these skills.

THE ORIGIN OF BREEDS

Anyone who has owned a purebred dog knows, of course, that his particular breed is of ancient and assuredly romantic lineage; it served as guardian of temples, hunting companion to the czars, war dog of Roman legions, sacred pet of Egyptian pharaohs or Aztec kings, lap dog of Chinese empresses. Modern dog fanciers fancy they can see in Arctic sled dogs signs of direct descent from the North American wolf, while the oriental toy breeds are heirs to an entirely separate ancestral line tracing back to the smaller Asian wolves, and the Pharaoh dog is the descendant of an ancient crossbreeding with jackals.

The idea of unique, ancient, and separate ancestral lines of modern dog breeds is obviously immensely appealing. It is also a pure anachronism. Virtually all of the more than three hundred modern breeds of dogs meticulously registered by kennel clubs today are of extremely recent origin, most dating to the last century or two. It was not until the 1870s that kennel clubs were even founded and began to keep closed registries of separate breeds. Up until then there was nothing to prevent a lot of crossbreeding. That is precisely what happened, on a scale that is almost unimaginable by today's standards.

The physical changes that begin to appear in dogs around 14,000 years ago, as evidenced by the fossil record, may be the first signs of diversification into new roles as permanent settlements arose and the transition from hunter-gatherer society to agricultural ways of life began. Some subset of the unselected scavenger dog population might have begun to be more deliberately culled or selected by humans for certain desirable traits or behaviors. But the earliest clear indication of a separation of dogs into distinct body types or behavioral types does not come until well into historic times. Between 4000 and 3000 B.C. something that looks pretty much like what we would call a greyhound or a saluki starts to show up on pottery and paintings in ancient Egypt and western Asia. Later, other distinctive—or at least different—types appear in ancient Egypt.

By Roman times, Pliny was able to divide dogs into six groups: *villatici* (house or guardian dogs), *pastorales pecuarii* (shepherd dogs), *venatici* (sporting dogs), *pugnaces* and *bellicosi* ("pugnacious" or war dogs), *nares sagaces* (scent hounds), and *pedibus celeres* (sight hounds). But even much more recently, as recently as a few hundred years ago, dogs continued to be categorized by such general type or function, much more than by specific "breed." Any large dog was a mastiff, any dog that hunted small vermin underground was a terrier; there were foxhounds, and sheepdogs, and pointers, and retrievers, but pointers were just pointers, they weren't German shorthaired pointers and Vizslas and Weimaraners.

All of which is not to say that Pharaohs or Chinese empresses didn't keep dogs, nor that those dogs weren't of a distinctive type. But to believe that one can trace the ancestry of a modern-day saluki directly and exclusively back to the Pharaohs is a fallacy that says much more about nineteenth-century racial theories of noble blood than about the dogs themselves. It all rather smacks of those mail-order genealogies one can buy (complete with authentic coat of arms) that show one's family tree going straight back to Charlemagne.

Wayne's DNA data show that the family trees of dog breeds are actually a tangle of intertwined branches. Virtually no dog breed can claim a distinctive ancestry that sets it apart from any other breed. The largest of the four groupings of mitochondrial DNA sequences the researchers found included both representatives of supposedly ancient breeds, such as the greyhound, the African basenji, and the New Guinea singing dog, *and* many common breeds such as the collie, the German shepherd, the boxer, the springer spaniel, and the Alaskan husky.

The promiscuous parentage of modern breeds is equally evident in the wide diversity of DNA sequences found within individual breeds; indeed in some breeds, including the dachshund, the Norwegian elkhound, the Siberian husky, and the Mexican hairless, certain individual dogs' sequences place them in an entirely different DNA grouping from others of the very same breed. Essentially no breeds have breed-unique sequences; for example, one particular sequence shows up in a Siberian husky, a chow chow, an English setter, a Border terrier, an Icelandic sheepdog, a Japanese spitz, a rottweiler, a papillon, a poodle, and a Mexican hairless—in other words, in representatives of what the American Kennel Club would consider the totally unrelated groups of sporting dogs, herding dogs, working dogs, nonsporting dogs, terriers, and toy dogs. The family tree of breed relatedness that emerges from DNA data bears no discernible resemblance to any family tree of presumed breed relations based on outward appearance, functional type, or AKC grouping.

The only breeds that show even a hint of having an ancient and independent origin separate from the rest of dogdom are some of the Norwegian breeds, whose DNA sequences appear to define a highly divergent group that does not directly overlap with the other dog DNA sequences. But on the other hand, even breeds that by every reason *ought* to display an ancient and independent origin turn out to be as much ancestral mongrels as are modern-day mutts. The Mexican hairless, or Xolo, was described by the Spanish conquistadors, and it is depicted on pottery dating from centuries earlier—from the Colima culture of western Mexico, which flourished from 250 B.C. to A.D. 450. Following the destruction of native civilizations by the invading Spaniards, the Xolo was hidden in mountain villages in western Mexico and bred in secret there; thus it is unlikely that the modern representatives of the breed reflect any recent crossbreeding in the last half millennium. Yet the DNA sequences from Xolos are diverse, falling into three of the four DNA groupings. Nor do the Xolo sequences reveal any close relationship of this indigenous North American breed to indigenous North American wolves. The wolf sequence that most closely resembles any found in the Xolo is one that occurs only in wolves from Romania and western Russia. Similar analysis carried out by Japanese scientists who examined Asian dog breeds reached exactly the same conclusion: extensive interbreeding occurred among the ancestral stocks of modern breeds.

Likewise, the dingo, which has a mystique all its own, turns out to be nothing terribly special genetically. The dingo is the feral dog of Australia; it was observed by nineteenth-century white settlers to be kept (and occasionally hunted) by the aborigines, but for the most part dingoes ran wild. There has been all sorts of speculation that the dingo is even a separate species from the dog, or the remnant of the missing link between dogs and wolves. Yet its arrival in Australia now appears to be not that ancient at all; the oldest dog fossils in Australia have been dated to about 1500 B.C., and in any case it certainly was not in Australia before about 12,000 years ago, as no dog fossils have ever been found on Tasmania, which separated from the rest of the continent at that time. The DNA sequence analysis places the dingo in the same large category with many other breeds, old and new.

The point, then, is that the founding populations of nearly all breeds, including those with a long recorded history, were genetically diverse, and were not descended from any one exclusive population of ancient dogs or wolves. Had any of the dog breeds that exist today diverged from one another in ancient times into separate, genetically isolated populations, they would have had time to develop unique, breed-specific mutations in their mitochondrial DNA that would set them apart genetically from other breeds. Such is not the case. Rather, for thousands upon thousands of years of dog evolution, the dog gene pool has actually been a single, well-mixed ocean of global dimensions. Genes drifted from one end to the other and back again, with the wolf populations from widely separated parts of the world contributing to the mix at several points along the way.

Even when local magnates in the late Middle Ages and thereafter began developing locally distinctive breeds of hounds and retrievers and pointers for the hunt, clearly a great deal of exchanging of sires, crossbreeding, and generally mixing things up continued. As late as 1848 one English bloodhound fancier was complaining that few of his fellow bloodhound owners followed the "principles of keeping the breed to themselves" in matings.

Only with the establishment of breed clubs in the late nineteenth century did this begin to change dramatically. In the name of developing and maintaining "purebred" animals, the kennel clubs in Britain and the United States set up closed breeding books: a dog could be registered as a bloodhound if and only if both of its parents had been registered as bloodhounds. The number of recognized breeds grew by leaps and bounds. In 1800 a British writer could identify only fifteen specific breeds; a century later the number was more than sixty; today there are something like four hundred breeds recognized worldwide. A number of those were created by the further splitting of a breed into separate types, each with their now separate and closed gene pools: springer spaniels split into English and Welsh springer spaniels; Welsh corgis into Pembroke and Cardigan Welsh corgis; cocker spaniels into English and American cocker spaniels; a variety of basically similar Belgian herding dogs into the Belgian Tervuren, Belgian Malinois, and Belgian sheep dog; the Swiss mastiff-type dog into the Bernese mountain dog and the Greater Swiss mountain dog.

There was more than a passing element of Victorian racist thinking behind all of this. Books and articles about animal breeding from the turn of the last century are full of exhortations to eliminate "weaklings" and to invigorate the race by maintaining the "purity" of its "blood lines." There was much excoriation of "mongrels" and "curs" and "half-castes," and much talk of the evil tendencies shown by "badly bred" specimens.

Virtually all such advice about "purity" is directly contradicted by modern genetic knowledge; in fact it is hybrids that show vigor, purebreds that tend to exhibit debilitating inborn diseases. But eugenics was the intellectual fad of the early years of the twentieth century, and its scientific trappings gave it considerable influence in everything from criminology to dog breeding. Look up any bibliography of dog books, and the name Leon Fradley Whitney is sure to appear—he was the author of *The Complete Book of Dog Care; This Is the Cocker Spaniel; Bloodhounds and How to Train Them;* and *How to Breed Dogs*. He was also author of a book you won't find in any dog bibliographies, *The Case for Sterilization*, a paean to eugenics published in 1934. It was such a definitive treatment of the subject that the author received a personal letter of appreciation from no less an authority on the subject than Adolf Hitler. (Whitney in turn publicly hailed Hitler's "great statesmanship" for ordering the sterilization of the feebleminded and insane. In an unpublished autobiography written four decades later, Whitney still defended his stance, explaining that "no ruler ever before had had the courage or knowledge to put sterilization to work." He did, however, offer the not entirely convincing excuse that at the time he made his original statements about Hitler he was not yet aware "what a vile human being" the führer was.)

I am not trying to suggest that modern dog fanciers are crypto-fascists. But they have inherited a breeding paradigm that is, at the very least, a bit anachronistic in light of modern genetic knowledge, and that first arose out of a pretty blatant misinterpretation of Darwin and an enthusiasm for social theories that have long been discredited as scientifically insupportable and morally questionable.

Inbreeding does make for greater uniformity of offspring, and to be sure it is not always the evil it is sometimes made out to be by animal rightsniks and others who seek to find proof of man's greed, immorality, and exploitation of the animal world in every inborn disease that appears in dogs. Inbreeding is a perfectly legitimate tool in scientific breeding; indeed it is a part of the breeding programs used by all livestock breeders. But it is only a part: the importance of outcrosses to bring in desirable new traits, and the recognition of the great significance of hybrid vigor, go back many decades in the scientific breeding of plants and commercial livestock.

And it is abundantly clear that, all of those myths of ancient and noble lineages that dog-breeder groups love to relate notwithstanding, the modern notion of a dog "breed" is very modern indeed. For perhaps 95 percent of the dog's 100,000-year history, breeding was largely undirected, with an interchange of genes occurring on a global scale; for 98 percent of the remaining 5,000 years breeding was steered toward the development of general types designed to fulfill general roles, but with continued genetic mixing in the form of continual crossbreeding and outbreeding; only in the last century or two has the idea of breeding purity for purity's sake seized hold.

SOURCES OF VARIATION

Genetic-marker studies suggest that the genetic differences between dogs of even radically different breeds are extremely small. Yet dogs come in an immense range of physical types, and display an equally great range of breed-specific innate behaviors. No other animal, wild or domestic, shows such a range of individual characteristics within the confines of a single species. Dogs vary in size from Chihuahuas, papillons, and Pomeranians that can weigh as little as a few pounds to mastiffs and St. Bernards that can approach two hundred. They have coats that vary from silky to rough to wiry to stringy to nonexistent. Ears run from fully erect to pendulous; tails from long to curly; faces from the squashed-in Pekinese to the elongated borzoi's, which seems to have just grown and grown.

Especially striking is that dogs exhibit many physical traits that are *never* seen in wolves, not even in the form of rare recessive traits. Most wolves are gray, some are black; rarely they are almost white. Most dogs, by contrast, have broken-colored coats, which never occur in wolves. Nor do the yellows, reds, blues, merles, brindles, spots, dapples, and other myriad color combinations that are routinely seen in dogs the world over.

Some of these alterations could of course be the result of genetic mutations, randomly generated chemical alterations that change the identity of one rung in the DNA double helix. Mutations are akin to garbling one letter of a coded message. Sometimes the result is nonsense; the mutation results in a gene that does nothing. (The "words" of the DNA code each instruct the cell's machinery to string together a specific sequence of amino acids, the building blocks of protein molecules. Those proteins in turn form the key structural components of the cell, and many also act as enzymes, chemicals with remarkable geometrical properties that facilitate further chemical reactions: they are just the right shape to bring the reactant chemicals together, sort of like a jig a cabinetmaker uses to hold two pieces of wood in the right position while he glues them. A garbled word usually produces an impossible instruction that the cell's machinery just ignores, and so no protein is manufactured at all.)

Much more rarely the result of a garble is a readable word that means something else, and the result is a novel protein that might, for instance, result in a different hair color. But such changes are a very long story. Mutations occur slowly, and the overwhelming majority of mutations either carry no significance whatsoever or are deleterious and are quickly weeded out by natural selection. The chances that all of the myriad physical changes observed in dogs over the past 14,000 years are a result of accumulated mutations is well nigh impossible. There just has not been enough time.

Equally unlikely is that these variations were inherent in

the wolf population, but merely hidden, waiting to emerge in chance matings between carriers. So where did they come from?

A source of dramatic variation is inherent in all organisms, and that is the astonishing changes that occur from conception to adulthood. An organism begins as a single fertilized cell and turns into something so utterly different as to make the difference between an elephant and a mouse seem almost trivial by comparison. Even after birth many organisms continue to undergo major changes. The degree of change that occurs during maturation from a juvenile to an adult varies from species to species; it is huge in the case of the dog. A two-day-old puppy is not a miniature version of an adult dog; in fact it is barely recognizable as a dog at all. Its proportions are all different, and for the first hundred days or so of its life those proportions change in a highly nonlinear fashion. The skull of a young puppy is almost as wide as it is long. By the time it is four months old or so, the skull has undergone a stunning change of proportions and is pretty much set in its adult form. From that point on, growth occurs proportionately: the skull gets bigger, but it keeps its same shape.

During the critical period of disproportionate growth, in other words, the pieces of a puppy are growing at different rates in different directions. Biologists call this allometric change (the prefix *allo* means "other"), as opposed to isometric change, in which proportions are preserved (*iso* = "same"). Development of a growing organism is a hugely complex process about which many mysteries remain, yet studies in many organisms have shown that even very minor changes in the genes that control and guide the process can result in astonishing alterations in adult form. A relatively few genes control overall body plan, and biologists have found genes in fruit flies the alteration of which results in offspring with some extremely bizarre forms, such as flies whose eyes are on the ends of their legs.

Likewise, alterations in genes that determine the timing or rate of periods of allometric growth can result in vastly different adult forms. One way this might happen is, for example, if a particular juvenile growth period were simply truncated. Such incomplete growth could in theory result in an adult that is a "snapshot" of one phase of juvenile growth. In other words, adult dogs might look like wolf puppies. Alternatively, the relative rates of growth of various structures during these critical periods of allometric change might be altered, giving rise to entirely novel forms—adult dogs that are not precisely like *any* form that their ancestors, puppies or adults, have ever had. That is what appears to have happened in the case of dogs. In some ways dogs are physically indistinguishable from their wolf ancestors: the ratio of snout length to total head length, for example, is pretty much constant in all adult dogs, and for that matter in all members of the dog family. (Thus dogs are not, as is often said, short-faced wolves. The only exception are breeds like the Pekinese, which have such distorted faces that they may be the product of outright mutations.) But in many physical parameters dogs show a degree of novel variation without evolutionary precedent at all. The ratio of head width to total skull length, for example, is all over the map in dogs. During the allometric growth phase, length grows faster than width, as the puppy skull shape changes to adult shape. In breeds like borzois and collies, either this period is prolonged or the rate of growth in total skull length that occurs during this period is accelerated. In small breeds the period is truncated or the growth rate retarded. So much is happening during this critical phase of disproportionate

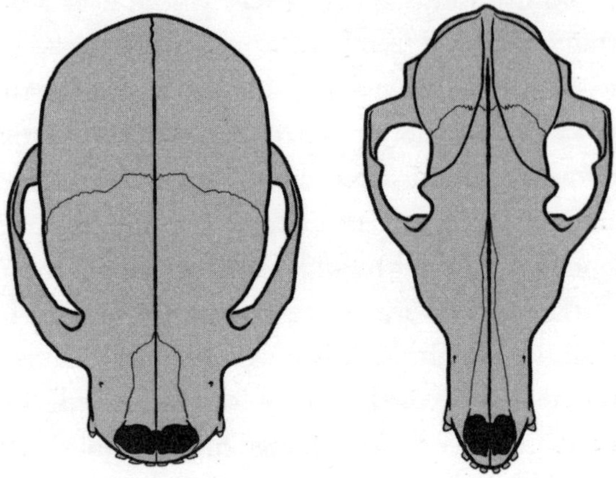

Skulls of very young puppies (left) are almost as wide as they are long, in contrast to the elongated shape seen in most adult dogs (right). Small variations in growth rates during the first four months of life account for the wide variety of head shapes found in different dog breeds.

growth that even a very small tweak in its timing can produce a very dramatic change in the final result.

The vast difference in size of breeds is also set very early in the course of development, and this too is the result of a tweaking of proportional growth rates. Robert Wayne, measuring hundreds of dog limb bones, found that virtually all of the size differences between breeds are the result of proportional differences that emerge before the first forty days of life. From that point on, the growth rates of limb bones—that is, growth per day expressed as a percentage of limb length—is virtually the same even in breeds as different in final size as the Lhasa apso (15 pounds) and the Great Dane (120 pounds).

Once you start messing with genes that control timing and rate of development, you can get all sorts of novel things happening, nearly all of which are unpredictable. Genes responsible for the manufacture of various bodily structures turn on and off in a complex, highly orchestrated pattern over the course of development, and many feedback mechanisms control this regulation of genes to make sure that growing body components all manage to fit together properly. Thus a small change in the "master switch" that affects timing of developmental periods can result in many cascading changes in physical shapes that are simply the result of the growing body's attempt to get everything to match up. But the result can be totally novel forms. Ray Coppinger has proposed, for example, that many of the proportional differences in the shape of skulls between small and large breeds of dogs are the product of such accommodations between bones of the growing skull. The size of the eye sockets tends to vary relatively little even between large and small dogs; small dogs thus have to end up with proportionately wider skulls just so the eyes can fit.

The point is that neither natural selection nor even deliberate artificial selection by people is necessary to explain the original emergence of the huge variety of physical traits that are now an established part of the identity of many different breeds. Indeed, it is difficult to see how they could have been produced by deliberate selection. If Coppinger's notion of accommodation is right, then simply selecting for a small dog, for example, gives you other novel traits such as a wide head—and does so automatically. Other novel traits such as spotted coats, silky hair, curly tails, and floppy ears likewise were surely part of an entire package of novelties that resulted from disruption of the timing or rate of juvenile growth stages. None of these traits is under simple, direct genetic control;

rather they are the result of extremely complex interactions of many genes, together with the laws of geometry that guide the feedback mechanisms during development. Once these traits emerged, people could of course have favored them and chosen to perpetuate them by keeping the animals that showed them, while culling those that did not. But how could you have selected in the first place for a trait, such as floppy ears, that had never appeared before?

Changes in the master genes that control development frequently produce even more surprising and unpredictable linkages between traits. This is especially so when early stages in the process of fetal development are disrupted. For example, in horses it has long been recognized that a rare recessive trait produces a true white hair coloration—and also usually results in death of the embryo. This appears to be because the cells responsible for skin pigmentation emerge early on in development from a structure known as the neural crest, which also gives rise to the brain stem and spinal cord. The recessive gene that is responsible for white hair color also is responsible for a fatal neurological flaw. This is just a coincidence, a chance byproduct of the master plan that the embryo follows in the course of development. But it is just one of myriad such coincidences that must occur, given all that goes on as a embryo grows to an adult. Thus many novel traits in dogs, such as broken-colored coats, floppy ears, and the like, may also be more the chance product of odd linkages that occur in development than the product of deliberate, trait-by-trait selection in the classic Mendelian sense.

Coppinger notes that dog breeders indulge in all sorts of post hoc explanations of the "purpose" behind the traits their favored breed possesses. The Romans seem to have led the way here, claiming that sheepdogs were white so that they could be distinguished from wolves, while other farm dogs were black because they have "a more alarming appearance." It is certainly undeniable that many breeds exhibit apparently useful adaptations to their assigned tasks; but it is at least worth considering the possibility that rather than being evidence of man's purpose and conscious intent, such "adaptations" might instead have appeared first and the assigned task only later. (In some cases the rationalizations are not even very convincing. Some Border collie enthusiasts claim that the dogs are mostly black because sheep move away from a black dog better than a white dog, a claim that seems dubious at best.) It is always tempting—the paradigm of consciousness at work again—to see every novel physical characteristic in a domestic animal as the direct end result of intentional human selection. That in turn leads us irresistibly to cooking up some explanation of the human purpose behind that intention. But some traits simply *are*. It is entirely possible that Border collies are black primarily because Border collies are black.

A few extremely odd characteristics in certain breeds may be the product of outright mutations. The very short legs of dachshunds, for example, or the hairlessness of the Mexican hairless may be examples of such traits that showed up and were eagerly seized on by dog fanciers precisely for their oddity and rarity. But the rapid emergence of novel traits that had never been seen in the dog's ancestors, and the emergence of such a remarkable variety of these novel traits, seems best explained by the ability of relatively small changes in the genes that control development to cause wholesale shifts in structure and form.

MIXED-UP INSTINCTS

Dogs show signs of a disruption of their natural developmental process in another way: their behavior. Very broadly, dogs display some seemingly juvenile behavioral characteristics even in adulthood. They beg for food, they are often submissive in puppylike ways, they bark excessively, they are ever playful. More specifically, they have clearly lost the full adult hunting pattern of their wolf ancestor. The village dogs Coppinger observed did occasionally eat wild animals, but their hunting pattern was much closer to scavenging than what wolves do: it was "more of a gathering activity than a display of predatory motor patterns." They tended to grab small animals like crabs rather than stalk and chase more elusive prey. That is similar to what happens when pet dogs go after small mammals; their victims frequently die not from a killing bite but simply from rough handling. Some free-ranging pet dogs may stalk, chase, pounce, bite, and even kill prey such as domestic livestock, but even in these cases they often lack the final wild behavior of "dissecting" the kill and consuming it—which in the wild, after all, is the whole point.

Many breeds of domestic dogs show little or no interest in getting even that far. Successful livestock guarding dogs show a total lack of interest in chasing livestock, or anything else for that matter, no matter what environment they are raised in; dogs of these breeds raised as pets often cannot even be trained to chase a ball. Ancestral hunting patterns are also disrupted in herding dogs and many sporting dogs, which show as their characteristic behavior an extreme, exaggerated emphasis on one isolated component of the wild-adult hunting behavior. The Border collie's "eye"—its fixation (there is no other word) on staring at sheep—is a hyperexaggerated slow stalk. So, in a different way, is the bird dog's point. Retrievers will endlessly chase but will not bite hard on the object of their pursuit.

The interesting thing about all such breed-characteristic behaviors in dogs is that they are removed entirely from their original, purposeful context. A wolf interrupted in its pursuit of prey typically halts the whole sequence of stalk-chase-pounce-grab-kill-dissect, and has to start over from the beginning. Dogs, on the other hand, repeat their favorite piece over and over endlessly. And the behavior is its own reward. Sheepdog handlers say that the way you reward a Border collie for doing a good job herding sheep is to let him do it again. Border collies indeed will find or even generate their own action if not provided with any—staring at the water dripping from a faucet, tossing objects and then following their motion, even chasing totally imaginary objects if necessary. Retrievers likewise have an incurable fascination with, surprise, retrieving. Sled dogs will "chase" for hours, and indeed days, on end with nothing to chase.

These behaviors very much resemble the juvenile patterns of play, in which bits and pieces of adult behavior—chasing, expressing dominance and submission, sexual mounting, stalking, mouthing objects, biting and grabbing—are run through in seemingly meaningless order and without any immediate purpose. Thus the disruption, selective exaggeration, or truncation of juvenile developmental stages may be at work here, in behavior, too, just as it appears to be at work in generating the distinctive physical characteristics of dogs. In some ways dogs seem like wolf puppies that never grew up; in some ways they seem like wolf puppies that did grow up but with various instinctive behaviors out of sync with one another. Just as the disruption and distortion of juvenile growth periods can generate novel combinations of physical traits, such as the borzoi's elongated head, so these alterations may produce novel combinations of behavioral traits, such as the foxhound's instinct to bark while trailing a scent. This is not a juvenile trait, nor is it a trait found in any wolves; indeed it would be distinctly maladaptive in wolves trying to stealthily stalk prey. Rather it seems to be the product of snipping out, distorting, and recombining ancestral behaviors that are present singly in the wolf but never displayed in this combination or sequence.

As we have seen, there would have been a natural selective pressure operating on scavenger dogs from the start that favored the disruption of the full adult hunting patterns. Those pressures would have intensified with the first human settlements. And some intriguing evidence suggests that merely through the favoring of tameness and the discouragement of predatory instincts, sufficient changes in the timing of juvenile growth periods could have been activated in protodog to bring about the appearance of a whole package of doglike behavioral traits. Experiments in Russia in which silver foxes were selected solely for a single criterion—the loss of their natural fear response to humans—brought about within twenty generations a population of foxes that had broken-colored coats, drooping ears, doglike barks, and submissive, soliciting behavior toward humans. This would seem almost certainly to reflect changes in the genes that regulate development, inasmuch as there was no deliberate selection for any of these other doglike traits at all. And given how quickly these traits appeared, the total amount of genetic change could not have been very large in the population. Genes that control development affect the timing of the critical phases of growth, as we've seen; they do this at least in part by switching on and off many other genes, which is part of why a small genetic change in one part of the genome can have such far-reaching consequences. Rather than change twenty genes, we are changing one gene that affects the operation of twenty genes.

Further selective breeding aimed at refining physical traits or particular behaviors may, however, be aimed more at those twenty genes. Starting in the 1930s, there was a great enthusiasm for trying to find single-gene inheritance patterns to explain all sorts of dog behaviors. A "nervousness" gene ("N") was said to determine whether gun dogs were under- or over-sensitive to loud noises or being touched. Another gene was said to control whether bloodhounds barked while trailing or were silent. In fact, the inheritance patterns are far more complex and indicate that many genes are involved. Elaine Ostrander, a molecular geneticist who has played a leading role in the effort to map the dog genome, carried out a preliminary experiment that attempted to isolate the genes responsible for the herding instinct in Border collies and the water-loving instinct of Newfoundlands. Puppies that resulted from crossing the two breeds were just about halfway between the two in their behaviors. The next generation, however, showed a rich assortment of the two behaviors; dogs that herded and liked water; dogs that herded and didn't like water; dogs that didn't herd but did like water; dogs that did neither. The statistics implied that perhaps a dozen or more genes were involved. (And also that it would require a pedigree containing several hundred dogs, with genetic samples from each, to actually begin to map the genes responsible for these behaviors.)

We of course realize now that it is absurd to think that a single gene could be completely responsible for a specific, fine-tuned, and complex behavior. Yet the fashion these days is sometimes to go to the other extreme and rail against "genetic determinism"; one can find quite a few passionate denunciations of the very idea that behavior is in the genes at all. This is equally absurd, and dogs offer some of the best proof of this. Breed-specific behaviors are irrefutable. Border collies win sheepdog trials; not a single other breed ever comes close. Foxhounds trail foxes and beagles trail rabbits, not just by training but by inclination. One of Ostrander's colleagues developed a behavioral assay to quantify such innate breed-specific behavioral differences and found, for example, that Border collies would stare at a remote-control toy car for the entire 120 seconds during the test that the car was moving, while Newfoundlands would pay attention to the car only if it ran directly into them. Hormonal studies have found highly significant differences in the levels of neurotransmitters in different breeds, which may account for at least some of these behavioral divergences. Border collies, for example, had much higher levels of norepinephrine and dopamine in their brains than did Shar Planinetz dogs, a livestock-guarding breed. These neurochemicals have been found to have a major effect on overall arousal and in the activation of instinctive motor behaviors.

Some of the precise behaviors that show up consistently (and completely reproducibly) in certain inbred lines are downright eerie. Certain strains of Siberian huskies and pointers have a strongly inherited shyness of or aversion to humans; when kept in identical conditions in identical kennels, the shy dogs will stay back (or, in the case of the pointers, actually freeze and quiver when humans approach), while the normal dogs come up to be petted. Breeders have succeeded in producing lines of Dalmatians that do or do not take up the proper "coaching" position, trotting under the front axle of a carriage very close to the heels of the rear horses. Researchers have even noted lines of miniature poodles that do or do not shake hands.

None of which is to deny that training, environment, and experience have huge effects on behavior, human and canine alike. But just to prove the point, Ray Coppinger tried raising Chesapeake Bay retrievers or Border collies as livestock-guarding dogs, and livestock-guarding dogs as Border collies. The result was a total flop. A lot of things really are in the genes.

CHAPTER 3

Social Etiquette, Doggie Style

LONG BEFORE a pseudo-intellectual feminist social theorist began advising an American presidential candidate to act like the "alpha male," just about everyone had encountered some such pop-psychology insight drawn from the supposed lessons of wolf society. There are certainly some striking similarities in the social rules that govern wolf society and human society. We are both territorial, up to a point; we both communicate with our fellows using similar types of threatening and supplicatory gestures, and similar tones of voice to accompany them; we are both intensely status-conscious and both suffer the vexation of inveterate social climbers in our midst; we are both suspicious of strangers; we both gang up on, and pick on, the weak and insecure; and through it all we are both surprisingly cooperative.

But there are plenty of ways in which we humans wouldn't be caught dead acting like wolves, or vice versa. Human communities do not generally restrict sexual intercourse to a single male and a single female within each group; they do not urinate to mark territory; they do not regurgitate food for their young; they do not sniff one another in greeting.

Dogs straddle two worlds. Dogs possess a template of behaviors, inherited from their wolf ancestors, which they attempt with varying degrees of success to overlay upon human society; unsurprisingly, the template does not always line up very well with what now lies beneath. But it is a template that has itself been hammered, bent, refashioned, dropped, run over by a few passing trucks along the way: it doesn't even line up very well with *wolf* society anymore, either. It is commonplace for would-be elucidators of dog behavior these days to invoke the wolf at every turn; they confidently assert that what the dog does is what its wild ancestors did thousands of years ago. But that goes only so far. Dogs are undeniably still wolves in many ways, following the social etiquette of a lost world. Sometimes it works, and we are charmed; sometimes they and we are left to stare in bewilderment at each other. But dogs, no less than people, do things wolves wouldn't dream of. To interpret all of the dog's instinctive behavior as a sort of throwback to a distant past is to miss half the story, and often the most interesting half. Dogs go in a flash from suave and worldly connivers to altruists, wheedlers, rubes, ingenues, bullies, terrific naïfs, artless innocents. The combination is maddening, bewildering, intriguing, and charming.

DOGS ARE WOLVES (FORTUNATELY)

Many of the things dogs carry over from wolf society are useful to their new role; many are not. The most clearly useful—though only up to a point—is the wolf's innate sense of social rank, and the system of communication that supports this rank structure. Social rank is a consequence of adaptations that many group-dwelling animals have made to the inherent contradictions of living in a group. Being part of a group gives an individual advantages and access to resources he could never commandeer on his own. It also puts him in immediate and constant conflict with members of his own species for those limited resources. Competition with one's fellows for limited resources is a nearly universal fact of nature. In species in which individuals can forage and defend themselves successfully as loners, it is generally the case that individuals seek to maximize their distance from one another. Males, or females, or mating pairs, set up and furiously defend exclusive territories and keep out all other comers. Whoever is best at seizing and holding ground—whoever manages to keep the other, competing members of his own species the farthest away from him—is the most likely to reproduce and raise viable offspring who will in turn pass on their parents' genes. The relentless logic of evolution admits no other outcome: every Carolina wren alive today is the descendant of a Carolina wren that succeeded in fighting off the competition. The nice guys did not merely finish last; they dropped dead, and their nice-guy genes died with them.

In group-dwelling animals, undeniably self-interested forces hold the group together, but it's still every wolf for himself when it comes to the struggle to pass on one's genes to the next generation. Every wolf in the pack has an evolutionary mandate to claim a mate, produce offspring, and see that his offspring survive—and that inevitably means survive at the expense of the other guys. And in the wolf pack, the other guy is not over the next hill; he's lying a few feet away. The situation is inherently explosive. The wolf pack is a tightly packed powder keg of competing interests. Every member of the pack has an interest in being the only member to breed and produce offspring.

At the same time, wolves need the pack. Wolves that hunt

very large prey such as moose may form packs with as many as twenty or thirty members, but even when the food supply consists of smaller game, cooperative hunting by smaller packs of four to seven brings in more food than the sum of those four to seven wolves operating on their own could manage. There is also an evolutionary bootstrap process at work in favor of group formation: groups themselves become a force that favors groups, for packs can defend large territories, and only other groups then have the wherewithal to resist that otherwise superior force. When everyone else is a member of a territorial group, the lone wolf is in big trouble, for he now doesn't have a prayer of claiming and holding any substantial territory on his own.

It is often suggested that members of the pack selflessly subordinate their own interests to the greater interests of the group, but this is really not an honest description of the evolutionary forces or motives at work. In wolf packs the males and females of the group each establish their own social rankings. The top male and top female furiously disrupt any attempts by their inferiors to breed. These rankings are often stable for long periods, and when this is the case the lower-ranking animals readily give way to their superiors without a fight. The alpha male is greeted with fawning, even puppylike, submissive gestures of face licking; if an inferior-ranking male is challenged by the alpha, he will roll over on his belly and submit. All members of the group, male and female, participate in the care and rearing of the young, regurgitating food for the puppies and being generally solicitous of them.

Why do the inferiors put up with this role? The honest answer is really that it is just an expedient. The group would erupt in constant aggression, and quickly disintegrate, if the pack did not acquiesce to the demands of the most assertive members among them. Yet if all that inferior wolves got in the bargain was room and board and the chance to play nanny for someone else's children, evolutionary logic would bridle at the arrangement. All wolves are offspring of alpha wolves. The instinct for submission must serve some purpose that helps a wolf not only eat but also reproduce—at least eventually. For how else would the instinct for submission ever be passed on to the next generation? The evolutionary calculus, then, is not that subordinate wolves are naturally peaceful, selfless caregivers; they are rather just biding their time. Subordination is a way to avoid getting killed or driven off by a larger or stronger or older and more experienced member of the group while awaiting one's turn to challenge him. It is a very good strategy to play the fawning courtier until one is strong enough to depose the king. It is a very bad strategy to be obnoxious or hostile to the king before the moment to strike has come.

The acceptance of social rank is thus a way to avoid constant fighting, and it is something built into every wolf, and dog. The innate grasp of social hierarchy by dogs is the sine qua non of their compatibility with human society, too. Without this instinct, dogs would simply never have been.

Wolves understand social rank, and accept it, and it is the source of long periods of stability in wolf society. Dominant and subordinate wolves go for months enjoying friendly relations, with no overt fighting, and indeed few overt signs of hostility. Subordinate animals have an endless capacity to deflect incipient aggression by their superiors by submitting to their will and temporarily repressing their own self-interested drives. It is no coincidence that wolves became house pets but raccoons did not.

But lest we get too carried away with the gentle wonder of

it all, it is worth quickly pointing out that while the social hierarchy is what made dogs possible in the first place, it is also what has made them an endless source of trouble to us. Wolves, and dogs, are all social climbers. They are always on the lookout for signs of weakness, hesitation, or a loss of self-confidence in their social superiors. In a wolf pack, when challenges do come from inferiors, they are often extremely violent. Dominance challenges in which one or both wolves in the struggle are seriously wounded are not unusual. A fight often triggers a general rise in aggression throughout the pack as well, spawning other challenges. The very disruption of the established social order that occurs when one wolf moves up is in itself a destabilizing force that requires members of the pack to sort out anew who falls where in the rankings.

Social rank is a result; it is not a state of mind. It is in a sense a measure of inherent aggressive tendency and willingness to use force, if necessary; it is maintained by threats and self-confident bearing. The rank order itself is not so much an inherent feature of wolf society as it is the consequence of a series of one-on-one encounters within the group. Many struggles of course take place all the time within groups. Even puppies wrestle over bones or just in play, and the winner of such minor struggles may change frequently, depending on the circumstances of the moment (for example, who is hungrier). But the wolf biologist Erik Zimen found that the true social hierarchy that emerges in the pack is much more the consequence of an assertion of freedom of movement at the expense of others. In that sense it resembles, in a stylized or miniature form, the territorial and mate struggles that exist in solitary species. Young wolves secure a place in the hierarchy only as they reach sexual maturity and begin to challenge others in this fashion.

When an alpha wolf is deposed, he often suffers what Zimen terms the "nosedive" effect. He seems to undergo a complete loss of confidence, and other members of the pack quickly seize the chance to pick on him. He can become a scapegoat, and the end result is usually that he is driven out altogether by repeated, violent attacks from all members of the group. Likewise, when a subordinate wolf succeeds in challenging a high-ranking member, he seems to enjoy a surge of almost arrogant confidence. Zimen relates a hair-raising incident involving one of the wolves in the pack he had kept in a large enclosure. When an older alpha male was removed from the group, Alexander, one of three young males, emerged as the new alpha as the result of a furious and violent dominance struggle. In the wake of that triumph, Alexander suddenly turned on Zimen one day, leaping up on him, placing both paws on his shoulders, snarling, and baring his teeth. As Zimen's coworkers rushed to the windows to watch, Zimen succeeded at last in talking Alexander down ("probably to the disappointment of some of my colleagues, who would have liked to have seen more action," he noted), but the relationship between them was never the same thereafter.

Submission on the part of a subordinate is largely just an act, a ritual that serves to deflect immediate aggression by a superior. It may have the temporary effect of reaffirming the social hierarchy and thus the stability of the group, but it is important to realize that that is not its "purpose." Its purpose is to save the subordinate's skin long enough that his genes will have their day.

Still, the net effect of all this is that it allows the group to do the things it needs to do to survive—hunt and defend a territory. To a certain extent, but only a certain extent, these tasks are successfully accomplished as a result of the willingness of the group to follow the management directions of the alpha male. The alpha does often act as a leader, and not just a bully. He is the first to enter or leave the den, he often leads the group when hunting, and the other wolves will often follow his cues in lying down and getting up. When two wolves interact, it is the dominant wolf that usually initiates it. All of these are characteristics that dogs clearly emulate in their acceptance of human leadership, in everything from going for walks to lying down for the night.

But there is a cohesiveness and cooperation in the pack that runs deeper than obedience. Hunting in wolves is always highly cooperative. David Mech, a wolf biologist who spent years studying the wild wolves of Isle Royale, Michigan, observed that the pack does have a component of "democracy" in its governance: its movements are sometimes the result more of a majority vote than of blind following-the-leader. Mech once observed a group of sixteen wolves traveling across jagged ice; although the lead wolf kept returning to the group and trying to get them to follow him, a majority clearly aimed to turn back, and eventually succeeded in getting the group to head home. Whether it is because of their more linear social hierarchy, which suppresses independent self-interest, or instead because of such democratic give-and-take as Mech witnessed, wolves are considerably more cooperative than many group-dwelling animals (such as chimpanzees, who are always cheating and picking on one another).

Wolves are also more adaptable than just about any other group-dwelling animal, and that is another natural social bond between our species. Wolves live in a great range of social groups, from the occasional loner to large packs. With the sole exception of man, wolves are the most widely distributed land mammal on earth, with a range that extends from North

America through Europe to Asia, encompassing semi-deserts, tundra, and subtropical forest.

DOGS ARE WOLVES (UNFORTUNATELY)

Many of the wolflike social behaviors of the dog are not, however, things that endear them to us, and many have lost their original social purpose to the dog as well. They are vestiges, appendages that evolution hasn't managed to shake yet. Like the human appendix, they range from merely useless to downright awkward.

The elaborate eliminatory patterns of the dog are a source of puzzlement and grief to many a dog owner, but if it is any consolation, they don't make a great deal of sense for the dog, either. In wolves, both the alpha male and the alpha female generally urinate with a raised leg; all other members of the pack merely squat. The raised-leg urinations involve depositing relatively small amounts of urine in prominent places and on conspicuous objects. This of course has almost nothing to do with the needs of elimination per se and everything to do with territorial markers. Many people have come to believe the frequently repeated tale that wolves only mark the perimeter of their territory in this fashion, as a "keep-out" signal. (This seems to have started with Farley Mowat's heavily fictionalized and liberally embellished account of his own limited adventures in the wild with wolves, *Never Cry Wolf*.) But would that it were so, for the sake of our yards, gardens, and sometimes curtains. In fact, careful studies by David Mech in Minnesota found that wolves urine-mark throughout their territory. They do the same with their feces (or "scats," as biologists like to call them) which are frequently deposited on prominent spots, too, such as snowbanks, stumps, shrubs, and even empty beer cans. Wolf scats are also frequently found at trail junctions, especially in the immediate vicinity of rendezvous sites where growing wolf pups are left while the adults go off to hunt. Scent glands on either side of the anus probably serve to add an individually distinctive odor to scats, reinforcing their function as scent markers. The scratching of the ground that sometimes follows elimination by socially dominant wolves, and which some but not all dogs exhibit, appears to be aimed at reinforcing the scent mark with a visual mark, or possibly to reinforce it more directly with odor from glands in the paws. (Wolves are careful while scratching up dirt or leaves during this action not to aim the debris directly at the site of their eliminations.)

Puppies from the age of a few weeks do have an instinct to keep their immediate nest area clean, and will go outside the nest to urinate and defecate. And in housebreaking dogs it is no doubt this basic instinct that is being built upon. The trouble puppies have is generalizing the concept of the den to an area as large as a house, and this is pretty clearly why housebreaking is a process fraught with accidents. Dogs not only have no instinct to keep such a large area clean; on the contrary, they have a definite instinct to thoroughly mark their immediate vicinity with both urine and feces. Wolves apparently do this so that pack members can know at any time whether they are in their home territory. The primary stimulus for raised-leg urination in wolves is not, as is often said, the smell of a strange wolf's urine, but rather the presence of the wolf's *own* mark: there is a strong instinct to mark and remark sites along frequently traveled routes within the wolf's own territory. Indeed, it may be an almost automatic response to the odor of urine. Laboratory studies have found that when the nasal lining of dogs is electrically stimulated, it triggers an immediate relaxation of the urinary sphincter muscles.

The functional purpose behind the dog's scent-marking has largely vanished as the fifty- to one-hundred-square-mile territory of a typical wolf pack has shrunk to the average dog's territory of a quarter-acre suburban lot. It is possible with a lot of training and consistency to teach dogs to defecate in one spot; it is much harder to get them to confine their urinations. Still, it could be worse, and it is worth noting that many species are not even as fastidious as the dog. For example, some species of loris, a lower primate, continually urinate on their hands and feet in order to spread their odor completely through their territory.

Digging is another vestigial behavior that most dog owners would happily do without and that dogs could readily do without, too, for that matter. In wolves and coyotes it is a highly stereotyped pattern associated with caching food for later consumption. Wolves always perform the action in exactly the same way, digging a hole with the front paws, placing the object in, then pushing the loose dirt or snow back in with the snout. In over a hundred videotaped observations, wolves never used their snout to dig or the paws to fill in the hole, even though there was no obvious reason in many cases why they should not: it is a classic hardwired motor pattern. The fact of its being so hardwired and stereotyped may explain why it is so readily triggered even in dogs for whom it rarely serves a purpose anymore.

It is comparatively rare for domestic dogs to regurgitate food for puppies, though bitches sometimes will carry food to their pups. But some dogs do regurgitate, and a few unfortunate dog owners possess specimens that not only retain this wolf instinct but apply it in novel circumstances, such as the dog that in an earnest if mistaken act of solicitousness would vomit regularly into his owner's shoes.

DOG AREN'T WOLVES

Some instinctive social behaviors of the wolf may be left unexpressed in the dog simply because the opportunity never arises for them to *be* expressed in a new social milieu. But even when dogs range freely in wild or semiwild circumstances, they show distinct divergences from their wild ancestors. As part of his behavioral study of the wolf, Erik Zimen raised a pack of poodles and a pack of wolves under quite similar conditions. While the wolves ran free inside an enclosure, the poodles had free run of the rest of the property. Zimen and his colleagues catalogued 362 specific behaviors displayed by wolves, everything from yawning and stretching to howling and tail wagging. The poodles displayed 64 percent of those behaviors with little or no change. About 13 percent of wolf behaviors had vanished altogether, and 23 percent persisted but in markedly modified form. Zimen found that in performing many of these modified behaviors, the poodles lacked a seriousness of purpose; compared to the wolves, the poodles were more playful or simply inept. As Raymond Coppinger observed with his village dogs, Zimen's poodles were incapable of hunting large prey. The poodles readily chased things, but their choice of "prey" was indiscriminate—birds, leaves, bicyclists—and it was clearly a game, an end in itself, very much as with young wolves at play.

The most striking differences seen in the poodles was in their expressive behavior—or rather, lack thereof. Wolves exhibit a rich array of facial expressions, ear movements, tail positions, and body postures. In poodles many of these expressions were greatly simplified, and many were absent altogether. The lip curling, snarling, and baring of teeth displayed routinely by wolves in defensive and aggressive situations was considerably muted and simplified in poodles. In part, this is simply because poodles are generally less fearful and less aggressive and tend not to mind invasions of personal space as much as wolves do: they just have less of an impulse to act annoyed. Starting as early as four weeks, wolf cubs begin to sleep apart from one another more and more often. By the time the cubs are four to six months old, they are like adult wolves, and almost never make contact with another wolf when sleeping. The poodles, however, continued to frequently lie together through the age of eight months or older, and even as full-grown adults did so about a third of the time, and even in hot weather when there was no conceivable reason for huddling to preserve body heat. Dogs are, in other words, simply more pacific and easygoing by nature.

Studies of poodle-wolf hybrids suggest that there may be more than one behavioral component to dogs' milder dispositions. When Zimen recrossed poodle-wolves ("puwos") together, these second-generation hybrids came in a mixed assortment of behavioral types. Some were timid about approaching humans but were very affectionate when they did; others were tame and not disposed to flee from novelties but were emotionally aloof. Zimen suggests that a reduction in the flight instinct and a greater capacity for socialization and bonding may be separately inherited traits, though both are necessary for wolves to become dogs.

Other studies of free-ranging dogs have documented the ways in which wolf behavior has been attenuated or extinguished over the course of evolution. In cities and villages, dogs that wander freely generally do not form packs, and while each dog has an identifiable home range that he sticks to, these ranges overlap almost completely with those of other dogs. Free-ranging dogs do engage in wolflike urine marking throughout their range, but they show almost no inclination to defend their territory against intruders. Even when feral dogs do form into packs, as they do sometimes in rural areas or in and around garbage dumps, these do not behave like wolf packs. Feral dog packs will sometimes more actively defend a territory and kill dogs that intrude, but they lack many of the more developed cooperative behaviors of wolves, such as care of the young by all adult members of the group. Reproductive behavior is also much looser, or at least certainly much more variable. Ray Coppinger observed a huge range of sexual behavior among village and feral dogs around the world. At one extreme, male New Guinea singing dogs are fiercely competitive, but in a very unwolflike way; they behave more like the males of species that occupy and defend individual territories, and the mere sight of another male provokes attack. At the other extreme, and perhaps much more typical of dogs, were the village dogs he encountered in Venezuela who "were observed to line up and breed a female sequentially, with little aggression between them."

There is certainly no simple or unicausal explanation for all of these behavioral differences between wolf and dog. Changes in neurotransmitter and hormonal levels, disruptions of the juvenile stages of development in which behaviors are molded, and the persistence of juvenile traits into adulthood are all factors in the transformation. The overall picture that emerges is that dogs are less confrontational and fearful, and while they retain a capacity for asserting dominance (as well as for acquiescing in subordination), their social interactions lack the urgency or insistence that one sees in wolf society. There is simply less at stake. The social pressure cooker of the wolf pack has been replaced with a tepid cauldron. Dogs have no need and no inclination for the packed and charged social world of their ancestors. That essentially all male dogs mark their home range with raised-leg urinations (as do the relatively unsocial male coyotes), that no male or female dog is inhibited from breeding by other dogs, and that most free-ranging dogs do not form coherent packs suggests that dog society has fragmented from a group of fiefdoms to a rather more democratic polity, or perhaps more accurately a world in which every citizen is a slightly delusional lordling. But they are a happy band of lunatics. Each imagines himself a potentate, and is untroubled by his neighbors' imagining the same. They are like an insane asylum full of inmates, all of whom believe they are Napoleon. Every once in a while they ask the guards if they can get together and have a Napoleon convention.

Beyond the hormonal and developmental changes that lurk behind all of this, some dog–wolf differences in social behavior reflect frank physical constraints. Poodles have droopy ears; they are simply incapable of the range of communicative expression that occurs in wolves. A wolf's ear carriage expresses a range of emotions and intentions, from dominance and hostility to fear and submission. Judging by the ears, a poodle looks like a wolf in a permanent state of submission.

In some breeds, physical changes have interfered to an even greater degree with the communicative structures that wolves use, especially in the expression of aggression or dominance. An all-female group of Cavalier King Charles spaniels was observed to show no intragroup aggression at all, and extremely little wolflike visual signaling. There was some subtly

The erect ears, hackles, and long snout of the wolf have vanished in many breeds of dogs, limiting their ability to communicate visually as wolves do.

expressed competition for food or access to desired spots in which the apparently more dominant dogs pushed aside the others, but that was about it. This breed has undergone very substantial modifications in not only ears but jaw, hackles, and tail as well. Dogs such as foxhounds and beagles that are bred to hunt together in packs show a quite similar lack of overt aggressive tendencies; they too have faces ill equipped for signaling dominance to anything like the extent the wolf, with its complete repertoire of nose wrinkling, fang baring, ear pricking, and tail and hackle raising, can.

EARLY EXPERIENCE

In his famous experiments in which geese followed him around like demented adolescents in love with a rock star, the animal behaviorist Konrad Lorenz demonstrated that newborns of many species will form lasting attachments to any animal they are placed with in the first weeks, days, or even hours of life. In precocial species such as geese, which are able to walk and swim within hours of hatching, there is a clear adaptive value to this behavior, which Lorenz termed "imprinting." It ensures that they learn very quickly who their mother is, and that they don't get left behind in all of the to-ing and fro-ing that occurs almost from the moment they set foot on the earth. In geese, imprinting is so powerful a force that goslings will form an attachment to the very first moving object they see. That is usually the gosling's mother, but it can equally be a zoologist, a cat, or a tractor. In many species of birds, hatchlings reared by foster parents of another species will not only form odd attachments but absorb a lifelong lesson in what constitutes a desirable mate: upon reaching sexual maturity, they will direct courtship behavior at members of their foster parents' species in preference to their own. Many hand-reared birds imprint sexually on humans, and forever shun their own kind as they futilely court the people in their lives.

In species such as dogs, which are born deaf, blind, and helpless, newborns have a longer time to learn the identity of their mother, and there is not quite the same urgency. Puppies are confined to a nest for the first three weeks of life, so there is little danger of them blundering off. Growing dogs do pass through a period in which they are particularly susceptible to forming social bonds, and which is also critical to their learning to recognize and relate appropriately to members of their own species and mastering the basic rules of social conduct. But though the learning that takes place during this period may often be described as imprinting, too, it is less absolute and of a less sharply defined form than in geese.

Several landmark experiments on imprinting in dogs were carried out as part of a huge project on animal behavior that took place in the 1940s and 1950s at Jackson Laboratory in Bar Harbor, Maine. More than a hundred litters of dogs of five quite different breeds—Shetland sheepdogs, basenjis, cocker spaniels, beagles, and fox terriers—were raised and studied under varying conditions. The most famous of these studies, published in 1961, came to be known as the "wild dog" experiment. Litters of puppies were reared in large outdoor fields with essentially no direct human contact. For a period of one week each, the puppies were brought in to the laboratory for daily sessions of human contact and interaction. The age at which the puppies had their week of human contact was varied from two weeks to nine weeks; a control group had no contact at all until age fourteen weeks, when all of the puppies were brought back to the lab for testing.

Puppies who were brought in at five weeks showed the least initial fear, as measured by how long it took them to approach and make contact with a person sitting quietly in the room with them and by how the puppy reacted to a handler's attempts to approach it. Those puppies whose one week of human contact occurred between the ages of five and nine weeks also performed the best when the tests were repeated at fourteen weeks. They scored highest, too, on another test given at fourteen weeks, which was designed to measure how the puppies would react to being put on a leash for the first time and led around to unfamiliar places.

The control group, and the puppies whose week of human contact had occurred at age two weeks or three weeks, did much worse, repeatedly balking when led on a leash. The control-group puppies were in fact so fearful that they would never voluntarily come anywhere near a person sitting on the floor. One of these fourteen-week-old puppies was given an additional month of intensive human contact and improved only very slightly. The experimenters found that these dogs "were like little wild animals and could be tamed only in the way in which wild animals usually are tamed, by keeping them confined so that they could not run away and feeding them only by hand, so that they were continually forced into human contact."

By contrast, other experiments have shown that puppies that are removed from all contact with littermates before four weeks of age often fail to develop normal social behavior toward other dogs and may sexually imprint on humans. They definitely show a marked ineptitude in mating behavior upon reaching sexual maturity. Three-quarters of male puppies removed from contact with other dogs at age three weeks were unsuccessful in achieving intromission during mating as adults; almost half failed because they attempted to mount the female from the wrong end, which would seem to reflect a rather basic misunderstanding.

The results of the Bar Harbor studies brought about something of a revolution in puppy raising. The idea was firmly established that dogs experience a "critical period" between the age of three weeks and twelve weeks during which primary social bonds are permanently imprinted, and many dog experts began recommending that the ideal time to adopt a puppy was when it was six to eight weeks old. Many dog books indeed seem to suggest that if a puppy is adopted later than eight weeks, it will never properly bond with its new owner and will be warped for life. But that is not what the Bar Harbor experiments showed at all. What is crucial is for puppies to have *some* human contact, preferably beginning at around three weeks but at least by seven weeks or so, in order to become used to humans and not react fearfully to them. That definitely does not mean that puppies must be moved to their final, permanent home by six or eight weeks of age. Puppies that have been kept in kennels without any substantial human contact past about twelve weeks of age do show a fear of humans—and indeed of new situations—in general. But puppies over twelve weeks get along just fine with the move to a new home and a new owner so long as they have had some initial exposure to humans, which inures them to the novelty of new people and new experiences. Studies have found that as little as twenty minutes of human contact twice a week can be enough to do the trick during these early weeks.

Recent evidence shows that removing puppies from their mothers and littermates at six weeks is in fact detrimental to their health and social development. Puppies moved to their new homes at that age showed significantly more signs of distress than did puppies adopted at twelve weeks, as well as a loss of appetite and susceptibility to disease.

There is increasing doubt among scientists about whether the "critical period" in dogs is that critical at all. Many scientists now use the less prescriptive term "sensitive period," but even that term embodies an assumption that may not stand up to scrutiny; it suggests that some biologically unique process is taking place, akin to that which (undoubtedly) occurs during imprinting in goslings. It may much more be the case that puppies simply develop an increasing fear of novelty around twelve to fourteen weeks. That older dogs (and wolves) *can* be socialized to humans if their natural flight instinct is controlled supports this interpretation. Thus it is not that puppies have some small, magical window during which their instinct to socialize is activated; rather, they retain that capacity into later life, but fear begins to intervene and overpower it.

RANK ORDER

There is no doubt, however, that puppies acquire some vital knowledge of social etiquette during their first two months of life. Beginning at two or three weeks, when puppies start to move about on their own and make exploratory contact with their littermates, they begin to learn what various canine social signals mean, and they learn the consequences of aggression and appeasement. As with socialization, the timing of this onset of social learning may have less to do with some inbuilt imprinting instinct than with the fact that this is simply the first opportunity puppies have to learn anything about society. But if people are part of that etiquette course, it may ease the way for good relations later on.

Puppies have an innate drive to make contact with other beings at this age. Experiments in which puppies were rewarded for approaching humans, and indeed in which they were actually punished for approaching humans, showed it made essentially no difference to their attempts to do so; the instinct to explore and make contact was so strong that it was its own reward. Some puppies begin playing and play-fighting almost as soon as they can move around; by six weeks essentially all are engaging in interactions with their littermates. They begin to exhibit the stereotypical postures of dominance and submission in the course of these tussles, but often don't seem to read one another accurately, or at all. Erik Zimen noted that at first wolf pups seemed almost oblivious to the snarls and threats from older wolves of the pack whom they pestered and chewed on. The older wolves, however, exercised considerable self-restraint and limited their expression of annoyance to threats. Puppies start to pay attention to the meaning of social signals when their littermates begin to use their sharp teeth with little inhibition. From these interactions they also learn how to turn real bites into "inhibited" play bites.

A possibly more important source of instruction in social conduct occurs during weaning. This is the first point in the puppies' lives when their interests begin to diverge from their mother's. When the puppies are four or five weeks old, the mother starts to walk away as the puppies try to nurse. No doubt the immediate stimulus for this is the increasingly sharp teeth and powerful jaws of the puppies. As the puppies grow increasingly active, the mother often begins growling and baring her teeth at the puppies as they try to nurse, eventually escalating this threat by seizing a puppy's muzzle in her mouth in a checked bite. By the fifth week, many of the puppies learn to respond to these threats by rolling over in the classic "passive submission" pose, baring their belly and lying helpless. The mother then typically responds by licking the fur of the puppy. These interactions typically peak around age seven weeks. This is a real object lesson in threats, appeasement, and submission.

Many authors have asserted that puppies at these early ages already begin to establish a dominance hierarchy among themselves as well. Indeed, the notion has become popular in dog-breeding circles that it is possible to test puppies for dominant behavior with "temperament tests" at age seven weeks to predict whether a particular dog will be dominant as an adult. The idea is to match individual puppies to prospective owners, presumably assigning the hard cases to confident, assertive humans (preferably FBI agents or middle-school vice principals), while the wimps get the less dominant puppies. The Bar Harbor experiments found that puppies eagerly tussle with one another over possession of a bone from a very early age, and that by age five weeks one puppy sometimes will succeed in repeatedly taking a bone away from another and holding it for almost all of a ten-minute test period. By eleven weeks this "bone-in-pen" test yields such a clear-cut winner much more frequently, about half the time. On the basis of these experiments, the researchers assigned puppies to a spot in the dominance hierarchy, and these and similar experiments have been cited ever since as proof that rank order emerges, and may even be fixed, during the "critical period."

But there is considerable evidence that the squabbles between puppies at this age are not at all predictive of future rank. The apparent rank order that emerges from these tests changes frequently from five weeks to twelve weeks. The puppy that is rated the most dominant at six weeks may be the least at twelve weeks. The order can change in a day, or even in a few hours.

Although a fairly stable precedence order for access to food or possession of bones and toys does emerge in groups of dogs by the time they are a few months old, even this may in truth have little—or nothing—to do with actual dominance status. That may sound like a contradiction, or like splitting terminological hairs, but Erik Zimen's studies of wolf cubs and poodle puppies strongly support the conclusion that the priority order that dogs exhibit in access to food really is fundamentally unrelated to the much more serious business of social status. In dogs, contests over access to food or desired items result in a priority order that includes males and females, with males usually taking precedence over females. The order also appears to strongly reflect physical differences in size and strength among the puppies. Together with the fact that the order changes frequently in the first months of life, this all implies that the priority order in dog society has much more to do with immediate motivation and immediate conflicts of interest than with some larger sense of social status—which in wolves is sorted out through deadly serious challenges that take place only among same-sex individuals and only upon reaching sexual maturity.

Wolves within a pack are actually considerably more cooperative over sharing resources than are dogs; they eat side by side with little dispute, at least when food is plentiful. Cubs do have frequent fights, but Zimen saw no evidence that these had any consequences for social dominance status, at that time or in the future:

> There were frequent violent squabbles [among the cubs]. . . . These fights were not always between two cubs; two or even three would sometimes attack a fourth. Nevertheless, a few minutes later they might all be huddled together, sleeping peacefully, and by the time the next squabble broke out three new friends might have formed an alliance. . . . No permanent attitude could be deduced from the current expressive behavior of two cubs engaged in combat. Their expression always reflected the relations of strength existing at that moment, and in a new situation a few minutes later it could be totally different. All this is in complete contrast to the aggressive behavior of older wolves. Cubs in their clashes seem to be concerned only with momentary conflicts of interest and not with any question of status. They make no attempt at long-term suppression of their siblings, and so—apart of course from sat-

isfying their immediate needs—they have no expansionary tendency aimed at extending their own freedom of action at the expense of others.

Dogs, less constrained by the cooperative forces of the pack, in a sense have more liberty to turn these contests over immediate interests into a more permanent test of wills for access to food or possessions. The much more serious business of establishing social status, however, is motivated not by such immediate conflicts but by long-term interests. When wolves engage in contests over true dominance, they are not fighting over a bone or even a mate; they are expressing a very basic genetic behavioral imperative to suppress the free action of their fellows, which in the long term is their only chance of mating and passing on their genes. Thus dominance struggles take place for their own sake. Dogs are less serious and less driven; they are also less constrained, and so tend not only to make more of a game of it but to indulge in dominance-like tussles in many more circumstances than wolves do.

FAKING IT

Dogs of some breeds, as a result of a general lack of motivation, or a lack of the physical apparatus required for visual signaling, or both, tend to live placidly in groups, and true dominance contests over status simply never erupt. Foxhounds and beagles have a reputation for being rather untrainable in household settings and heedless toward their owners, but that is probably not because they see themselves as top dog; rather, they don't particularly give a damn about *anybody* being top dog. Other breeds clearly have a much stronger motivation to assert social dominance and may repeatedly challenge their owners with increasing violence, up to and including attacks and biting, unless firmly put in their place. A good many actually succeed in their challenge, or believe they have anyway, which is all that matters, and as a result, owners scurry around catering to the dog's wishes all day long. Dogs that are more status-conscious are also much more sensitive to the group dynamics that arise in multi-person and multi-dog households, and these are the dogs that may get along fine for years, then suddenly make a move to assert themselves when a human or canine member of the household moves away or when an old dog begins to lose physical strength. (I will come back to this whole fraught issue of dominance aggression toward people and other dogs, and the many and fascinating problems this causes, in chapter 8.)

The normally calculating social behavior of dogs, however, is also behind much of their day-to-day acceptance of and trainability within human society. Dogs are easily trained to sit, lie down, and stay because those are precisely the sorts of submissive postures or actions that subordinate wolves display toward dominant individuals, who, as Zimen notes, fundamentally seek to limit the freedom of action of their fellow pack members. Dogs seek to make contact with, lick, greet, and lie near their owners in almost precisely the same way members of the wolf pack behave toward the alpha male.

Is this love, or perhaps loyalty? It is certainly expedient, and evolution has equipped dogs and their ancestral relations with a near boundless capacity for ingratiation. In a sense it may not be too far off to call it love, for it is an instinctive behavior that is expressed, in the immediate context, for its own sake; it is a powerful drive that has no other immediate reward than the continued nonaggressive behavior of a social superior. Dogs have a powerful instinct to be with and to be compliant and mild toward those they view as their social betters.

In the evolutionary sense, however, it is hard not to see all of this behavior as cynical in the extreme, for it is nothing but an expedient: change the balance of power ever so slightly, and all bets are off. Wolves simply would never have acquired these instincts at all unless they paid off from time to time by greasing the path to power. If we are going to call this love and tenderness (love and tenderness shown only to a social superior, one needs to underscore), we have to be prepared to call it cruelty and sadism when wolves pick on and drive off a scapegoat.

Well, we are fickle in love, too, and again there is something about the very elemental—"pure"—instinctiveness of this drive that does make it different from just, say, a trick like barking to get a dog biscuit. So perhaps love it is.

Loyalty, though, is a tougher proposition, for it implies some grasp of a larger sense of purpose. In a very superficial way dogs are loyal—in the sense that they like to hang around us. But all of those tales about dogs that stick with their masters in the blizzard, or that rescue them from burning houses, or that risk their own lives to protect their master's property from wolves and bandits, run into serious conceptual difficulties. Our reliably anthropomorphic selves are ever ready to project human motives upon an animal so amenable to anthropomorphic projection as the dog, and the narrative of the dog that saves its master is so compelling and so fixed a part of the journalistic canon these days that even the most routine and obvious actions by dogs routinely appear under the headline "Dog Rescues Family" in newspapers. Sometimes these turn out, when one actually reads to the bottom of the story, to be rather disappointing, something like a dog having heroically barked when the smoke alarm went off, waking his master, who, having passed out in an alcoholic stupor, is thereby roused to stagger to safety.

Dogs that lie down next to injured people in the snow are almost certainly not doing so "to keep them warm"; they're simply doing what dogs do. (Lie down on your living room floor and see what happens.) Dogs that "guard" objects, like an owner's purse or shoes, from other people are behaving indistinguishably from the way a dog tries to keep a dog chew toy from another dog. That the owner is usually in possession of these objects may make them especially prized—it must seem to the dog that he has at last succeeded in wresting the bone away from no less than the top dog.

Dogs that run to their owner's side and growl menacingly at an intruder are inevitably seen to be "protecting" the owner. But that is not what wolves are doing in such circumstances; they are rather *seeking* the protection, or at least the reassurance, that comes from proximity to a more dominant member of the pack. This phenomenon manifests itself in the veterinarian's office in what is clinically called "facilitated aggression": a dog that may be perfectly tractable by itself becomes emboldened by its owner's presence to attack the vet. (This is why veterinarians would generally prefer to have someone other than the owner hold a dog that is being examined.)

Many of the seemingly loyal things that dogs do reflect a similar ready misinterpretation on our part of basic canine instincts that have been subverted to our cause but whose purpose, as far as the dog is concerned, remain unchanged. Search-and-rescue dogs that find people in collapsed buildings have no more awareness that they are rescuing people than narcotics-sniffing dogs are aware that they are enforcing the nation's drug laws. As far as search-and-rescue dogs are concerned, they are playing fetch. The dogs are first taught to fetch one special object only. The next step is to have people go and hide—with the object. When the dog finds the person, his reward is he gets his toy back. At the scene of genuine disasters, the dogs have to be rewarded several times a day by having someone play the role of (toy-bearing) "victim" so the dogs don't get frustrated and give up.

Ray Coppinger, in his extensive study of livestock-guarding dogs, found that far from having any sense of protecting sheep from wolves or coyotes, the dogs owed their effectiveness to their general goofiness. When a predator approaches, the livestock guard dogs react in completely out-of-context and inappropriate ways—barking, wagging their tails, and even trying to play with the intruder. They do not so much intimidate the predator or chase it off as confuse it and disrupt its hunting sequence.

Dogs unquestionably enjoy our company; they unquestionably find reassurance when they have a stable place in the social hierarchy of human society; they unquestionably are on occasion of service to man as a result of their sensory prowess and peculiar habits and fixations; but we are guilty of that worst of human traits, our limitless self-centeredness, when we see every useful thing they do for us as proof that they are doing it all for us.

CHAPTER 4

Canine Kabuki

In a close-knit society operating in conformity to strict rules of conduct, it saves no end of trouble and embarrassment to be able merely to hint at one's intentions—and likewise, to be savvy enough to pick up on the mere hints of others.

Social hints can take several forms. They can be rituals (like lifting one's hat or shaking hands) that have long since lost whatever direct purpose they originally served, and have come to assume a conventional meaning. Or they can be more tangible vestiges of the deliberate behavior they connote (like shaking a fist), or even vestiges of reflex reactions (like cringing to avoid a blow). Social hints may be dropped consciously or unconsciously; they may be visual or vocal; they may be true or false. But to qualify as hints, the one essential quality they must possess is that they stop short of the outright action they stand in for. The whole point is that they are a way to avoid a good deal of rough stuff that might otherwise be required when individuals with often sharp divergences of interests are crammed together in close quarters.

The dropping of hints and the reading of hints are the germs of communication. Being only human, when we think about communication, we naturally think about communication as humans do it. Even biologists, it turns out, are only human; for decades it has been practically de rigueur to approach animal communication from a linguistic point of view, to take as a given that animal sounds and displays "stand for" something just as sounds do in human language. The usual approach has been to watch what an animal is doing at the moment it makes some sound or visual display, and then to slap on a corresponding semantic label. Thus certain animal sounds were said to be "food calls" or "alarm calls" or "mating calls" and so on. Like human language, animal language was seen to be a sort of abstract code in which information was replaced by symbols, transmitted, and then decoded on the receiving end. The best explanation anybody could come up with for *why* animals would do such a thing was that it was a sort of general good for the group as a whole; animal communication was, as one biologist attempted to explain it, the product of "a synergistic interplay between participants, both of which are committed to maximizing the efficiency of the interchange." We might term this the "knowledge is good" theory of animal communication: individuals share information because the more freely information is shared, the better off everyone is.

More recently this view has been sharply questioned on both theoretical and practical grounds by a number of evolutionary biologists and field zoologists. For one thing, most animal displays and sounds, it turns out, are clearly *not* semantic. Many signals—the wolf's howl, the chicken's cluck, the raven's caw—are each used in many different contexts. One signal doesn't seem to "mean" any one specific thing. More damning is the critique from evolutionary theorists, who pointed out that unless the sender of a signal gained some direct benefit from doing so, the signal could never have evolved in the first place. Animals don't have some abstract commitment to the efficiency of the information-sharing process; what they have a commitment to is the efficiency of saving their own necks.

As biologists increasingly began to look for the evolutionary motive behind communicative signs, it became apparent that far from being abstract code symbols, animal displays and sounds are tied functionally, and very closely, to their biological purpose. Dogs don't use some arbitrary symbols to represent ideas, like Morse-code dots and dashes or semaphore flags or letters of the alphabet; they use highly ritualized and stylized signals—signals that are tuned very precisely to exploit strong, preexisting dispositions in their fellow dogs. The sounds of a word in human language rarely have any functional connection to their meaning. There is no reason we need to call a rose a rose; we could have called it gzorneplatz, and it not only would have smelled as sweet, it would have meant exactly the same thing. Dogs have no such freedom of invention in the sounds and physical gestures they use to communicate. They use the "words" they do for a very good reason: making these sounds helps them get what they want. It is a cause that has everything to do with self-interest, and essentially nothing to do with the "knowledge is good" motive that drives the syntax and semantics of human language. Dogs are more Machiavelli than Webster; their communicative style is more kabuki than Shakespeare.

ACTING OUT

There are some things a dog can't help doing. If he is going to bite someone, he needs to look at his target, and he needs to bare his teeth. If he is going to defend himself, he has to tuck his ears back and his tail down and turn aside. In the dark unrecorded mists of wolf history, wolves that had the wits to notice these things had an edge over their more obtuse pack-mates. Being on the lookout for the fangs or the intent stare of a more powerful member of the pack was a way to avoid unnecessary physical injury from a wolf one had no intention of challenging anyway; being on the lookout for the cringe or the averted gaze of a weaker member was a way to avoid the unnecessary trouble and danger of fighting with a wolf who was prepared to give way without a fight anyway.

Once wolves were on the lookout for unintentionally dropped hints, it became possible to start dropping them intentionally. A wolf that can accurately read a fang or a stare as a threat can avoid a fight: a wolf that can show a fang or fix a stare can then express a threat without a fight. This evolutionary feedback loop between receivers and senders is what was almost surely behind the development and ritualization of the visual signals that wolves, and now dogs, use.

Most of these signals are directly related to the very serious wolf business of dominance and submission within the pack. Dominance and threatening signals include baring the teeth, pricking the ears, and staring. Submissive and nonthreatening signals include laying the ears back, averting the gaze, approaching obliquely rather than head on, tucking the tail tightly under the belly, and (the ultimate gesture of passive surrender to superior force) rolling over and lying belly-up.

Over sufficiently long time, these signals become ritualized. Every time a wolf lifts his lips and shows his fangs, he is not literally about to bite; rather this is a symbol of threatening intentions, and, at this point in the evolutionary history of the wolf, read as such by other wolves. Wolves are predisposed

Active Submission

Passive Submission

Dominant Stance

Submissive "Smile"

Play Bow

Tooth-baring Threat

to read it that way because of the indisputable fact of evolutionary history that fangs really *do* bite. Wolves became in turn disposed to use a show of fangs as a threatening gesture precisely because wolves were predisposed to react to fangs *as* a threat.

Just about all vertebrate animals long ago acquired an innate appreciation of another biological fact that is frequently exploited in visual communication: big things out there are more dangerous than small things. Thus threatening or dominance-asserting wolves try to literally look big. They stand erect, sometimes astride the animal they are attempting to impress, they raise their tails, they stiffen their hackles. Submissive or fearful dogs try to look small by crouching low, sometimes even dragging themselves along the ground. It is important to realize that this does not mean that the big-looking wolf is conscious of how big he looks, nor that any other wolf is fooled into thinking he really is big. Again, these are rituals. But they ultimately derive from the fact that wolves have been wired to react in ways that make these rituals effective.

A number of submissive displays in wolves and dogs derive from uniquely puppylike behaviors. Puppies do all of the submissive things that are related to trying to look small and nonthreatening, but they do a couple of additional, specialized things that reflect their unique needs. Wolf cubs beg for food from all adult members of the pack by licking them on the corners of the mouth. This stimulates the adults to regurgitate partially digested food, which the cubs rely upon as they begin to be weaned but before they are able to tackle real meat on the bone. Nursing puppies also display an instinctive tendency to "knead" their mother's udder with their paws, which stimulates the milk letdown response. Both of these behaviors have become highly ritualized as submissive displays that adult wolves put on when greeting the alpha male, and they are unquestionably why dogs greet their owners by licking their faces and by leaping up or lifting a paw to them. Adult wolves show what is clearly a very strong, innate forbearance toward the cubs of the pack. They refrain from biting back at the cubs even under grave provocation, even when the cubs fail to heed warnings and threats. The ritualization of puppy-like food-begging gestures into a more general submissive signal exploits this hardwired predisposition to put up with a lot of crap from the younger generation.

The point is that signals are more likely to be adopted if they take advantage of a preexisting sensory or behavioral bias. Some signals, to be sure, are fairly arbitrary, and may reflect a certain degree of coincidence in their evolutionary history. While many species show visual signals that are based on perceptions of size or vestigial threatening motions, something like the dog's tail wagging does not seem to follow any obvious or general principle. But it is not completely arbitrary. It is certainly an attention-getting motion, which may in part explain its origin, and the height of the tail as it is wagged still conforms well to the general rules that relate tail carriage with motivation: held high and waved it is a dominant gesture, low it is submissive, and at medium height a general expression of friendly greeting.

The "play-bow" is another dog-unique signal. Dogs (and wolves) that want to engage another in play will bow down with the front paws outstretched, and this is universally understood to signify that what follows is not to be taken seriously. It is clearly derived from the submissive crouch, yet it is much more specific in the precise way it is executed and in the "meaning" it implies. During the actual play that follows, both dogs often engage in dominant and submissive gestures regardless of their actual dominance status. A more dominant dog may roll over on his back as a way of inviting the more subordinate dog to playfully "attack" him.

Finally, some signals may simply reflect in their origins nothing more than flukes in the mechanical assembly of nerves and muscles. People who are nervous will clear their throats or blink their eyes or exhibit facial tics or shudder; these have nothing whatever to do with the predispositions of "receivers" to read such signals (though it does not prevent them from observing and drawing deductions). Wolves and dogs when nervous or very submissive retract the corners of their lips, pulling their mouths into a shape that often looks to us like a "smile." (It can even result in the teeth showing, which can be confusing; but the dog "smile" is invariably accompanied by other submissive visual signals, such as flattened ears or a bowed neck. The fang-baring threat involves lifting the forelip to expose the canine teeth, which does not happen in the "smile.") But if receivers come to correctly interpret even such automatic, nervous reflexes as indicative of an underlying emotional state or intention, there is nothing to prevent its becoming a useful and even ritualized signal.

Some dogs, by the way, are inveterate smilers. Because it is a naturally submissive gesture, it is one that is easily reinforced in dogs by their human owners, and can come to be used far more frequently, and in far milder situations, than it is in wolves. The most avid canine smilers may be dogs that are not only good and submissive, but whose owners are also unconsciously rewarding them when they smile with petting and attention, precisely because they find it an appealing facial expression. Likewise, many of the common things that we find easy to teach dogs (shake hands, lie down, roll over), and even some less common tricks like crawling along on the belly, are all instinctive submissive signals in dogs. Dogs come ready-wired to do these things. It's not hard to subvert these behaviors to slightly different ends from the ones they were originally designed for.

For a signal to evolve at all, sender and receiver must both derive some direct personal advantage from the exchange. The advantage to each may, however, be very different. The receiver aims to "read the mind" of the sender; the sender aims to manipulate the behavior of the receiver. And that means that bluffing is well within the possibilities of the game. There is no doubt that a wolf or dog that acts cool and confident can assume a position in the social hierarchy he could never defend if it came to pure brute force. This is a phenomenon not unheard-of in human society, either; a swagger works wonders, and sometimes indeed the apparent threat of violence is even more potent a persuader than violence itself. Game theory suggests that any system that permits bluffing guarantees bluffing, for the simple reason that someone who calls a bluff is always taking a chance that it is not a bluff, and will get walloped. As long as signals are *usually* honest, a certain amount of bluffing will always piggyback on that honesty. And as any poker player will tell you, someone who never bluffs is as likely to come out a loser as someone who always bluffs. If you watch dogs interacting, you will see that they often will ignore even rather elaborate lip curls from another, yet at other times give way to much more subtle threats. A certain amount of probing and testing is probably going on all the time. Visual signals are only a first approximation of the truth.

SOUNDING OFF

Dogs, as Erik Zimen found in his wolf and poodle studies, have a more limited repertoire of visual signals than do their wild forebears. This is no doubt in part because dogs are generally less concerned about the social hierarchy, which most of the wolf's visual signals are very directly aimed at; it is in part because of the physical differences that simply make it impossible for dogs—some breeds more than others—to pull the faces that wolves do.

By way of compensation, dogs appear to be much more vocal than wolves. (This is especially true when it comes to the bark—about which more later—which the dog has made uniquely its own.)

Just as with visual displays, the sounds that wolves and dogs make have the character and form they do for a reason. Some sounds are designed to conform to laws of acoustics, others to appeal to or exploit preexisting biases on the part of their intended recipients. Just as it is an age-old fact of life on Earth that big things are dangerous, it is equally true that big things make low noises. (Verification of this law of physics can be obtained by reference to any handy tuba or string bass.) Probably nearly all mammals and birds have an innate grasp of this fact, a useful survival skill in a world full of big things that eat smaller things.

So just as a threatening animal may try to look big by standing erect and raising its hackles, it can also get the job done by sounding big—that is, by using a low-pitched sound. Likewise, a submissive animal can try to sound small, using a high-pitched sound. Note that none of this implies conscious intent to convey information; it does not even imply that the animal making these noises is aware that he is conveying information at all. All that it requires is that it produces results. And that it does, for the simple reason that animals are predisposed to interpret big sounds as threatening and small sounds as nonthreatening, and to react accordingly.

This relationship between pitch and motivation is so innate a part of the mammalian and avian vocal communication package that it is as near a universal law of communication as one can find. Species from the chickadee to the hawk, the pocket mouse to the wombat, all follow this same rule. Humans do so as well, usually quite unconsciously. Although the sounds of words themselves are unrelated to meaning, we instinctively adjust our tone of voice to convey friendly, neutral, or hostile intent. A threat uttered in a squeaky falsetto just doesn't carry much conviction. On the other hand, if you listen carefully to yourself the next time you talk to a baby, you will find not only that you are saying the most idiotic things (which you probably knew already) but also that you have automatically adopted a tone of voice that resembles Tiny Tim far more than Clint Eastwood.

Dogs follow these conventions so faithfully that they could be the prototype that all other species follow. A growl is a low, harsh tone that clearly conveys a threat. A whine is a high-pitched tonal sound that conveys appeasement or submission. We don't usually think of birds, kangaroo rats, or wombats growling and whining, yet it is uncanny how much like a dog's growl and whine many bird calls sound if you record them and play them back at half speed.

Some researchers who have been particularly eager to impute humanlike cognitive abilities to other animals have clung tenaciously to the idea that animal sounds are true analogies of human language, cooperative projects in semantic information transfer. They have ridiculed skeptics by suggesting that the only alternative to the "knowledge is good" theory of animal communication, which they advocate, is what they call the "groans of pain" school: animal sounds are nothing but involuntary blurps that escape unbidden. But the evolutionary approach that seeks to explain the self-interested purpose behind animal signals implies something far more sophisticated at work than groans of pain, even if it is far short of semantic information-sharing. Eugene Morton, a researcher at the National Zoo in Washington, D.C., who made an extensive survey of animal sounds in many species, and who first noted the universality of growls and whines, has argued that the important thing is to ask not what sounds mean but rather what they *accomplish*. Growls and whines undeniably reflect underlying motivation, but the real reason dogs growl is because growls work: the growlee often backs off as a direct result. Dogs whine because whiners get walloped less often.

Whines and growls vary in intensity and pitch, and it is usually not difficult to see a correlation between the urgency of the motivation and the pitch of the signal. Whines shade into whimpers, growls into snarls, as urgency grows. Not surprisingly, dogs and wolves use whines and growls, and all variants thereof, under many different circumstances. Wolf cubs whimper when they are hungry or are seeking attention. Mothers use much the same sound to call cubs back to the den. Males whine to solicit sexually receptive females. Dogs of all ages whine when threatened by a social superior. Trying to assign semantic meanings to different shades of tone is not only futile but wrongheaded. A particular kind of whine does not mean "Feed me" or "I'm lonely" or "Come home" or "Hubba hubba." A whine is used *whenever* the aim is to signal a nonthreatening status and to seek the nonviolent approach of a social partner. A growl is likewise used whenever the aim is to get another to back off. This is why calling your dog in a high-pitched voice, and telling him to lie down (or saying "No") in a low-pitched voice, is much more effective than the opposite.

At times a whine can take on the rough and strident quality of a growl even as it rises in pitch and becomes something like a shrill squeal. This usually happens when a dog is extremely fearful and may be about to bite in fear. It is in effect a superposition of the two extremes of emotion.

The one dog and wolf sound that does not lie on this spectrum of motivation is the howl. Howls are long, melodious sounds that sweep through many different pitches. As such they don't fit into the growl-and-whine scheme very logically. But that is because their pitch qualities have more to do with environmental acoustics than with innate size judgments. Sounds that travel long distances must run a gauntlet of sound-absorbing obstacles, particularly trees and their leaves. Different kinds of trees absorb different pitches. A sound that sweeps the sound spectrum thus has a better chance of getting through under differing environmental conditions than does a sound confined to a single pitch. Wolves howl under many different circumstances, but always when the aim is to communicate across large distances. They will frequently howl when separated from the rest of the pack and trying to keep, or reestablish, contact. Howls are individually recognizable; indeed even human researchers can often track individual wolves by their howls, and even do a census of the local wolf population by counting the number of distinctly recognizable howls. The sound of one wolf howling frequently triggers a responding howl, and wolves are more likely to howl when near the edge of their territory. Again, just as with whines and growls, howls are used in many different "semantic" contexts. A howl might seem to mean "Over here guys" or "Where are you?" or "Keep out" or "Come here"; in fact the howl is used whenever there is a desire to establish one's presence over a long distance. That may equally be to locate one's own pack members and to deter an encroachment by members of a rival pack.

Compared to wolves, dogs are not great howlers. Some dogs never howl, and some, often to the great perplexity of their owners, howl only in response to the fire whistle or Aunt Bertha singing along with the piano. All sorts of ridiculous theories have made their way into dog books to explain this (including the absurd but apparently widely believed suggestion that dogs howl in pain because their ears hurt when they hear a loud noise). The simpler and more obvious explanation is that this is a largely vestigial behavior that has carried over from wolves. Howl-like sounds in the distance evoke howls in response. If the dog thinks anything about the fire engine siren, he thinks it is another dog announcing his location.

The dog that howls at Aunt Bertha may be performing a slightly different piece of vestigial wolf behavior. For reasons that still remain unclear, wolves within a pack regularly engage in a group chorus. This usually happens in the wild when the wolves begin to stir in the morning or evening, in conjunction with a sort of "group greeting ceremony" in which the younger and more subordinate wolves dash about and lick the older, dominant wolves on the face. Then one wolf starts to howl, and pretty soon all join in. Although this is frequently written about in popular books about wolves as a prelude to departure for the hunt (and is not infrequently described in rather mystical overtones), Erik Zimen observed it to take place at other times as well; the common factor was that it always occurred just after the wolves had awoken from sleep. Zimen has suggested that it serves somehow to reinforce the cohesion of the pack. In other words, Aunt Bertha can take heart that the household dog views her as a member of the family.

But in dogs, howling usually goes unreinforced, which may be one reason dogs don't do it very much. When a dog howls and gets no reply in return it must get discouraging. The urgency of purpose behind the wolf's howl is lacking as well in the less cohesive and less territorial dog world.

THE EVER-USEFUL BARK

Wolf cubs bark, but adult wolves and coyotes do so only very rarely. One study of thousands of vocalizations by captive wolves found that only about 2.5 percent were barks. Wolf barks tend to be single woofs followed by long pauses.

Dogs bark at the drop of a hat. They bark repeatedly. And they bark under circumstances in which wolves never do, such as while playing. Ray Coppinger once monitored a livestock guard dog barking for seven hours without a break. The Bar Harbor researchers found that there were substantial breed differences in the propensity to bark and in the number of barks emitted per session, and that both of these traits were clearly inherited, though probably independently. The record barker was one cocker spaniel that emitted 907 barks in ten minutes, or more than 90 a minute. Basenjis were much lower on both scores, Shetland sheepdogs and fox terriers fell halfway between the two extremes, and beagles were as likely as cockers to bark, but not to emit so many repeated barks at one time.

Barks are acoustically almost precisely halfway between

growls and whines, in both pitch and structure. Whines are high-pitched and pure toned, rising slightly then falling quickly. Growls are low-pitched and acoustically rough and noisy, a blend of many different pitches. Barks are medium-pitched and somewhat noisy, while having a definite pitch that rises and falls.

In function, Eugene Morton found in his cross-species survey of the animal vocal world, barks are also perfectly poised between the extremes of aggression and appeasement. Wolves, like many other species, use barks as a deliberately ambiguous alert. A wolf will bark when it spots something and is not yet certain how to react to it. It is in effect a temporizing move; it is a way to let whatever is out there know that it has been seen and to announce one's own presence without committing oneself. It is the functional equivalent of the sentry's "Who goes there?" Committing oneself prematurely with a growl at something that it's not smart to be growling at can lead to big trouble; sentries with itchy trigger fingers are only a menace. Likewise, whining in the face of the unknown is the equally bad strategy of preemptive surrender.

Barks, such as the wolf's woof or the chickadee's chirp, often serve to recruit the vigilance of fellow members of the group. The bark is an easy sound to locate in space, and by emitting a woof in response to some suspicious sound or movement, a wolf gains the advantage of having many other eyes and ears focused on a possible danger. The pack members who so respond to a woof each gain as well, by being placed on the alert. Barks and their kindred sounds have thus frequently been cataloged by animal behaviorists of the old school as "alarm calls." But many birds' so-called food calls and contact calls are, acoustically speaking, barks as well. Thus it might be better simply to call them "alerts," which can signify many different things. As usual, the cartoonist Gary Larson has provided the best summary of the matter. One of his cartoons shows a bearded, lab-coat-clad figure walking down a suburban street wearing a helmet bristling with electronic doodads. The caption reads, "Donning his new canine decoder, Professor Schwartzman becomes the first human being on Earth to hear what barking dogs are actually saying." In the background are dogs chasing cars, dogs sitting in their front yards, dogs following the professor down the street, while out of their mouths emerge the decoded words, "Hey!" "Hey! Hey!" "Heyyyyyyyyyyyy" "Hey! Hey! Hey! Hey! Hey! Hey! Hey! Hey!"

While many species have pressed the bark into service in multiple roles, dogs are the undisputed masters. Precisely because the bark is so content-neutral in its "meaning" on the aggression–appeasement scale, it can readily be used for any number of different functions. As the Bar Harbor researchers found when they crossed the barky cocker spaniels with the relatively mum basenjis, dogs have a strong genetically determined tendency to bark, period, which probably reflects the disruption of their adolescent development process: their barking proclivities resemble those of wolf cubs much more than those of adult wolves. Dogs bark when they are hungry or bored; they bark when they want to come into the house; they bark when they want to go out of the house; they bark when another dog has a bone; they bark when another dog barks; they bark when their Frisbee is out of reach on a shelf; they bark when their owner comes home; they bark when the UPS man drives down the driveway; they may even bark when a burglar tries to break into the house. The amount of energy dogs expend in barking is phenomenal, totally out of proportion to any benefit they can possibly derive from the activity, and that alone suggests that barking may not be so much a purposeful or consciously selected adaptation as something that just happened to tumble out (along with floppy ears and broken-colored coats and a certain amount of general goofiness) from the genetic mixup that took place when wolves became dogs.

But once barks became so readily available a part of the dog's vocal repertoire, there was nothing to prevent dogs from putting them to good use from time to time, even if dogs often bark for no real reason at all. Because barks do not come with any loaded significance, dogs are not constrained by social rules in applying barks to novel circumstances. And that is no doubt why it is so incredibly easy to teach dogs, consciously on our part or not, to use barks to "mean" specific things. Dogs readily learn that barks in certain contexts lead to certain rewards, such as food, or going for a walk, or getting their Frisbee. It is extremely easy to teach a dog to "speak" on command. It is by the same token extremely hard to teach dogs to shut up if they have not been trained to do so from a very early age. (Many dog trainers wisely recommend that dogs be taught in puppyhood a command such as "Quiet" and rewarded with a biscuit only when they are quiet for a set length of time that is gradually increased.) Owners who try to get their incessantly barking dogs to shut up often end up inadvertently rewarding their dogs, not merely for barking but for barking incessantly. This happens, typically, when the owners ignore the dog out on the front porch through fifteen minutes of barking and then finally, not being able to take it anymore, let the dog in. The dog learns from this that the longer he barks, the more likely he is to get the desired reward. Dogs that bark at mailmen are also a classic product of unintentional reinforcement. For they in fact have been repeatedly rewarded for this behavior. Every time a dog barks at the mailman who infringes on what the dog imagines to be his territory, the mailman subsequently buggers off; mission accomplished. Because dogs so freely apply barks to novel situations, they can convince themselves that their barking does all sorts of wonders, and so keep inventing new reasons to do it. The barking Shetland sheepdog who would be set off by toothbrushing or toilet flushing was admittedly an extreme case, but many dogs are adept at drawing what are to us bizarre connections between their barking and the events that ensue. One of my dogs, a Border collie, managed to identify the following sequence of events which he now executes his role in faithfully:

> person starts speaking on phone and ignoring dog →
> person's tone of voice changes in identifiable pattern it assumes toward end of call ("nice talking to you" "see you later") →
> dog starts barking →
> person hangs up phone and pays attention to dog once again

Dogs are indeed masterfully superstitious at drawing connections between the things they do and the things that happen, rather like the man in the tale who tore up little pieces of paper and threw them on the ground to keep elephants away ("Well, do you see any elephants around here?"). If you spend a lot of time barking, there are a lot of things that happen to happen while you're barking.

It is intriguing from an evolutionary perspective to note that, like barks, words in human language are by their very construction acoustically neutral on the emotional growl-to-whine spectrum. Almost universally, words in human language are well-mixed blends of percussive consonants and tonal vowels. (Recent studies have shown that consonants and vowels in speech are actually processed in separate parts of the brain, perhaps reflecting this fundamental and ancient distinction between growl-like sounds and whinelike sounds.) But when these two types of sounds are combined, the emotional import inherent in sounds is temporarily neutralized, as it were. Perhaps only by thus freeing sounds of any inherent emotional baggage could language begin to evolve as a semantic system: if every time you said "eggplant" or "aardvark" someone either punched you in the nose or cowered, communication wouldn't have gotten very far. The bark is not a word, but maybe it is a sort of proto-word, or proto-proto-word.

WORDS

Trained dogs can easily distinguish dozens of different words of human speech. It is always a temptation to believe that they actually understand what these words mean, yet given the nonsemantic nature of their own communication system, the odds seem strongly against it. Dogs have come to associate certain sounds with certain actions, but those associations are often extremely dependent upon other contextual cues that we may not be aware of. One way to show this is to try giving a dog a familiar command over an intercom. Even a command that the dog is highly motivated to carry out is often ignored unless it is accompanied by some additional cues in our body language. One of my dogs knows probably thirty commands, including commands for herding (lie down, here, get back, walk up), obedience (sit, stay), "fun" activities (Frisbee), and directions (go to the house, go upstairs, get out of here, excuse me—this last when he is standing in the way of the door). Yet if I say "Excuse me" to him in some place other than a doorway, all I get is a blank stare. It is safe to say that none of these words conjures up an image of the object or action in the dog's mind the way it would for us. Indeed, for all of the many continuities that link humans with nonhuman animals, one of the great discontinuities is the way we use language. Human infants, almost as soon as they begin to learn the names of things, take a manifest pleasure in using the name for its own sake. They will point to an object and say what it is—not because they want it, but for no other reason than to share the pleasure of calling the attention of another human mind to it. Even language-trained animals, such as chimpanzees, that have been taught to create "sentences" with computer symbols or sign language expend something very close to 100 percent of their utterances on demands for food, toys, or attention. There is no evidence that they have an independent notion of the symbols as standing for concepts. They have, rather, learned to manipulate series of symbols to get results. Dogs have certainly learned to look at us, or come, when we speak their name, but there is not a scrap of evidence that they grasp the notion that their name is *their* name, in the sense that it stands for or represents them.

Given all that, however, it certainly seems odd that dogs can distinguish words in human language. Studies by Russian speech scientists found that dogs can readily be trained to distinguish the vowels *a* and *i* produced by an audio synthesizer; even when the base pitch of the vowels was changed, the dogs had no trouble telling the two apart. (The dogs were trained by their good Pavlovian handlers to raise their left paw when they heard *a*, the right paw when they heard *i*.) Dogs may often be confused by substitutions of one consonant for another—try saying "Fly clown" instead of "Lie down," and your dog will probably react exactly the same; and indeed a hundred years ago the pioneering comparative psychologist Lloyd Morgan observed, "When I said 'whiskey' to my fox-terrier, he would at once sit up and beg; not because his tastes were as depraved as his master's, but because the *isk* sound, common to both 'whiskey' and 'biscuit,' was what had for his ears the suggestive value." But the ability to distinguish vowels depends on rather precise analysis of the higher-pitched resonances that accompany their base pitch. Dogs do not utter vowels themselves; why should they be able to tell them apart when we say them?

The simple and general explanation for this happy circumstance is that ears are older than speech. Mammalian ears have been around for tens of millions of years, and the ears of all mammals have much in common. Human speech, however, has been around for only 100,000 years or so, and the human vocal tract is a unique and late development. Only humans possess the vocal apparatus needed to generate the sounds of speech. (Attempts to get even our closest relation the chimp to speak were a total failure.) Thus it is not surprising that as the human vocal tract evolved, it evolved in a direction to make sounds that ears, which had evolved for other purposes for a lot longer, were already attuned to pick up and discriminate. It is not that dog ears are attuned to speech; it is rather that speech is tuned to ears, and dog ears and people ears already had much in common for reasons that had nothing to do with listening to human language. For most of human history, there was no such thing as language.

One reason dogs and wolves may be particularly attuned to the subtleties of pitch that distinguish vowels, however, is that such subtleties play a key role in maternal recognition. When recordings were made of the sounds made by adults and cubs in wolf dens, it was found that the fundamental pitches of the whines the adults of the pack made to the cubs as they entered did not overlap with one another. Thus they were individually recognizable—at least to wolves with a good enough sense of pitch to tell them apart.

A second evolutionary factor may have helped to make canines, and for that matter all mammals, attuned to even more subtle pitch components of sounds—components that turn out to be particularly important in distinguishing one vowel sound from another. The difference between vowel sounds has to do largely with changes in the higher-pitched overtones that accompany the fundamental pitch that the larynx generates. The vocal tract in effect acts as a series of filters, selectively amplifying or muffling various of the overtones coming from the larynx. The result is a series of characteristic pitches. Studies have shown that the relative pitches of the first two of these resonances that emerge from the vocal tract (they are known to speech scientists as "formants") are the most important in establishing the recognizable sound character of a particular vowel.

Formants also play a vital function in another sort of discrimination that is much older than speech. We have already encountered the physical law that big things make low sounds. But that of course is true only up to a point, as the growls and whines that emanate from a single animal themselves prove. A husky guy can talk in a falsetto. It is harder for a woman, or a field mouse, to make a low-pitched sound, but still there is a great deal of variation in pitch that the vocal apparatus of all mammals can produce: big things can fake it by sounding small, and vice versa. There are many individual variations in the shape of the vocal tract that can also affect pitch. But it turns out that animals cannot so easily cover up or alter one thing—the nature of the formants. An analysis of the relationship between the length of the vocal tract and the pitch of the resulting formants in dogs found that while individual quirks can cause changes in the pitch of any one formant, the *spacing* between formants is a very direct function of body size. The bigger the dog, the longer the vocal tract, and the narrower the spacing between formants. Thus being able to detect formant spacing would have been a way to cut through faking and individual vagaries to get an accurate fix on true underlying size of whoever was making that sound. Formant spacing is the basis of both size recognition and vowel recognition. Thus the reason dogs can tell the difference between vowel sounds at all—the reason they can so readily tell apart words like *sit* and *stay*—may ultimately lie in their ancestral skill at literally sizing up the creatures in their world.

LASTING IMPRESSIONS

Dogs have not, at this stage in their evolution, equaled man's feat of the invention of writing, but they have surpassed humans in the only other lasting communication medium widely available on Earth—communication by smell. Visual and vocal signals can offer a wealth of data about individual identity, location, and immediate emotional state and intentions, but they are fleeting. Smells exuded by individual dogs have a unique identity; they also persist in the environment for a considerable time. David Mech's study of scent marking by wolves found that they would respond to urine marks as much as twenty-three days old. It probably does not take a scientist to point this out, but he also noted that wolf scats were "powerful sources of odor." Scats were readily detectable, even by humans, from as much as thirty feet away even at temperatures of around 0° Fahrenheit.

Dog and wolf urine, as well as secretions of the odor glands between the paws and in the anal region, are individually recognizable. Male dogs that are sexually experienced are capable of telling the difference between the urine and vaginal secretions of females in heat from those not in heat. Because wolves react differently to urine marks of different ages, Mech concluded that they probably can extract useful information about how recently a mark was left as well.

Knowing who passed by, when, and whether it was a female in heat are all useful things for a dog or wolf to know about the world. They are things usually in the interests of the "sender" to advertise as well. Indeed, the trouble that wolves take to distribute their urine and feces clearly points to an adaptive purpose, for such action is definitely not universal in mammals. The bladder probably evolved in the first place as a way to conceal an otherwise telltale odor that might alert predators to one's presence. Instead of leaking urine out continually, animals with a bladder could store it up and get rid of it all in a conveniently out-of-the-way spot. Many species of mammals continue to follow this procedure; rhesus macaques, for example, typically empty their bladders upon wakening and then do not urinate again for seventeen hours. Wolves occasionally try to avoid sending an olfactory message with their eliminations: while members of a wolf pack usually defecate in prominent spots along trails, and especially at trail junctions, lone wolves frequently leave the path to defecate, presumably to evade detection. Dogs, who after all pretty much have nothing to hide, are not observed to adopt such behavior.

Scats, like urine, may be individually recognizable owing to the action of the anal sacs, a particularly odd pair of glands that often inject secretions onto scats as they pass. There is a small amount of evidence that the odor exuded by these glands may serve a more specific function, perhaps akin to the alarm and defensive purpose that the skunk has made famous. Some stalwart researchers who conducted an extensive study of the attractiveness that various bodily odors hold for dogs had the interesting experience a few times during their research of being hit directly in the face by a sudden discharge of anal sac secretions by a nervous dog. The anal sacs are a source of a certain amount of woe to owners of small dogs, as these breeds are particularly prone to blockages in the glands, which the dogs attempt to relieve by dragging their hind ends along the ground, and which the owners frequently have to attempt to relieve themselves by manually expressing their contents. As a colleague of mine who owns a Clumber spaniel once remarked, the only thing worse than unsuccessfully unblocking a Clumber spaniel's anal sacs is successfully unblocking a Clumber spaniel's anal sacs.

The ritual sniffing of rear ends that occurs when strange dogs meet is likely a way to match up individual smells with individual dogs, putting a name to a face, as it were, so that when either later meets up with a scent mark from the other, he will know whom it belongs to. As olfactory ignoramuses ourselves, we can only begin to appreciate the sagas that reside in canine by-products.

CHAPTER 5

Two Colors, a Million Smells

MAN IS A VISUAL ANIMAL, and has a hard time imagining any other way of being. We shut our eyes, and pictures of things from recent or distant pasts fill our minds; we dream, and our dreams are suffused with images, unreal though they may be, yet images surely; our very grasp of whos and wheres and whats, from the concrete to the most abstract, is a grasp of visual forms and relationships. A fragment of a melody or a whiff of a scent may evoke a memory, but these are not normally the stuff human memories are made of, nor the stuff of human understanding.

Yet dogs, like many other animals, inhabit a perceptual world where things are as likely to be understood and remembered by their smell as by their sight, where mental maps are assembled from avenues and topographies of odor, where the unseen is alive and vibrant and the seen is grayer and starker. If we could see through a dog's eyes we would be shocked and dismayed by what had happened to our most precious link with the world about us: detail lost, blurs that no amount of staring and focusing can alter, a world of washed-out hues and odd shifts of color. A dog would be equally appalled if he smelled through our nose.

But dogs are not merely Mr. Magoo with a big nose. To see through another's eyes or smell through another's nose, we would need not only a nose or eye transplant; we'd need a brain transplant as well. Anatomical studies of the dog's eye and ear and nasal lining can of course tell us something about the raw data he receives from his surroundings. Even before nerve signals reach the brain from the sensory organs, a lot of analysis has already taken place. Complex nerve cells in the light-sensitive retina at the back of the eye combine the pulses from individual light receptor cells to turn pixels into lines and shapes and motion. Nerves that line the membranes of the nose perform an exquisitely sensitive sorting of odor molecules by chemical shape.

But the real data-crunching that yields a final, fully formed perception takes place in the brain itself, and the vast differences between the amount of hardware devoted to different senses in different mammals makes it clear that there's more to smelling than a nose. A big nose doesn't just mean you smell a lot; it means you have a very different mind, too, one that inhabits a perceptual sphere that humans can only gropingly describe in words, never live and feel. Dogs and people don't see eye to eye, hear ear to ear, or smell nose to nose; all factors that explain at least in part why they don't always think mind to mind, either.

A DOG'S-EYE VIEW

Like tourists who assume everyone speaks English, or should, it is second nature to us to think that the world looks pretty much the same to all creatures, great and small. We rarely give much thought to the optical processes that turn light into vision; we assume that our visual version of reality *is* reality.

Even those of us who wear glasses fall into this way of thinking. Glasses bring things back into focus so they once again look like they are.

If those people who run around staging role-playing seminars on multiculturalism for business executives were to do the same for multispeciesism, I would suggest as the first group exercise they get everyone down on the floor with their eyeballs about six inches off the ground. Simply by virtue of visual perspective, the world looks very different to a Chihuahua.

Dogs also differ from humans in their ability to focus on near objects, to perceive and distinguish detail, and to see contrasts between light and dark. Some of these differences are relatively minor, but some must result in a highly altered version of reality. The most remarkable feature of the human eye is its extraordinary power of "accommodation." The lens in a normal eye, when relaxed, is of just the right thickness and curvature to bend incoming light rays from a far distance (equivalent to the setting of "infinity" on a camera lens) so that they converge in sharp focus upon the retina at the back of the eye. If the lens were incapable of adjustment, the light rays from close objects would end up converging at an imaginary point well behind the retina; the result would be a grossly blurred image striking the light-sensitive cells of the retina. But by squeezing the lens with muscles that are under unconscious control, we can make the lens thicker and alter its curvature, bringing close objects into proper focus. The greater the squeeze, the closer to our face is the focus. In young children, the eye's lens is capable of adjusting by as much as 14 diopters, an optical unit used in describing the power of lenses (and in prescribing eyeglasses). That degree of accommodation corresponds to being able to focus on everything from infinity to an object less than three inches away. By way of comparison, eyeglasses with a power of 14 diopters would look like the proverbial Coke bottle bottoms. (Most glasses for correcting nearsightedness in humans run about 1 to 5 diopters.)

Dogs have a much more limited power of accommodation, generally not more than 2 or 3 diopters, which means they can focus on close objects only if they are no nearer than a foot or two. Anything closer than that will unavoidably be a blur. That may well explain why dogs generally try to sniff or touch objects at close range: they simply cannot see them very well.

If the relaxed lens normally brings a distant object's image into focus behind the retina, the result is hyperopia or farsightedness. Accommodation can generally make up for the misfocus, but that means a corresponding loss of close vision. If the relaxed lens brings a distant object into focus in front of the retina, the result is myopia or nearsightedness, and in that case distant objects will always be blurry without the use of corrective lenses, as accommodation can only move an image forward, not back, relative to the retina. Optical measurements of dogs' eyes have found a surprising incidence of myopia in some breeds. A study of about two hundred dogs by veterinarian Christopher J. Murphy and his colleagues found the average canine refractive error to be pretty close to normal (within a quarter of a diopter of perfect, an amount that would not provoke any person to get glasses). Several breeds of sporting dogs, such as Chesapeake Bay retrievers, golden retrievers, Labrador retrievers, cocker spaniels, and springer spaniels, were on average a bit farsighted. But two-thirds of rottweilers and half of German shepherds and miniature schnauzers in this study were significantly myopic, by more than 1.5 diopters. The myopic rottweilers were close to 3 diopters nearsighted on average. Generally, people who have more than about 0.75 diopters of nearsightedness will complain of noticeable impairment and find they need to wear glasses or contact lenses to function in everyday life.

The animals in this study population were all pets. Interestingly, when Murphy and his coworkers looked at a second population of German shepherds—animals kenneled at Guide Dogs for the Blind in San Rafael, California—they found that the guide dogs had average normal vision, with fewer than a third showing even as much as 0.5 diopters of nearsightedness. The guide dog program did not specifically test dogs' vision in selecting animals, but they did flunk out any dogs that failed to perform well in training, which suggests that myopia results in a real impairment in getting the job done. The average farsightedness of sporting dog breeds suggests that there has likewise been selection at work in these breeds—that good distance vision has a demonstrable effect on making a good working dog. The researchers noted a tendency for severe nearsightedness to run in families, which suggests a strongly inherited component. In breeds that are not expected to perform anything more demanding than lying on the carpet, walking on a leash, and finding their supper bowl, there has no doubt been little selection for good vision, which has allowed myopia to sneak into the gene pool.

There are distinct breed differences in peripheral vision and overall field of view as well. Human eyes look straight ahead, giving us just about a 180-degree field of view, but with a lot of overlap between left and right eyes. Animals can see in true 3-D vision only when they use both eyes together, and the overlap in the human visual field thus maximizes the region in which we can perceive depth by using this binocular vision. The eyes of dogs are turned a bit to the side, which allows them to see a bit to the rear, with a wider overall field of

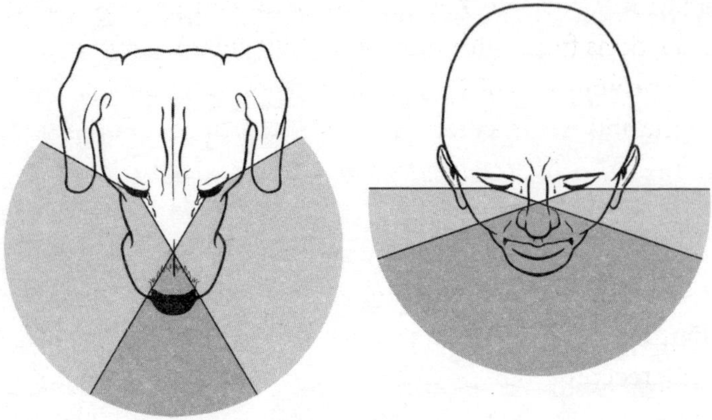

Dogs have a wider field of view than humans do, but the range of overlap of the two eyes is smaller, limiting three-dimensional vision to a narrower sector.

view—though at the cost of a smaller region of binocular vision. Short-faced breeds have more sideways-looking eyes, long-nosed breeds more forward-looking eyes. But in long-nosed dogs the nose literally gets in the way, which cuts down the total field of view of each eye, as well as its overlap with the other eye; long-nosed dogs especially have a problem when they try to look with both eyes at anything below the horizontal plane of vision.

Dogs generally do just fine with their more limited 3-D vision. The times they really need to perceive depth accurately are when they are looking straight ahead at a single item of interest (rabbit, Frisbee, and so on), and that is well within the binocular field of view of almost all dogs. Studies on puppies have also shown that even with one eye covered they can pick up depth "cues" that allow them to make pretty accurate judgments about how far away an object is. Shadows, relative motion, relative size, and other such features of objects all convey depth information that the dog brain can process and draw deductions from, with or without binocular vision.

The ability to pick out detail at a distance depends in part on the ability to focus sharply, but it also depends on how fine-grained the light sensors in the retina are. In general, the more densely light-sensitive cells are packed into the retina, the greater the ability to resolve small details. It also matters how these cells are wired up. Dogs have excellent night vision, but one way they achieve that is by ganging multiple light receptor cells together and coupling them to a single ganglion, the nerve cell that transmits the resulting signal to the brain. The result is exactly analogous to what happens in high-speed camera film: each grain in the film is more sensitive to light, but each grain also covers a larger area, resulting in a coarser-grained image. In primates, one light receptor cell plugs into one ganglion. In carnivores, such as dogs, it is typical to find four light receptors converging on each ganglion. Overall, the density of ganglion cells in dogs is considerably lower than in humans, and the total number of nerve fibers running from the eye to the brain is about 170,000 in dogs, versus 1.2 million in people.

The highest density of ganglion cells is found along a horizontal streak that runs across the center of the retina; this is where an image from the distant, level horizon would fall when the eyes are looking straight ahead, precisely the situation in which picking out fine details is most needed. This visual streak is much less pronounced in many breeds of dogs compared to wolves, however. The visual streak in wolves has about 14,000 ganglion cells per square millimeter; some dogs equal that, but others have fewer than half as many.

There are several ways to measure the acuity of an animal's

vision; one method is to train the animal by presenting it with two cards, one containing alternating black and white stripes and the other a solid neutral gray, and rewarding it for picking the striped card. Once the animal does this reliably, it is then given a series of choices in which the stripes on the black-and-white card get narrower and narrower each time. When the stripes reach the point that they blur together in the eye into an undifferentiated gray, the animal's chance of picking the right answer falls to 50–50. A similar experiment has been performed by monitoring the animal's brain waves as it is shown increasing narrow striped patterns; when the blurring-together point is reached, the brain waves show a characteristic change. Normal humans can pick out a stripe that fills as little as one-sixteenth of a degree of arc in their visual field. Dogs cannot see anything narrower than about a sixteenth of a degree of arc, which corresponds to 20/75 vision: what a normal human can see at 75 feet, a dog would need to be 20 feet away to see. (The sharp-eyed bluejay, by comparison, has about 60/20 vision—it can see at 60 feet what a normal-sighted human needs to be 20 feet away to see.)

Dogs have made other trade-offs between sharp vision and night vision. Like many other primarily nocturnal animals, dogs possess an unusual layer of cells at the back of the retina known as the tapetum lucidum; these cells act like a literal mirror, reflecting incoming light back out through the retinal cells, giving them in effect another shot at detecting each incoming photon of light. But this process inevitably means further blurring, at least in dim light. (The tapetum is also why the eyes of dogs, cats, horses, deer, and many other animals glow so brightly yellow when caught in a flashlight or headlight beam. The "red-eye" in humans that is the bane of flash photographers results from the less intense reflection of light off the blood vessels at the rear of the retina.) There are some interesting hints that the tapetum may not be a completely passive mirror, and that its particular chemical composition may cause the color of incoming light to shift slightly as well. Blue light is absorbed by riboflavin molecules in the tapetum and then reemitted at a color closer to the center of the spectrum. These reemitted colors coincide with the wavelengths at which the eye's black-and-white receptor cells, known as "rods," are most sensitive. Thus the blue-black of the dark evening sky may well appear much brighter to a dog than to us; this would exaggerate the contrast between dark sky and dark objects on the ground.

Only a few studies have been made of how the dog's higher-level visual processing machinery puts together data from the retina to form a perception of shapes and motion. Studies in which dogs are trained to discriminate between shapes have found that they can rapidly learn to tell horizontal lines from vertical lines, but have a harder time with more complex geometries, such as upright and inverted triangles. Dogs are acutely sensitive to motion, however: in one test, a stationary object that dogs had to be within a quarter of a mile of to notice could be spotted in motion a half mile away.

CANINE COLOR BLINDNESS

Early studies of color vision concluded that with the exception of primates, most mammals, the dog included, could not perceive color at all. This is still an apparently widespread belief among dog owners. However, careful studies by Jay Neitz of Wisconsin Medical College and his colleagues have established definitively that dogs do possess color vision, albeit of a limited kind, similar to a form of color blindness in humans.

Humans are able to distinguish the full spectrum of colors in the rainbow because they have three different sets of color receptors in the retina, each with a peak sensitivity to a different wavelength of light. These three wavelengths correspond roughly to yellow, green, and blue. When light strikes the retina, the brain in effect compares the relative strength of the signal coming from each of these three types of receptor cells—known as "cones"—to obtain a precise fix on its wavelength. Light that stimulates the blue and green cones equally, for instance, is perceived as blue-green. The combined response of the yellow and green cones sorts out whether a color is red, orange, yellow, or green; red light, for example, would stimulate the relatively nearby yellow cone much more than the green cone, farther down the color spectrum.

Dogs, and in fact most nonprimate mammals, have only two kinds of cones. In the dog these cones have their peak response at wavelengths that correspond to the colors of yellowish green and violet. That means that while dogs can see both red–orange–yellow–green colors and blue–violet colors, and can tell that any of these colors *are* colors as opposed to white or gray, they cannot tell the colors apart within these two broad groupings. They cannot tell red from yellow or green; they cannot tell violet from blue. In other words, in contrast to the approximately one hundred distinct hues that humans can discriminate in laboratory tests, dogs can distinguish but two.

Intermediate colors in the dog's spectrum, those in a narrow band in the vicinity of bluish green, would not look like any color at all to a dog, but would rather be indistinguishable from white or various shades of gray, since these medium colors would stimulate both types of cones equally—just as does white light. This narrow colorless band in the middle of the spectrum is known as the neutral point, and it occurs only in animals that have only two kinds of cones.

Neitz was able to demonstrate color vision in dogs by training two greyhounds and a poodle to nose display panels on which colors were projected. The dogs were given a choice of three panels and were rewarded for nosing the one that looked different from the other two. It was a straightforward, if time-consuming task, to show that when all three panels were illuminated with white light, the dogs could usually tell when a specific colored light was added to one panel but not the other two. But when the colored light reached the vicinity of bluish green, the dog's ability to detect its presence plummeted quickly to the level of chance. And when two colored lights equally spaced on either side of the neutral point were blended together, the dogs also failed to distinguish that mix from white light.

A practical consequence of Neitz's findings is that many of the things we make for dogs are the wrong color. A bright red-orange dog toy stands out dramatically against the lawn to us, but to a dog its color is not readily distinguishable from the green of grass at all. A violet object would probably be a much better choice when the background is green. Trying to teach a dog to pick out different-colored objects is probably going to be a losing proposition when the colors are, say, red and yellow or orange and green. Likewise, it is probably impossible to train guide dogs to tell apart the red, yellow, and green colors of a stoplight on the basis of color alone.

Dogs, like most mammals, probably lack full color vision as a result of evolutionary pressures that go back tens of millions of years. When mammals first appeared at the end of the dinosaur age, Neitz points out, the only niches available were nocturnal ones. So the first mammals had a need above all for night vision. The cones that provide color vision are not, however, very responsive to dim light. The much more sensitive rod cells in the retina, by contrast, cannot discriminate colors at all. So the trade-off in the early mammals favored giving up some cone cells for more rod cells. The three-color vision in primates was apparently only "reinvented" much more recently as an adaptation to their special place in nature. Wolves, being essentially nocturnal, still gained more from having a preponderance of rod cells to boost night vision than they lost from having a lack of full-color vision. (They also appear to be able to distinguish shades of gray that are imperceptibly different to the human eye.) The two-color vision of wolves and dogs provides some insurance against being too easily fooled by camouflage, which would be the fate of an animal that could see only in black and white (black-and-white camouflage has only to match the overall brightness of the background, not color at all). But beyond that, it is safe to say, wolves lacked full-color vision for a simple biological reason: they simply didn't need it to get the job of being a wolf done.

SHARP EARS

Differences in hearing ability also strongly reflect adaptive need. The legendary ability of the dog to hear high pitches has been verified by laboratory tests. Dogs can hear sounds up to about 65,000 Hz, or cycles per second. A healthy teenage human being (or, to be more precise, one who has not already blasted his ears out listening to a Walkman at full volume) can hear sounds up to a maximum of about 20,000 Hz. To produce the top note a person can hear would require adding about twenty-eight extra keys at the right-hand end of the standard piano keyboard, or about two and a third octaves; to get to the top dog note would take forty-eight keys, or four full octaves.

Dogs do not themselves produce any sounds this high, but small rodents do, and thus their hearing range may reflect a predatory adaptation to finding high-pitched things to eat. Dogs, like most predators, also possess a fairly precise ability to tell the direction a sound is coming from. Humans can tell which of two possible sources a sound is coming from when they are separated by as little as 1 degree of arc. Horse, cows, and goats have trouble figuring this out even when the sound sources are separated by as much as 20 or 30 degrees. Dogs do well down to about 8 degrees of separation, on a par with cats, ferrets, opossums, sea lions, and monkeys. Sound localization is accomplished by a combination of acoustical physics and brain computation. In general, the brain calculates the answer by comparing the relative loudness of the sound reaching the left and right ears, or by measuring the time delay between the arrival of the very start of a sound at each ear. A big head helps, because it maximizes the distance between the ears, thus increasing the difference in arrival time and volume between left and right. But a lot clearly depends on the brain circuitry, as some very large animals such as the horse are very bad at sound localization, while relatively smaller-headed animals (notably man) are quite good at it. Dogs obviously came equipped with the more advanced circuitry needed to do this well. Careful measurements have shown that the sound localization ability of dogs corresponds to an ability to distinguish arrival times in the left and right ears of as little as 55 microseconds.

Dogs, and humans, possess another sort of sound localizer that relies completely on brain wiring. One difficult problem in sound localization is what to do about echoes. A sound coming from the right might bounce off a tree or a wall to the listener's left, creating a reflected sound wave that arrives at the ears from the opposite direction from the waves that arrive directly from the source. Human infants up to about age four months are confused by such echoes and are unable to tell where a sound is coming from when it is accompanied by reflected sounds. But older infants have no trouble turning toward the actual source of the sound even when there are reflected waves coming from a confusing direction. Studies have shown that the brain's circuits actually shut out the delayed signal of the echo: the brain in effect can recognize that this second signal, which arrives a millisecond or more later, is an echo, and actively suppress it from notice. Studies in dogs have shown that this ability to filter out reflected sounds appears during the course of development in puppies, too.

THE CALCULUS OF OLFACTION

Like the eye, the nose is both sensor and computer. The eye's retina is actually an extension of the brain; in computer terms, it is a networked PC, not just a dumb terminal. The primary nerve cells of the retina that respond to individual "pixels" of incoming light are wired to a series of more complex nerve cells—all still within the retina—that begin to do the job of making sense of more complex geometric patterns, like lines and shapes.

The nose is a networked PC, too. A large bundle of nerve cells known as the olfactory bulb rests directly above the mucous lining of the nose; its full-time job is processing the smell signals relayed by the primary receptor cells, whose long thin filaments extend directly into the mucous lining of the nose.

The olfactory bulb in the dog is dramatically larger than it is in man. The canine nose also has something like twenty times as many primary receptor cells as the human nose. How all of this works to detect odors is one of the great scientific wonders of the world. Studies in a number of species have found that different regions of the mucous lining within the nose have different chemical properties, more readily absorbing chemicals of one particular molecular shape or another, or preferentially absorbing in one region chemicals that are more water soluble and in another chemicals that are more fat soluble. The ability of the nose to make precise chemical distinctions is truly extraordinary. Some pairs of chemicals that exist in nature are identical in every way—they are made up of exactly the same elements, joined together in exactly the same three-dimensional sequence—except that one is the three-dimensional mirror image of the other. Yet such "stereoisomers" frequently have a dramatically different odor, indicating that the nose can sort them out by their complex shape alone. The molecule carvone, for example, has the odor of caraway in one of its stereoisomers, the odor of oil of spearmint in its mirror-image form.

Measurements of the acuity of the dog's nose suggest that the dog is many times more sensitive than man to the presence of minute quantities of odor molecules wafting in the air, but the data are all over the map. This is probably in part because the threshold for detecting different chemicals no doubt varies dramatically according to the particular chemical involved. Some comparative studies have found that dogs can detect certain organic chemicals at concentrations a hundred times less than people are able to; for other compounds the dog's edge may be a factor of a million or more. In police and security work, dogs can detect the odor from natural gas leaks, concealed narcotics, explosives, and currency, all at levels well below the threshold at which humans are aware of the odor. In controlled studies dogs could detect human scent on a glass slide that had been lightly fingerprinted and then left outdoors for as much as two weeks, or indoors for as much as a month; they could pick which of six identical steel tubes had been held in the hands of a person for no more than five seconds; they could distinguish between T-shirts worn by two identical twins who ate different foods, or by two nonidentical twins who lived in exactly the same environment and ate exactly the same foods.

More than such a remarkable sensitivity to trace odors, it is the ability to pick out particular odors of interest from a welter of competing smells and to match and distinguish them that is the dog's most impressive olfactory feat. This ability is surely a reflection of the dog's superior olfactory computing powers, for it requires not just smelling but analyzing. Dogs have no innate interest in the smell of people, narcotics, or hundred-dollar bills; but if trained repeatedly to focus on certain categories of smells, they can perform mind-boggling feats of cross-matching. In the twins and T-shirt experiments, the dogs were first trained by presenting them for fifteen seconds with a sample T-shirt doused with an artificial smell; they were then allowed to approach a small trough ten feet away and fetch whichever of the two shirts placed there matched the sample. The experimenters found that the dogs did better when the two T-shirts were placed fairly close together in the trough—a foot and a half from one another—which permitted the dogs to smell the two simultaneously. In the actual test the dogs were given as a sample a shirt worn by one of the twins for one twenty-four-hour period and had to pick from the trough the shirt worn by the same twin during another twenty-four-hour period.

With a lot of practice, dogs can perform the even more difficult task of matching the odor from one part of a person's body to another part—pants pockets to hands or crook of the elbow to hands. When presented a sample odor from a person and then given a choice of six different tubes, one of which had been rubbed on a different part of the body by the same person, trained dogs did significantly better than chance. But they made a lot of mistakes, too; the average performance for the elbow and hand cross-match was about 1 in 3 correct (versus 1 in 6 expected by chance). On the other hand, when the "suspect" was a person already known to the dog, the correct response rate shot up to 73 percent. Part of the difficulty dogs have with this task is that while person A's hands smell different from person B's hands, person A's elbow also smells different from person A's hands in some ways. At the same time, some odors are common to all humans. The dog is clearly capable of detecting and distinguishing all of these smells; the challenge is for the dog to learn which comparisons are the ones its seemingly fickle human handlers are interested in. They are not necessarily the comparisons of innate biological interest to the dog.

An extraordinary combination of sharpness of nose and olfactory computation is also involved in the amazing ability of dogs to find and follow tracks. A series of simple but brilliant experiments by Norwegian and Swedish scientists have provided some wonderful insight into how dogs perform this task, which probably seems the most incomprehensible to us of all their olfactory feats. The scientists were inspired in part by a thirteenth-century Icelandic saga that tells of two Norwegians who, attempting to elude their Swedish captors, tie reindeer hooves backward to the soles of their boots. Intercepting their trail, the Swedes' dogs follow in the wrong direction, ending up at the empty hole in a pigsty where the prisoners had been held. The scientists first tried the same ruse, having a person walk either forward or backward across pavement or grass. Twenty minutes later, a trained tracking dog and its handler, neither of whom knew which way the person had actually walked, were allowed to approach the midpoint of the track, and the dog was set to work. The dogs consistently were able to follow the trail in the actual direction the person walked, regardless of which way the toes and heels were pointing. So much for Icelandic sagas.

The dogs' performances were videotaped, and the dogs were also equipped with wireless microphones taped to their noses to record their sniffing. When the scientists reviewed the data, it was clear that the dogs had almost no trouble making up their minds which way to go; in fact they made virtually snap decisions. The dogs would sniff from two to at most five of the footprints, for a total of three to five seconds, then strike out in the correct direction almost every time. Further tests confirmed that, as incredible as it seems, the dogs were apparently able to determine which of the footprints had been left the most recently by the strength of its odor. The odors the nose is capable of detecting are all by definition volatile; that is, they are the product of chemicals that evaporate into the air and thus can be inhaled into the nose. Thus the older a track is, the more its volatile components have already evaporated, and the lower the concentration is that remains. The scientists found that the dogs could readily detect and follow the trail left by a bicycle, but were unable to determine its direction. But when they fastened leather strips around the rear tire of the bicycle, thus laying a trail more like footprints—discrete patches of scent at spaced intervals whenever the leather strips struck the ground—the dogs once again were able to determine direction of travel. Again, that supported the notion that the dog is making a direct comparison of relative strength, and thus relative age, of the odor from two or more adjacent prints. The continuous track of the bicycle provided too smooth a gradient of odor strength to allow such comparison. Finally, the researchers tried smearing sausage on the leather strips, the clever idea being to leave a scent track that would be an odor version of the Norwegian prisoners' false trail: as the sausage wore off, it would produce an increasingly weak scent. Thus the strongest smell would be at the start, the weakest at the finish—the opposite of what happens with a normal trail. Sure enough, the dogs were consistently fooled, and tracked the sausage-modified bicycle the wrong way.

Dogs generally find it impossible to determine the direction of a trail more than three hours old, even if they can still follow the trail. That suggests that the overall odor has faded to the point that the difference from one print to the next is just too small to discriminate. On a thirty-minute-old trail left by a person walking one stride per second, the relative age of two adjacent footprints differs by one second out of 1,800 seconds. Assuming smell fades at a constant rate, that means that the dog nose must be capable of detecting a difference in odor strength of at least a like ratio, one part in a couple of thousand. That boggles our minds, but by way of comparison, the human visual system is perfectly capable of similar feats of discrimination. If you hold two needles out at arm's length, one above the other, your eyes and brain can tell if one of the needles is a fraction of a millimeter closer to your eyes than the other. That is less than a part in a thousand. It is all a matter of what the brain is wired to do.

CHAPTER 6

If They're So Smart, How Come They Aren't Rich?

IN THE REFLEXIVE IMPORTANCE we attach to vision, we are, as I said, something akin to ugly American tourists venturing forth upon a tour of the animal world. But this is a genteel prejudice compared to our notions about intelligence. On the inflammatory issue of mental ability we are Father Coughlin, Senator Bilbo, and the Imperial Wizard of the Ku Klux Klan rolled into one. As is so often the case, it is those who profess to love the quaint locals who are the worst bigots.

Surveys of human attitudes toward the intelligence of animals reveal a remarkable consistency in the ranking of species. People of widely varying background and education agree that apes are the smartest, followed by dogs, cats, pigs, horses, cows, sheep, chickens, turkeys, and fish. Interestingly, for decades, both those who have tended to be skeptical about imputing humanlike intelligence to animals and those who have been extremely eager to do so have willingly played this ranking game. The classic experiments in animal intelligence in the early part of the twentieth century all involved putting rather abstract learning or problem-solving tasks to various animals and scoring their performance; after reading over many of these studies, one modern-day researcher mused that "it was almost an account of how one would select animal candidates for the British civil service."

A small but attention-getting cadre of other modern-day scientists who do research mainly on primates (TV is always a sucker for young women palling around with big hairy apes—television producers may not know much about cognitive science, but they have all seen *King Kong* and know a good story line when they see one) have taken a remarkably similar tack, drilling apes to construct things that look like sentences and to perform tasks that seem to resemble arithmetic calculations, and thereby drawing conclusions about how far above other species and how close to human beings chimpanzees or gorillas fall on this grand animal IQ scale.

The idea that intelligence is a quantifiable substance that the gods doled out in greater or lesser quantities to the various representatives of the animal kingdom suits too many human purposes to be easily gotten rid of. It certainly fits our notions of what human intelligence is all about. Quickness in catching on to new ideas or skills is, after all, what supposedly separates the kids who get into Yale (well, the ones whose last names are not Bush, anyway) from the rest of the pack. And certainly animals do differ dramatically in their ability to learn the things *we* want them to learn. Teaching a sheep to fetch the newspaper might just be within the realm of the possible, but is unlikely to prove a very happy experience along the way.

Yet just as human IQ tests have come under fire for being culturally biased, so many of these supposed measures of animal intellect may actually be measuring a lot of things besides innate brain power. The apes that perform all of those spectacular mental feats have been drilled for years in the lab and bribed with carloads of M&Ms along the way, and have learned, if nothing else, that whatever strange new things their telegenic female handlers ask of them are sure to be worth trying because the result is a handful of M&Ms at the end. They have had one heck of a Head Start program, in other words. Animal species differ dramatically in their ability to see and to use their hands; they differ dramatically in their fear of novelty or their willingness to explore; they differ even in how hard they're willing to work to get an M&M or a biscuit as a reward. We may think we're probing the depths of an animal's mind when all we're really probing is the depth of his stomach.

DOGS AS UNDERACHIEVERS

All animals are capable of learning, forging new mental associations that link events or actions on their part with other events. Indeed, virtually all animals *have* to be able to learn if they are to survive: learning is a way of dealing with the rather annoying fact of life that things change. Hardwired instincts can only go so far in preparing a wolf for a world where sources of food and water and shelter are always shifting, where potential rivals and mates come and go, where trees fall and block trails, where rivers freeze and thaw. Learning is a broad common denominator that links all species of mammals and birds, and a good many more as well (to name three: goldfish, earthworms, and squids).

Intelligence is such a complex and emotionally loaded matter that views on the subject have tended to be couched in extreme positions over time. The behaviorists, epitomized by the psychologist B. F. Skinner, viewed intelligent behavior (and indeed all behavior, human and animal alike) as the product solely of "operant conditioning"—an animal's learning to respond to stimuli that lead to a reward. The behaviorists completely discounted genetics as a significant factor and insisted that such learned responses accounted for essentially everything organisms did. In principle, one could thus teach any animal to do almost anything by applying an appropriate pattern of "reinforcement" to its behavior.

The first nagging doubts arose when two of Skinner's disciples, who had rationally concluded that there was good money to be made applying their mentor's scientific discoveries in the world outside of the laboratory, set up shop training performing animals for television commercials, fairs, zoos, and other public exhibitions. They were extremely successful, but, as they later wrote, "our backgrounds in behaviorism had not prepared us for the shock of some of our failures." One of their most interesting failures, they revealed, occurred when they tried to train raccoons to put coins into a piggy bank for a TV commercial. The raccoons had no trouble handling the coins, and were in dutiful Skinnerian fashion rewarded with food when they happened to drop them into the piggy bank. But instead of getting better at this task, the raccoons got worse and worse as the training went on. The raccoons began rubbing the coins and holding on to them. Their trainers were forced to conclude that the animals' innate food-washing instinct was such a powerful force that no amount of operant conditioning could overcome it.

A basic notion in traditional learning theory is that animals experience a "learning curve": as a test is repeated over and over and the animal is rewarded for a correct response and/or punished for an incorrect response, it tends to produce the correct response more and more often. Differences in the rate at which different species learn have then been taken by many scientists as evidence of differing degrees of innate mental capacity. For example, monkeys learned readily to pick one of two differently patterned cards to get a food reward, while rats learned this task much more slowly. But later someone had the wit to give the rats another chance; this time they were set the task of learning to choose one of two odors rather than one of two pictures, and with that small change in the experimental protocol the rats' score zoomed up to the monkeys' original level. In other words, the test had simply been biased. Rats smell very well but don't see well at all. Likewise, goldfish did rather poorly on a test in which they had to reverse a pattern they had already learned—the fish seemed to be very slow in catching on to a new reward pattern. But when the test was redesigned with a more stimulating reward (a food paste instead of fish pellets), the goldfish's performance shot up. It turns out it is rather hard to get a goldfish hungry enough to really want to do well.

These discoveries were symptomatic of a much more sweeping problem with all cross-species intelligence tests. *All* animals have the capacity to learn. They also have adapted over millions of years of separate evolution to *very* different, indeed unique, ecological niches. Each species has certain instinctive motor patterns; it has certain instinctive likes and dislikes; it has certain things that matter a great deal to itself and certain things that don't. Primate researchers make much of the fact that in some controlled laboratory experiments apes such as chimpanzees can learn the correct answer to a problem on the basis of a single experience. Well, dogs can, too, if it is a single instance of something that really matters to them. They can also find it well nigh impossible to learn things that require them to go against a basic behavioral inclination, whatever the reward.

An illustration: In his classic book on training Border collies, *The Farmer's Dog*, John Holmes tells of a dog who, running through an open gate, collided head on with another dog. It was an accident. But forever after, the dog would never go through that particular gate if that particular other dog was nearby. In classical learning-theory terms, this is a rather sophisticated "conditional" task of a kind that primates are supposed to be adept at mastering, and "lower" animals such as canines less so. (In a conditional task, an animal must learn a rule that specifies one choice under one condition and the opposite choice under different conditions; for example, pick the triangle and not the square when they are red, but the square and not the triangle when they are blue.) But here was a case of a dog learning on one go. Logically, there is no difference between the gate/no-gate dog/no-dog problem and the square/triangle red/blue problem. Yet the first is charged with a canine psychological significance that is absent in the latter: Dogs are intensely attuned to social interactions, and being collided with by another dog—probably a dog that occupied a dominant position in the social hierarchy—made a lasting impression that colored blocks would never have.

Interestingly, humans are not immune to this phenomenon either. There is a whole class of problems that consist of pairs of logically identical puzzles, one of which we grasp the answer to immediately, the other which tends to stump even intelligent people. The "easy" version is always one in which the problem is posed in terms of rules of social conduct; the "hard" version is posed in terms of abstract relationships. The classic example, which you can try on your friends, goes like this: (hard version) Four playing cards are lying on the table, and you are supplied the following information about them. Card one is a club. Card two is a queen. Card three is a diamond. Card four is a seven. What additional information do you need to determine whether the following rule is being obeyed: All red cards must be ten or less? (easy version) There are four people sitting at a bar. One is an elderly man. The second is drinking a beer. The third is a young boy. The fourth is drinking a ginger ale. What additional information do you need to determine whether the following rule is being obeyed: No one under age twenty-one may have an alcoholic beverage? Many people when presented the hard version of the problem incorrectly answer that one needs to know what color the seven is, or miss the fact that one needs to know what color the queen is. Few people have the slightest difficulty with the logically identical, easy version of the problem—correctly concluding that one needs to know only the age of the beer drinker and the beverage of the boy.

If it is easy to teach dogs (and people) rules that have social implications, it can be extremely hard to teach them rules that require that the social variables be ignored, or that go against other basic adaptations to their special environmental niche. Trying to teach a dog not to dig in the garden by yelling at him whenever he does so almost invariably succeeds in teaching the dog the following rule: Do not dig in the garden whenever a person (or one particular person) is present. Likewise, trying to teach a dog to perform certain highly instinctive behaviors such as yawning or scratching to obtain a reward is essentially impossible. (People have actually tried.)

It has also been shown that many animals whose ecological niche involves foraging among patchy and ever-changing food resources are instinctively slow learners for a very good biological reason. It doesn't make for a good foraging strategy to be either too fixed in one's ways or too quick to drop old habits, unless the evidence is really compelling that an old source of food has dried up once and for all and a new source of food is providing a consistent bounty. If you teach a dog to find food in one spot and then subsequently teach him that the food is in another spot, the dog will not shake his earlier belief entirely. If later on you retest him, giving him a free choice of where to look for the food, he will split his choice about 50–50 between the two possible spots. That is an efficient strategy in a world of fluctuating gifts; just because food or water was available at one place yesterday doesn't mean it will be there tomorrow. From our point of view, we may think a dog is being terribly slow to learn to perform some behavior like coming to the door reliably when called, even when he gets a dog biscuit as a reward. But if a dog has earlier learned that not coming to the door has its rewards, too (a chance to chase the squirrels, perhaps), he is bound to take that into account—to split the odds, as it were. It makes sense to drop one sometimes-rewarded choice entirely only if repeated evidence shows that another choice is consistently better.

So attempts at measuring the "pure" intelligence of an animal run into much the same problems as human IQ testing, only a lot more so. Even if one can filter out all of the sensory biases, one is left with huge social, psychological, and ecological biases. These biases can be extremely subtle yet extremely surprising in the huge effect they have on the outcome of tests. For example, dogs do not do well at all on a so-called delayed non-matching to sample (DNMS) test. In this test, the dogs are first presented the "sample": a tray holding, say, a blue Lego block in the middle. The dog gets to push the Lego block out of the way with his nose and eat a piece of hamburger hidden underneath. Then after a delay of ten seconds, he is presented the tray again. This time the blue Lego block is on one side and a novel object (such as a yellow coffee can lid) on the other. The dog's task is to learn that the reward is *always* hidden under the object that was *not* presented as the original sample. Dogs typically take a very long time to master this—it is not at all unusual for them to require several hundred trials before they get to the point that they will make nine out of ten correct choices in a row. And even after they have reached that point, they are almost always flummoxed if they are retested with a longer, variable delay (ten to fifty seconds) between the presentation of the sample and the choice of objects. Even the best dogs in one study scored scarcely better than chance when thus retested.

Monkeys do quite well on this task, so it would be the most natural thing in the world to conclude, as most people think they already know, that monkeys are smarter than dogs. But when the experiment was tried again with a slight modification, the dogs breezed it. This modified task was spatial as opposed to strictly visual. For the sample, the dogs were presented the tray with a red Lego block placed either on the left side or the right side. Then the tray was returned with two identical red Lego blocks covering both the left and right food wells. The dogs had to learn to choose the block on the side opposite from where it had first appeared. They learned this considerably faster and with fewer mistakes than did the dogs in the first experiment; moreover, the ones that learned it had no trouble giving 90 percent correct answers even when the delay was increased to twenty seconds, and many dogs in the study (the younger ones) did almost as well even with a seventy-second delay.

The original visual DNMS experiment had been specifically tailored to take advantage of the curiosity monkeys show toward novel objects. It is possible that dogs had trouble with it because their vision is not as acute; it is also possible that

In the delayed non-matching to sample (DNMS) test, a dog is first presented a "sample" object . . .

. . . and is allowed to nose it aside to obtain a food reward.

The dog is then given a choice between two objects . . .

. . . and must learn that the food is always hidden beneath the object that is not the previously presented sample.

they simply lack the monkeys' curiosity—and, on the contrary, may even be wary of novel objects, a problem that was avoided in the spatial DNMS experiment by presenting the same old red Lego block each time. In fact, one dog in the original visual DNMS study had to be dropped from the test because he showed an obvious fear of approaching the new objects that appeared in each subsequent trial.

So the moral of the story is that given the chance, dogs can be every bit as smart as monkeys, and sometimes even every bit as smart as chimpanzees. But asking them to do things that go beyond their ability to see, or that go against their instinctive natures, is guaranteed to make them into underachievers.

Another way we are often guilty of underestimating canine intelligence is with our tendency to be dismissive of anything that is instinctual. We tend to equate such behaviors with what wind-up toys do and sometimes don't even think of it as intelligence at all. But many highly instinctual behaviors in dogs, and other animals, nonetheless draw upon considerable computing power in their execution. A wolf when he is hunting exhibits a highly stereotyped sequence of behaviors; yet each has to be executed with split-second feedback from the sense organs to adjust to the motions of the prey, the terrain, the behavior of other members of the pack. Making a moose-hunting robot would be far from a trivial task; in fact it would probably prove much harder than building a computer that can beat the human world chess champion. Even making a four-legged robot that can run over rough terrain without falling flat on its face has proved enormously difficult. The amount of intelligence—that is, pure computational complexity—that goes on in the brain to coordinate the muscles involved in running with four legs is vast, and in many ways the dog's mental powers in these areas surely exceed our own.

MY DOG'S SMARTER THAN YOUR DOG

If trying to rank the relative intelligence of different species is a suspect exercise, then ranking the relative intelligence of breeds within a species is even more suspect. A trap we very easily fall into when assessing the intelligence of animals, dogs especially, is to rate as especially intelligent those particular animals that do the things we want them to. Working dogs such as Border collies and retrievers, breeds such as poodles and Shetland sheepdogs that do well in obedience trials, even dogs that are good at playing Frisbee, are all routinely accounted as "smart" in casual judgments. Dogs like basset hounds or St. Bernards that are relatively unreactive are deemed to be more than a bit on the slow side. The veterinarian Benjamin Hart carried out an extensive survey of veterinarians and other dog experts and ranked one hundred breeds on a variety of behavioral characteristics, including ease of housebreaking and ease of obedience training, and the findings probably wouldn't surprise very many people. The dogs most people would think of as smart—Shelties, German shepherds, Dobermans, poodles, Labradors—came in at the top of the obedience and housebreaking rankings. At the bottom were foxhounds, beagles, and Afghan hounds. A similar, though statistically far less rigorous, survey of obedience judges in Canada and the United States by the psychologist Stanley Coren came up with similar rankings. Coren went further, though, and explicitly claimed that his list was a ranking of the actual intelligence of the various breeds.

In obedience trials dogs must walk at heel, sit and stay, lie down, and come when called; in more advanced competition they must fetch a dumbbell and jump over hurdles in response to hand signals. These are certainly fair tests of a dog's trainability—that is, whether we can get the dog to do what we want him to, in accordance to some narrow and highly arbitrary criteria. But is this really a test of intelligence at all? In his book *The Intelligence of Dogs*, Coren hedges his bets by devising all sorts of tests of all sorts of "intelligences," proposing that canine smarts is divided up into innate intelligence, adaptive intelligence, and obedience or working intelligence, and within each of these categories broken down further into "crystallized" intelligence and "fluid" intelligence. A "Canine IQ Test" he proposes is, I suppose, no more arbitrary than many human IQ tests, but that may not be saying much: your dog gets five points for immediately coming when called by his name and not coming when called in the same tone of voice by a different word ("language comprehension"), he gets three points if he notices that you've rearranged the living room furniture within thirty to sixty seconds of entering the room ("environmental learning"), he gets five points for wagging his tail and coming to you when you smile at him without saying anything ("social learning"), but only four points if he comes without wagging his tail, and so on and so forth. You then add up all of these points, rather like those quizzes in women's magazines ("Rate Your Sexual Confidence Quotient!"), to determine whether your dog is "brilliant," "superior," "borderline," or "deficient."

The variety of problems that dogs are asked to tackle in this test at least acknowledges that intelligence is not a one-dimensional trait, but none of this is scientifically very convincing. For one thing, it is the height of human self-centeredness to propose that there is such a thing as "obedience intelligence" in the first place; dogs hardly evolved to win obedience ribbons in dog shows. It is undeniable that breeds, and individuals within those breeds, vary dramatically in how quickly they will learn obedience commands or other tasks we set them. But many studies in dogs and other species have shown time and again that what we take for intelligence differences are almost always differences in motivation, temperament, alertness, and even basic sensory ability. There is good reason to doubt whether any of Coren's "Canine IQ" questions are measuring intelligence per se. How well dogs do on many of these problems will invariably reflect nothing but differences in training and routine that the dogs have been exposed to. True differences in intelligence might explain why some dogs notice that the living room furniture has been rearranged while others do not, but differences in a great many other things that have nothing whatever to do with intelligence are just as likely to be behind such behavioral differences.

How easy it is to confuse intelligence with more mundane qualities was first underscored a half century ago in studies on maze-learning rats. Strains of rats were selected and separately bred based on how well they did in learning their way around a maze. Over time, the researchers had a strain of smart rats and a strain of dumb rats. It was all very impressive, until one of the students on the project decided to retest the rats on different kinds of mazes. It turned out that the slow learners were actually not slow at all; they were simply afraid of the particular maze that had been used in the original experiments. Rather than breeding for intelligence, the researchers had bred for emotional reactivity and fear.

The overwhelming role that fear plays in determining learning ability in dogs was demonstrated in a classic experiment by the Bar Harbor researchers. The scientists had noted that when puppies were reared in isolation from humans for the first four months of their life, they became virtually untrainable, impossible to housebreak, and unable to acquire obedience commands. This "kennel dog" or "isolation" syndrome could, however, have several different causes. It could have a cognitive basis—the dogs lacked the ability to learn because, not having had any early training, they had never acquired the mental skills needed to learn; that is, to relate actions to rewards or punishments. Or it could be a purely emotional syndrome: the dogs were simply too fearful of new situations and people, and that emotional reaction overwhelmed the effects of any rewards and punishments administered. To find out, the researchers rigged a test apparatus that would allow puppies to be given training without a human handler present. The dogs were brought into a room, and a choke collar was attached to a leash that ran through pulleys on the ceiling. The dogs were placed on a wooden board in the center of the room and were taught to stay on the board by being given a mild remote-control tug on the leash if they tried to walk off it. The dogs were divided into several groups and were trained starting at different ages, with the last group not receiving any training until sixteen to eighteen weeks, the age at which all of the dogs were retested. All of the dogs were given the same amount of social contact with human handlers at other times.

When the scientists analyzed the results, they found that the age of initial training made no difference in performance at sixteen to eighteen weeks. "It follows," the researchers concluded, that "the lack of trainability seen in the kennel dog and isolation syndromes is probably largely produced by emotional factors arising from either lack of socialization to human handlers or lack of familiarization with the physical environment in which future training takes place, or both."

The huge emotional and motivational differences between

breeds are likewise almost surely of vast significance in explaining the apparent differences in intelligence that people impute to them. Working dogs are highly motivated to perform their characteristic behaviors, and there is considerable spillover from these behaviors to other areas. Border collies are extremely attentive to moving objects—indeed they are very alert in general—and so simply have more opportunities to draw connections between the things going on in their environment. (Going on a long car trip with a Border collie can be an exhausting experience, especially somewhere around the 127th time he swings his head quickly around to follow a car passing in the opposite direction.) They are also frequently stirring things up themselves, so they equally have more opportunities to draw connections between their own actions and consequences. A dog that is highly motivated to go outside where the sheep are and to pay attention to sounds and movement is going to quickly learn to leap up at the sound of the door being opened. A dog that is less motivated is not going to make such a connection because it simply doesn't matter as much to him. Dogs such as beagles and foxhounds that have been bred to work in packs, to concentrate on tracking smells without being distracted, and to be relatively inattentive to matters of social dominance are naturally going to be less interested in pleasing, or heeding the cajoling of, their human owners. Most of the livestock-guarding dog breeds won't even look at a thrown ball, so attenuated is their stalk-and-chase instinct. It is a physical fact that smaller animals have a higher metabolic rate than large animals; they dissipate heat faster and so, simply as a matter of thermodynamics, have bodies that must work at a faster pace to stay warm. That means they are more active, and tire or become overheated less quickly. On the other hand, certain small breeds such as terriers tend to be highly excitable or nervous and so are easily distracted. The point is that many facts of physics and biology determine how alert and keen a particular breed will be. (Largely unexplored is the possibility, not at all unlikely, that some differences in dogs' performance on tasks that matter to us reflect basic differences in visual acuity.) It is probably no surprise that the more active, motivated, and alert herding and sporting dogs dominate the top ranks of obedience trials, while hounds and guard dogs like mastiffs and Great Pyrenees are near the bottom. Border collies are "smarter" than basset hounds in the same way that someone who is full of pep and who avidly tries new things works out problems quicker than some lazy bum who lies around on the couch watching TV all day long. But in terms of innate ability to learn, it is very hard to make the case that any breed of dog is truly smarter than any other. Their brains are probably far more alike than most people usually assume.

Behavioral differences between breeds are, of course, "in the brain," at least in a qualitative sense; different breeds have had the wolf cognitive development track knocked off course in different ways to produce their breed-specific temperaments and motor patterns. It is difficult to find any convincing trend in relative brain size between breeds, though one quantitative trend is inescapable, and may possibly be significant in making a true comparison in overall intelligence between dogs and wolves, at least: the brains of dogs are about 25 percent smaller than those of comparably sized wolves.

One other sort of interdog difference in intelligence also seems to reflect a genuine difference in computing machinery: old dogs really can't learn new tricks, and not only that, they frequently exhibit symptoms strikingly similar to those of human Alzheimer's patients. Commonly reported problems in older dogs include wandering and disorientation, an inability to recognize familiar people, disturbed sleep and nighttime pacing and restlessness, difficulty negotiating stairs, and urinary or fecal incontinence. As with Alzheimer's patients, these symptoms appear in the absence of any physical disorders such as muscle degeneration, urinary disease, or vision loss that might otherwise explain these problems. The spatial DNMS experiments showed that dogs over ten years old had much greater difficulty learning the task, and their performance on the variable-delay retest fell off sharply. (The old dogs nonetheless remained just as highly motivated as young dogs. They answer just as quickly—they just keep getting the wrong answers.) Old dogs get set in their ways, and any change can be confusing.

THE BOOBY-TRAP METHOD OF EDUCATION

The few socially oblivious breeds aside, most all dogs are, as I have mentioned, acutely sensitive to social interactions and their consequences. Given a choice between a materialistic interpretation of events and a social interpretation, they will choose the latter. Luckily, many of the things we seem to think it worth our while to teach dogs—sitting, lying down, coming when called, getting out of our way—inherently involve social signals or some inferences about social relationships. (Of course, the reason we teach dogs these things is mostly that these are things dogs can do in the first place. It is not as if we scoured the animal kingdom looking for an animal that would sit, having decided that this was just what the world needed.) Likewise, the working behavior of working breeds draws upon self-rewarded instincts that we channel to our ends. It is not as if dogs have separate compartments of their brains for learning about social relationships, or about herding, or about what it means when the doorbell rings. Rather, they are biologically predisposed to notice certain things (like moving objects or threatening gestures from social peers) and to perform certain actions (such as chasing prey or cringing), and so it is much easier for them to make firm connections when one end of the link is anchored to one of these biologically weighty items.

The dog's readiness to interpret its environment through the lens of its species-specific concerns and proclivities often causes much trouble when we try to shape behaviors. Laboratory studies of learning certainly prove the effectiveness of punishment in eliminating behaviors. But in practice the problem with punishment is that the dog is so acutely attuned to the social scene that an aggressive act from a social superior is too psychologically potent a signal for the dog to place it in any context other than an assertion of social dominance. Whacking a dog for eating a book or digging in the garden or defecating on the floor is often merely puzzling to the dog, because eating books and digging in gardens and defecating are not socially significant actions. The whacked dog naturally responds submissively, cringing and trying to be appeasing by whining or licking, but he may totally fail to make the connection to his own behavior that seems so obvious to us.

Benjamin Hart points out that really the only time such "interactive" punishment as hitting or grabbing the dog by the collar is effective is when the issue on the table is dominance and dominance alone: when a dog growls or threatens or bites its owner in an unmistakable attempt to claim higher status. At such times physical force gets the message across very powerfully. But when the misbehavior involves a property crime rather than lèse-majesté, the success rate of interactive punishment is dismally low. In such cases, remote-control punishment, if it can be rigged, is always much more effective. The more impersonal the punishment—the more it seems to be an objective law of nature rather than anything carrying social import—the better. Hart suggests, for example, placing mouse traps in the garden or on trash cans to cure a dog of digging holes or ripping open the garbage. Squirts from a water pistol by a person in a concealed emplacement, or mild electric shocks delivered by a remote-control collar, are other effective remedies for such situations.

Laboratory studies in learning theory certainly have their limitations—it is not always clear that teaching rats to press levers has much to do with real behavior in the real world—but they do carry some important, and often ignored, lessons about other problems with punishment. One clear take-home lesson is that timing is crucial. For a punishment to be effective, it normally must be administered almost instantaneously. Even a few seconds can be too late for the animal to draw the connection between its own behavior and the consequences. Another key lesson is that if punishment is to be employed, it had better be effective. Otherwise, instead of teaching the animal not to do something, all we're teaching him is to ignore the punishment. An owner who is reluctant to punish his dog in the first place often falls into a pattern of employing a wimpy reprimand, having it ignored, then trying an ever so slightly stronger reprimand and having that ignored, and on and on. This is precisely the classical method for teaching an animal to become habituated to an otherwise painful stimulus. Starting with a tap on the nose and slowly building up to knocking the dog on the head with a baseball bat makes for a hardheaded dog that still ignores reprimands. An effective punishment applied from the start—and you know if it is effective enough, because by definition an effective punishment is one that works—avoids this process of escalation and habituation altogether. A dog that will respond only to a baseball bat by the end of this unintended toughening-up process would usually have responded to a much more moderate, yet still firm, reprimand applied from the very start.

Ill-timed punishment can simply be puzzling to a dog, but repeated ill-timed punishment can lead a dog to try to draw a more general inference from whatever information it can grab hold of: that the thing to be avoided is not the particular behavior we have in mind but rather the person delivering the punishment, or the place where the punishment usually occurs, or in some extreme cases *any* behavior at all. In this last case the dog gives up trying to do anything, a condition known as "learned helplessness." Badly timed punishment can also sometimes end up punishing, in the dog's mind, the behavior we actually want to encourage. Whacking a dog who doesn't come when called, once he finally gets within whacking range, is a proven and highly effective way of teaching a dog never to come when called.

Even when punishment is well timed and judiciously applied, it runs up against a basic law of entropy: there are an infinite number of ways to do something wrong, but only one way to do it right, so just as a practical matter it is usually a much more efficient method of teaching to reward the correct behavior than to try to punish misbehaviors.

But rewards have their own pitfalls, too, and to be brutally frank there are probably more dogs ruined by ill-judged rewards than by ill-judged punishment these days. Jack Knox, a legendary trainer of Border collies, discourages handlers from saying so much as "good dog," because the dogs end up spending more and more of their attention and time looking to the handler for what is, to a dog, the overwhelmingly potent and distracting force of social acceptance by a dominant member of the group. (Laboratory studies with timber wolves have shown that social rewards are more powerful reinforcers than even food rewards are.) Just as interactive punishment often makes the dog forget what he did that brought on the punishment, so praise can do the same; the dog gets so excited and goofy over being petted that it drives from his mind what it was all about in the first place. Watching some currently popular dog-training videos, one cannot help harboring a slight suspicion that the instructor is getting kickbacks from multinational dog biscuit conglomerates; every couple of seconds the dog is having another treat shoved in his mouth. It may be effective reinforcement, but it is not terribly dignified to see adult dogs that are constantly performing for tidbits. The fact is, it is also unnecessary. The very impressive behavior of working dogs is almost entirely self-reinforcing: they do it because they like doing it for its own sake. Similarly, many of the day-to-day behaviors of a well-trained dog are inherently reinforced in dogs that are treated with quiet dignity; one of the greatest rewards to a dog is the company of and matter-of-fact acceptance by its social superiors. According to classical learning theory, a behavior that is not at least intermittently rewarded will eventually wither away of its own accord. Yet dogs that have once learned to come when called or to sit on command or to walk good-naturedly on a lead will continue to do so the rest of their lives without any obvious further rewards. The reinforcement is the inherent social reward of submission and companionship.

THE MENTAL LIFE OF DOGS

A century ago, Edward L. Thorndike, one of the first true experimental psychologists, complained with ill-concealed irritation about all of the popular books on animal behavior then flooding the market. Popularizers of science had grabbed hold of Darwin's ideas on the common ancestry of all life and run with them, and everyone was outdoing one another with tales of the humanlike reasoning displayed by animals. The trouble was, Thorndike noted, such tales were "all about animal *intelligence*, never about animal *stupidity*." He wasn't saying animals were necessarily stupid. He was just arguing for fair scorekeeping: if a marvelous anecdote about an animal finding his way home against all odds were counted as proof of intelligence, then it was only fair to chalk up a lost animal that never made it home on the other side of the ledger. But no one ever paid attention when animals didn't come home.

It is hard to deny that dogs on occasion do very stupid things. But there is a method to their stupidity that is highly revealing. A dog can find his way through a complex network of trails in a wood, yet get his leash wrapped around a tree and seem helpless to figure any way out of the situation. He can find his hidden ball by sniffing all over the kitchen and climbing up on a shelf to pluck it from behind a book, and then stand, as he does every day of his life, on the hinge side of the door waiting for the door to open. My Border collie can bring sheep from the field into the barn with scarcely a word of guidance, but if the sheep are in an open shed in the field, he will invariably run around behind the shed and lie down staring intently at the back wall of the building, as if that were the equivalent of running behind the sheep.

The common denominator in all such errors dogs make is

a failure to grasp an underlying mechanism. The associations dogs make between events in the environment can be extraordinarily subtle, and most of the time they are extraordinarily smart because of the richness and saneness of the environment itself. Our everyday actions are accompanied by a welter of cues, most of them unconscious, that provide fertile material for the dog's learning ability to act upon; we jangle our keys as we prepare to go out, we head for the closet when it's feeding time, we put on one pair of shoes when we go for a walk with the dog and another when we leave for work. The intelligence—that is, the seeming insightfulness—in the behavior of dogs that pick up on these associations is really intelligence that resides in the cause-and-effect rationality of the world at large. The world by and large *is* a rational place, television game shows and children's taste in music notwithstanding; when two things happen at the same time, they usually really are linked by cause and effect. A dog has no need to grasp the underlying notion of cause and effect in order to be right most of the time by associating things that happen simultaneously.

But the readiness of dogs to develop superstitious associations is pretty strong evidence that their grasp goes no further. Sometimes two things happen together by mere coincidence (John Holmes's dog collision is a perfect example), and dogs are just as convinced by these circumstances. Dogs will often refuse to deviate from a set route or routine even when the merest dose of common sense would point out the absurdity of their behavior. Dogs clearly have intentions, and one might even say thoughts, but where dog minds seem to reach their limits is where it comes to forming hypotheses, to thinking *about* their thoughts. Understanding why one thing causes another is really not possible without such an ability to hypothesize, to try out ideas both right and wrong within the confines of one's own mind. So too, imagining what others think—or even *that* others think—requires an ability to think about thoughts. I have a very resourceful Shetland sheepdog who has discovered all sorts of ways to make her intentions known; at a very young age she began standing in one certain position by the door when she needed or wanted to go outside. It is greatly tempting to think that she had grasped that this was a way to communicate with us, that she has an intention of alerting us to her desire, of making us aware of something we were not aware of before. Functionally that is what she is doing. But the fact that she will go and stand at the door in exactly the same way even when no one is there to see her rather deflates the idea that she even understands that other beings are beings with their own thoughts. She can certainly react to our behavior, but she seems to have no conception of what we know or don't know.

The same pattern appears in canine emotions. I would not hesitate to say that dogs experience fear, lust, hesitancy, curiosity, anger; contentment, perhaps; and, after a fashion, love. But they can demonstrably be shown not to experience emotions that require an ability to imagine the feelings or thoughts of others—concern, guilt, shame, loyalty, protectiveness, pity, empathy, compassion. Every time they display a behavior that convinces us they are showing some such emotion, some ability to put themselves in another's place, someone comes along and drives a truck over our convictions. Ray Coppinger once totally deflated me by describing a test his students had done with a bitch and her puppies. Young puppies that get separated from their littermates and mother will let out a distinctive, high-pitched distress cry. On hearing this, the mother will rush over, pick up the puppy, and carry it back to the nest in her mouth. Few normal people who witness such an action would hesitate for a second to call it a display of concern or protectiveness. The astonishing and rather disturbing fact, however, is that if you record a puppy's distress call on a cassette tape player, set the cassette player outside the nest, and switch it to play, the mother will do exactly the same thing—she will rush over, pick up the tape player, and carry the tape player to the nest. This tends to shake up our easy assumptions about what is going on in a dog's mind when it outwardly displays behavior that seems so similar to the things we do.

Many dog owners, I am sure, are gnashing their teeth at the previous paragraph, since it seems so commonsensical that dogs do display loyalty, protectiveness, and empathy toward their masters, and it would seem to be rather denigrating to suggest otherwise. But it is no more belittling a dog to point out that he lacks the ability to impute thoughts and feelings to others than it is belittling a person to point out that he lacks fur or the ability to follow a scent trail. Dogs are what they are; they are adapted to an ecological niche and a way of life that is uniquely theirs. It is a way of life that includes a rich and complex repertoire of social behaviors directed toward other members of the group, and it isn't their fault if the nature of the human mind makes such behaviors so amenable to anthropomorphic projections. Humans are obsessed with what others are thinking, especially what others are thinking about them; such transactional emotions as loyalty, fellow feeling, competitiveness, distrust, and sympathy are the stuff of our social interactions. Yet as social an animal as the dog is, dogs and wolves do not form the sorts of alliances that occur in some primate bands, alliances that require a careful bookkeeping of reciprocity. Dogs are ever assessing and reassessing their place in the social hierarchy; they are experts at appeasing their social betters and deflecting aggression; and they are experts at sensing an opening and social climbing. But they do so by attending to the actions and signals of others, and they do so fundamentally out of self-interest. We worry about what others think of us; dogs worry about what others do to them. Superficially, reacting to the behavior of another being and feeling empathy for that being can look a lot alike. A dog that approaches joyfully when his owner is in a good mood and that creeps up carefully when his owner is in a foul temper certainly looks like a dog that is empathizing. Yet a dog that is merely reacting, as dogs always do, to the welcoming or hostile tone and body language of a social superior will behave in exactly the same fashion.

I suppose it might sound as if I am suggesting that we humans always act out of noble impulses, while dogs are crass manipulators, or even automatons, but I don't mean that at all. It seems abundantly clear that dogs have thoughts and feelings and are acutely sensitive to the behavior of other beings. And it is also abundantly clear that while our own compulsive musing about the thoughts and feelings of others holds the seeds of morality and compassion, it is more often than not pressed into service for selfish or at least self-centered ends. There is nothing automatically noble or selfless in the mental exercise of putting oneself in the other guy's position. It's a terrifically useful mental tool to have, for example, if your life is devoted to nothing but ambushing and killing your enemies.

All I am saying is that the ability to have thoughts and feelings of one's own, and even the ability to be aware of and react to the actions and social signals of others, does not automatically imply an ability to grasp the concept that thoughts and feelings exist in others. Human infants and toddlers do not even have this grasp, nor do autistic humans. For example, up to the age of two or three, humans cannot seem to understand that someone who is out of the room when a toy is hidden would not know where the toy is. The ability to appreciate that others have *minds* is a distinctly human characteristic that emerges in the course of childhood development.

The phenomenon of canine "guilt" is a perfect illustration of how our tendency to project human social emotions onto dogs is so tempting—and yet demonstrably fallacious. Most dog owners have had the experience of coming home and being able to tell immediately from their dog's behavior that he has been at it again, ripping open the garbage, chewing on shoes, tearing up newspapers, or pooping on the floor. The dog acts unmistakably "guilty," hanging his head, or creeping up to his owner, or sometimes rushing out the door. If it were a person who behaved this way, we wouldn't hesitate to interpret it as evidence that the guilty party understands that he has violated a rule and has been caught. But the first piece of evidence for another interpretation in the case of the dog is that the dog's "guilty" behavior is identical to the submissive display dogs always exhibit toward a display of aggression by a dominant member of the pack. It also is invariably the case that "guilty" dogs have already had the experience of being punished, or at least spoken to in a disapproving tone of voice, when their owners return home and discover the shredded newspaper or soiled carpet. These facts in themselves raise the strong possibility that what the dog is exhibiting is not conscious awareness of its misdeed but rather a learned association between (a) reproving behavior on the part of the owner and (b) two visual cues: the return of the owner and the presence on the floor of torn-up newspaper or spilled trash or dog poop. The dog is putting on a submissive display in a learned anticipation of the owner's punishment or disapproving tone. The clinching piece of evidence that this is indeed the case is that it is invariably possible to evoke precisely the same "guilty" display by the dog by, for example, placing him in a room with newspaper that someone else has torn up. When the owner returns home, the dog acts just the same as if he had done the tearing himself.

Although we never actually punished our Border collie the few times we returned home and found he had defecated on the floor, he very quickly picked up on the annoyance in my wife's voice as she cleaned up the mess with newspaper. He thereafter would rush out of the room at high speed when all of the following ingredients were present: my wife, a piece of newspaper in her hand, dog poop on the floor. He did this on several occasions when another dog was the guilty party.

People who are convinced that their dogs are acting guilty often construct elaborate explanations for why their dogs would continue to commit acts that they must (as their guilty consciousness attests) know are wrong. Dogs are often accused of harboring spiteful or vengeful feelings toward their owners in these cases. In fact, the deeper cause of their misbehavior is sometimes something as simple as boredom or frustration at being cooped up for hours with nothing to do, and their hang-dog look on their owner's return is a simple learned response to getting whacked.

DOG ESP—NOT

There is so much intelligence wrapped up in the universe that the ability to form learned associations explains much of the intelligence that dogs manifest. Yet some intelligent feats dogs perform clearly cannot be explained by trial-and-error learning alone. That many mammals and birds can in fact perform tasks that require an ability to refer to and manipulate data not immediately available in an incoming stimulus shook up the behaviorist model when it was first discovered several decades ago, and led to a recognition that animals have mental "representations" of their world—stored visual patterns, for example, or conceptual categories—which can be formed and then later accessed to make novel decisions. The mental machinery for handling these representations can be quite specialized to particular tasks, however. Animals have a strong instinctive ability to make mental distinctions according to biologically important categories. Dogs, for example, appear to come prewired with the hardware needed to distinguish members of the group from strangers, males from females, dogs from nondogs, and things that move like animals from things that move like inanimate objects.

Another kind of special-purpose circuit, found in many mammals, is located in a part of the brain called the hippocampus. It acts as the navigation center. Laboratory experiments in rats have shown that when an animal enters a room that it has previously explored, different nerve cells in the hippocampus fire depending on where in the room it is at any given instant.

Field experiments by psychologist Nicole Chapuis have shown that dogs likewise can form such "mental maps" of their environment, and through a combination of recognizing familiar landmarks and dead reckoning determine their location and the relative orientation of sites of interest, even along unfamiliar routes. One test involved leading dogs from a starting point in a field on a straight line to a spot where some meat was cached, then straight back to the starting point, then along a second straight line to a second food cache, then finally back to the start again. The dogs were then released, and the question was, After they went to one of the caches, would they find their way directly to the second without retracing their steps to the starting point? The dogs' ability to make a novel shortcut clearly implies a grasp of the geometry of the situation, and in 96 percent of the tests the dogs did just that; only about 1 percent of the time did they ever retrace their steps to the start, sticking to the single route they had been shown.

The ability to form mental maps or other mental representations has sometimes been taken as evidence of conscious reasoning or even conscious self-awareness. But no one would say a computer is self-aware or consciously reasoning, and it certainly wouldn't be hard to write a piece of computer software that replicates what a rat or a dog does by way of navigation. The rat studies that related specific neurons in the hippocampus to specific map locations offer an impressive explanation for how the mammalian brain is wired to automatically perform such map exercises. I am not at all suggesting that all of a dog's individual psychology and behavior can be reduced to a mechanistic explanation based on a bunch of firing neurons. But mental feats that can seem amazing and even mysterious on the surface, feats that seem to demand some higher level of consciousness, become far less mysterious once we understand the underlying neural mechanisms at work.

Some people are so eager to believe in the higher consciousness of their pets, however, that they take their dogs' behavior as a sign not only of conscious abilities but of psychic abilities. But this, alas, says more about human psychology than animal parapsychology. The "psychic pet phenomenon" received much attention when the New Agey researcher

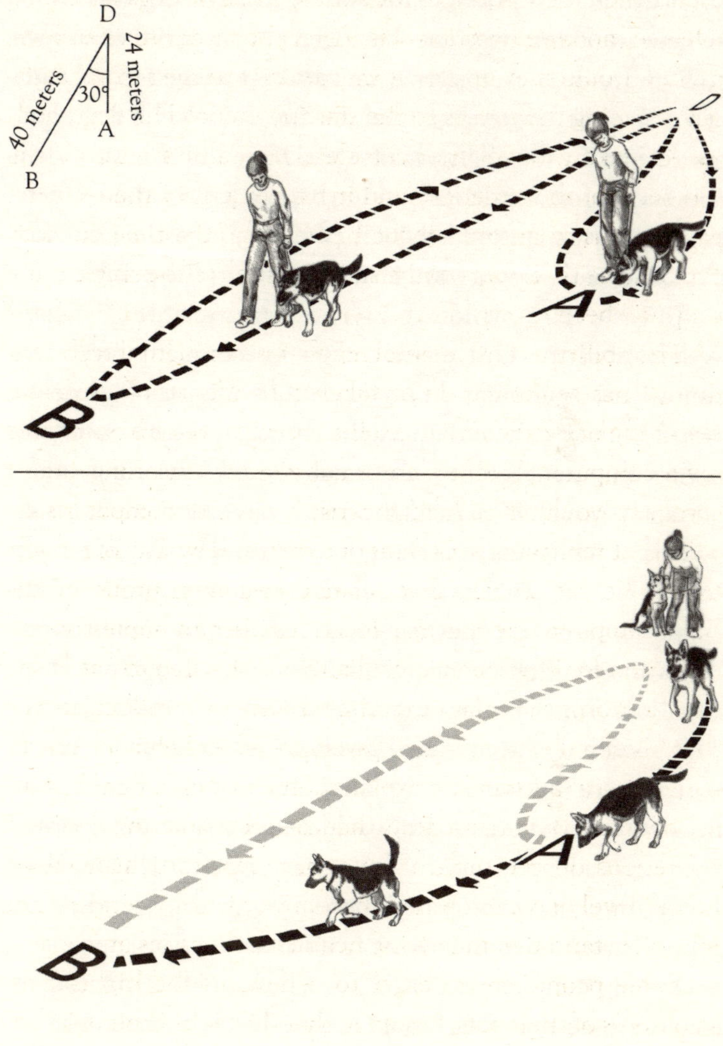

If led on a leash between two baited sites, then released, dogs almost always take a novel shortcut between the two locations—demonstrating an ability to navigate by dead reckoning.

Rupert Sheldrake claimed to have compiled substantial anecdotal evidence that dogs often know in advance when their owners are returning home. He urged people to test their own pets, and shortly thereafter a star exhibit emerged in the form of a dog named Jaytee, an inhabitant of the town of Ramsbottom in northwest England, who was filmed by an Australian television company demonstrating his psychic abilities. Whenever his owner started her journey home, Jaytee, a five-year-old terrier mix, would run outside and sit on the porch.

To his credit, Sheldrake invited a real scientist, Richard Wiseman of the University of Hertfordshire, to conduct a controlled experiment on Jaytee, and to Wiseman's credit he did. The first step was to eliminate any possible source of nonpsychic signals that Jaytee might be receiving. For example, some "psychic" dogs might simply have learned that their owners return home at certain times every day. Or they might be able to hear the sound of a familiar car engine at a considerable distance. Or they might be reacting to certain subtle behaviors of other people in the house who happen to know when the owner is planning to return on each particular day. The researchers accordingly designed an experiment procedure in which no one, including Jaytee's owner, would know in advance what time she would begin her return journey. One experimenter stayed at the owner's home and videotaped Jaytee throughout the period of the owner's absence while another accompanied the owner to a remote location and, using a random number generator on a handheld calculator, selected a time that they would return. Jaytee's owner was not told the return time until a few seconds before they actually began their trip back.

The other crucial part of the experimental design was to have an unbiased judge, who was not told of the time that Jaytee's owner began her return trip, review the videotape and decide when Jaytee first "signaled" his owner's return. The results were immediately quite revealing. During the first experiment, Jaytee ran to the porch a total of thirteen times. Even after eliminating all of the times Jaytee might have had some obvious reason to do so (a person walking past, a car pulling up), there were still three separate times that Jaytee gave his "signal," and the first of these occurred several minutes *before* his owner began her return trip. Subsequent experiments found exactly the same pattern. Jaytee ran to the porch repeatedly, almost always missing the correct time by many minutes with his first signal and on several trials failing to give a signal at all during a ten-minute block following the start of his owner's return trip. The researchers pointed out that several well-known statistical fallacies readily explain how Jaytee's family had convinced themselves of his psychic abilities. First is selective memory: Jaytee gives his "signal" repeatedly, many times during the day, and it is only human nature for the people at home with Jaytee to remember the ones that correspond with his owner's return and forget the others. A closely related foible is selective matching: Is it the time his owner thinks of returning home, or the time she actually gets in the car, that Jaytee senses? Is it going to the window or going to the door that is the signal? Is it standing there for ten seconds or a minute that counts? Unless these criteria are specified in advance, the number of possible matches between the dog's behavior and the owner's return can grow without bound. Again, it is simply human nature to match up after the fact the one that fit and ignore the others. "What is clear from our experiments," the researchers concluded with admirable scientific reserve, "is that the mechanisms . . . by which a pet might appear to be psychic without actually being so are quite plausible and that without safeguards to rule them out, a more informal study than ours could lead to a false conclusion."

Dogs can perform some truly amazing acts of sensing things unperceived and unnoticed by us. The evidence for extrasensory powers, however, is not terribly persuasive. And I have always wondered, too, why the reputed psychic powers of animals never have any practical applications. People who claim to be in psychic contact with their pets are always reporting on what their cat or dog is communicating telepathically about their social anxieties or emotional needs. If I have a psychic dog, I want one that can at least tell me which way the NASDAQ is going to move tomorrow.

CHAPTER 7

Odd, but (Mostly) Normal Behavior

THERE ARE DIFFERING DEGREES of weirdness to the weird things dogs do. Leaving aside outright pathological behaviors such as compulsive self-mutilation and hyperactivity that arise from neurological or hormonal disorders, most of the apparently odd things that most dogs do are perfectly normal; or at least as normal as is possible, given what dogs are. There are, for example, some perfectly natural, species-specific behaviors in dogs that seem outré to us only because we lead such sheltered lives. If it seems strange to us that dogs greet one another by sniffing each other's hind ends, it probably seems strange to dogs that humans greet one another by waving their hands. Sniffing hind ends is a highly adaptive behavior in wolves, and it remains so in dogs. It is a way to relate an individual to his odor and thus to scent marks left in the environment. It is no odder than us asking the name of someone we meet at a party. When we read about him in a scandalous story in the newspaper a few weeks later, we then have a face to match to the salacious details.

Slightly weirder are remnants of once-adaptive behaviors from the dog's wolfish past that have come to be rather out of place in the niche the dog now occupies. These include rolling in garbage, chasing cars, defending the yard against the UPS truck, and urinating in front of one's owner to signify submission.

Weirder still are behaviors that result from some wires getting decidedly crossed as wolves became dogs and the normal pattern of adult wolf development became disrupted—barking at the dishwasher, running off with underwear, and guarding shoes.

At the pinnacle of the weird yet still arguably normal are behaviors that are the product of an opportunistic blending of wolf–dog social instincts with the rich pageantry presented by human society. If you take a wolf, mix up and reassemble his normal adult behavioral patterns in a way that exaggerates juvenile characteristics such as play, and then throw him into a world of people doing very unwolflike things, all sorts of things can result, and do—from a dog that pretends to have a broken leg to one that eats his own scats for no other reason than to attract attention. These dogs certainly have behavioral problems as far as we're concerned but there is nothing literally wrong with them. They do not suffer from brain defects, nor hormonal imbalances, nor hallucinations. They are behaving according to a perfectly rational system of responding to rewards in the strange world that they find themselves inhabiting. The fault is not in themselves but in their stars.

The weirdness that arises from cultural conflicts, cultural misunderstandings, or simply cultural differences is admittedly not always easy to distinguish from the weirdness that reflects a genuine pathology—all the more so since some of what makes a dog a dog is a disruption of its wolfish neural wiring, development patterns, and hormone levels. So at a certain level, dogs really *are* weird. And some breeding practices may be unintentionally making them weirder still (particularly in abnormal aggression, which is the topic of the next chapter).

Yet the relentless pressure from the medical profession to medicalize behavioral problems that has been a feature of Western society for more than a century has now come to the veterinary profession and further blurred this line. One nineteenth-century physician saw a pathological mental condition in the phenomenon of slaves who wanted to run away from their masters. There is something equally clueless in veterinarians prescribing tranquilizers and Prozac for Border collies, sled dogs, or other working dogs that, kept as pets and confined to apartments all day, exhibit frantic or destructive behaviors due to sheer boredom and frustration at not being able to exercise their instinctive behavioral patterns. Border collies compulsively eye anything that moves, or failing that, anything that might move—that's what they *do*. Yet there have been cases of Border collies being drugged up because their owners think there's something wrong with them when they spend all day staring at or snapping at flies and dust particles. In fact, it's nothing that a flock of sheep wouldn't cure.

ANCESTRAL EMBARRASSMENTS

Many dog owners are mystified by the seemingly irresistible attraction that extremely foul-smelling things hold for dogs. Dogs will often seek out the ripest, most putrid, most godawful things (one of my dogs had a particular liking for week-old squirrel carcasses), and then with every sign of acute pleasure pull their lips back much like a horse smelling a mare in heat, and in a very stereotyped behavioral pattern do a shoulder roll right into the middle of the mess: they bend their forelegs and repeatedly rub the side of the neck and the top of the head into the object, sometimes switching sides and then finally rolling over onto their back and wriggling over the spot. This is almost certainly a holdover of a once-adaptive behavior in wolves, which have been observed executing precisely the same maneuver. Some other predators do the same.

All sorts of explanations have been proposed for this behavior; it is often suggested that it is an attempt by the wolf to disguise its own scent so that it can more effectively sneak up on prey, or even—a really bizarre notion that somehow seems to have been uncritically embraced by many writers—that by smelling weird the wolf, upon returning to the pack, is an object of greater interest to fellow pack members, who give him more attention in the form of sniffing. The obvious trouble with this latter explanation is that this behavior is highly instinctive and apparently self-rewarding, as it persists in dogs even when there is no social reward at all—quite the reverse, in fact. It is really hard to see how such a distinctive behavior, one that is so hardwired, could arise if its only purpose was so marginal and so displaced in time from the supposed reward. If it could be conclusively demonstrated that wolves that roll in stinky things somehow gain a real advantage in the social hierarchy compared to those who are less inclined to do so, then perhaps. But there is no evidence to support that so far.

Scent masking is a more plausible notion, but it is worth considering the possibility that something else entirely is going on. We are such olfactory ignoramuses that the only thing we really notice about this behavior is that the dog ends up stinking to high heaven, so we naturally assume that that is the point of the entire exercise. But in fact, ending up stinking may just be a coincidental by-product. Dogs and wolves are, after all, attracted to rotten things in the first place because they *eat* rotten things. Wolves in the wild will return to a carcass sometimes days later and finish it off, and have been observed on occasion eating extremely putrid meat. Another relevant fact is that in experiments in attempting to socialize wolves to humans, one of the first things wolves will do when they overcome their fear and begin to approach a human is to rub against his clothing and on objects that bear his scent. Finally, at times dogs and wolves will also go through their stereotypical neck rubbing on things that are not particularly stinky at all. Dogs and wolves have scent-producing glands on their head, and this raises the possibility that rather than trying to acquire the foreign odor themselves, they are instead attempting to leave their own odor on an object that simply happens to interest them in the first place. There may also be a component of claiming ownership or territorial assertiveness in leaving their scent mark on things that smell like other members of the pack or that are prized possessions. But just as wolves and dogs choose visually conspicuous vertical objects to urinate upon, and conspicuous spots like trail junctions at which to defecate, they may simply be choosing olfactorally conspicuous objects to leave their body scent upon. Foul- or unusual-smelling things are more likely to be investigated by other wolves; the result is like leaving an announcement on a bulletin board at eye level as opposed to dropping it on the ground. You leave it where other members of the social group are likely to find it. Dogs unfortunately don't realize that all of this effort is lost on us.

Also lost on us is another form of olfactory or visual communication frequently displayed by puppies and by especially submissive dogs. This is known to animal behavior experts by the rather clinical name of "submissive urination," though it amounts to having the pee scared out of them: a young or subordinate dog approaching a senior member of the group will frequently dribble out some urine, and this is apparently recognized as a mark of submissiveness and reacted to as such by a dominant animal. Why this should be the case is probably simply that a communicative function has piggybacked upon an autonomic nervous system response. Losing control of one's bladder is an automatic response to fear that, in evolutionary terms, probably had nothing to do with communication originally: it is a way to lighten the load and prepare for flight. But over time it could acquire a communicative function if other animals could make useful predictions about the behavior of an animal who is peeing nervously. (A good basic rule: a nervous pisher is unlikely to attack or threaten one's dominance status.) Wolves apparently do recognize submissive urination as such.

This leads to a certain amount of misunderstanding with people, however, who don't view wetting one's pants as an act of communication. Dog owners in fact frequently make the problem much worse by punishing a submissively urinating dog for his act, which then makes the dog even more fearful and submissive, and more earnest than ever in his endeavor to get across the fact by peeing when approaching his owner. Puppies usually grow out of submissively urinating, though sometimes they do not, and they are especially likely to exhibit this behavior when greeting a human—especially a human who is larger or more assertive and who the dog therefore perceives to be the more aggressive and dominant member of the family. The best cure seems to be to ignore the dog in the places and situations that tend to trigger urination. Benjamin Hart reports some success in rigging remote-control "surprise" punishment, but it is of course particularly important in this circumstance to make sure the dog does not get the idea that the punishment came from a person, as that would make the encounter even more about dominance and submission. One of Hart's patients was a toy poodle that had the particularly charming habit of urinating on people when picked up. The effective cure, along with desensitizing the dog by playing down the boisterousness of greetings, was to arrange for one member of the family, armed with a squirt gun, to give the dog a blast whenever he let loose while being picked up by another person.

Other relics of wolf behavior are equally incompatible with modern life. Wolves can go for days without eating, an adaptive trait in a hunter whose source of prey is not always steady or predictable. By way of compensation, wolves are capable of eating huge amounts of food at one sitting. Wolves in captivity that are starved for several days have been recorded to consume more than eighteen pounds of meat and fat in one go. Dogs have inherited such wolfish habits. The stomach of an average-size dog can hold more than a gallon of food, and like wolves they have a powerful and basic instinct to overeat. Dogs are less active than most wolves are, and so need far less food, but a more important cause of the very high rate of obesity in dogs is simply that they are genetically programmed to eat more food than they need no matter how much exercise they get. (A small amount of weight gain is associated with the hormonal changes that occur in spayed bitches, but this amounts to a couple of pounds at most. If allowed to eat all the food they want, spayed bitches will eat more than nonspayed bitches, but if they are fed a controlled diet, no weight change occurs. There is no evidence for any changes in appetite or weight in castrated male dogs.) Surveys have found that (like American humans) about one-third of all pet dogs are obese, and the proportion may be even higher among small terriers and toy breeds. The solution, of course, is simple: don't feed your dog so much. But given dogs' innate capacity for overeating and their strong inclination to do so, as well as their ability to get us to do what they want, that is of course easier said than done.

SURVIVAL OF THE WEIRDEST

Some of the genetic changes that occurred during the transformation of wolf to dog were clearly adaptive to the new niche of mooching off of people. There had to have been strong selective pressures that favored a loss of fearfulness and a reduction in the distance by which dogs would approach people. But other traits that emerged from the genetic pileup of domestication just happened. They are part of the dog's ancestral baggage, but unlike things such as scent rubbing and submissive urination, they don't even have the excuse of having once been useful.

Barking, or at least excessive barking, is one of these traits. Barking has been deliberately emphasized in some breeds, such as foxhounds and beagles that bark when they find scent, and a few herding dogs like Shetland sheepdogs that bark to intimidate sheep into moving (though barking is actively discouraged in Border collies, which are expected to get sheep to move by "eye" and stalk alone). But for the most part barking is bizarre, maladaptive, unwanted, and impossible to stop in dogs. In two random surveys in which owners were interviewed about their dogs' behavior problems, one-third of those responding complained about excessive barking. All sorts of gizmos are now on the market to attempt to deal with the problem, including collars that deliver an electric shock, a high-pitched sound, or a squirt of citronella spray into the dog's face whenever he barks. Some are equipped with computer chips that can be user-programmed to recognize the wearer's individual bark. The only trouble is that dogs frequently resume barking the instant the collar is taken off. Some dogs are resourceful enough to discover that if they modify the pitch of their bark, they can escape triggering the collar even when they're wearing it. The real problem, though, is that barking is such a rewarding activity that although punishment can inhibit it, punishment does nothing to reduce the drive that propels it in the first place. And in fact, precisely because barking is so annoying, it is frequently rewarded unintentionally or even unconsciously by humans: it is an extremely effective attention-getting device, and every time it succeeds in getting a human's attention, it is reinforced.

Playfulness is another very doggish trait that was probably produced more by an incidental clashing of genes than by any deliberate choice by people or adaptive strategy by dogs. Again, like barking, it is appealing to people in some ways, but it is often entirely out of hand and maladaptive. It is enjoyable that dogs like to play fetch or tag, but it is not so enjoyable that they repeatedly attempt to turn serious matters into a game. The repertoire of play behaviors is so innate in dogs that they can whip them out on all sorts of occasions and make new discoveries about how useful play can be: dogs often seek to deflect aggression (i.e., punishment) through play. They readily learn how to get a game going, or at least what seems a game to them, by doing things such as swiping articles of clothing or tools and running off with them. Many dogs discover they can avoid coming when called by initiating such a "game." Making a human run after them is a great way to get to stay outside longer.

The resourceful propensity that dogs have to reassemble

various ancestral behaviors into play makes for some particularly stellar kinds of weirdness, especially when in so doing they succeed in provoking a reaction that reinforces their discovery. Pointless digging, tail chasing, chewing up things, and stealing things are some examples. A more extreme syndrome, but not at all uncommon, is what is politely termed in the scientific literature "coprophagy." Dogs do have an instinct to eat the scats of large hoofed animals, which is a perfectly normal and adaptive scavenging behavior given their nutritional value. Bitches eat the excrement produced by puppies before they are old enough to walk; this is an adaptive behavior that keeps the puppies and the nest clean. Eating one's own feces, or the feces of other adult dogs, is however distinctly maladaptive, since it is a great way to pick up intestinal parasites. Yet a certain nontrivial segment of the dog population does exactly this. Sometimes it seems to be the product of boredom or a lack of bulk in the diet, but most of the time it probably comes about through one of these playful, or just confused, cross-wirings of ancestral instinct. Just as dogs like to steal pieces of paper and run off with them, especially if the result is the very satisfying scene of a human jumping down and running in pursuit, so a dog that eats feces is almost sure to provoke a very nice reaction on the part of its owner. That alone can be enough to reinforce the behavior.

The only real cure for any of these behaviors is to ignore them. Even yelling can be counterproductive, given the dog's propensity to turn punishment into play.

PEOPLE AS PEOPLE VS. PEOPLE AS DOGS

The only mental tool that a dog can use to relate to humans is the one that came in the tool kit with which evolution equipped dogs for dealing with other dogs. To put it another way, we subvert the dog's hardwired social instincts; we slip ourselves in during the socialization period, a time when puppies haven't yet fully learned what is a dog and what is not a dog, and thus dogs naturally learn to include people in the set of beings on whom dog social skills are to be applied. If dogs were raised in the company of humans who behaved in a completely doglike manner, dogs would undoubtedly relate to people precisely as they do to dogs. But of course we don't act very doglike. There is enough vague similarity in some of our important actions that dogs can somehow fit what we do into their dog social schema, particularly on matters of leadership and dominance and tone of voice and threatening motions. But there are many doglike rituals we either don't do or actively discourage. Most humans do not like having their crotches snorted into by dogs and teach them not to do it. While most humans do play with their dogs, they do not bite their dogs on the nose or neck, or wrestle with them on the floor, or play-fight with them over dog chews or bones. Dogs that have been socialized to people and that have learned some basic bounds about which things to try with people and which things not to try are still relating to people basically as they do to dogs—again, especially in matters of the social hierarchy—but they have placed people in a special category of dogs with an asterisk next to them. They have been specifically taught that certain acts in the dog repertoire are forbidden.

How big the asterisk is, is important, and trouble sometimes results when it's even a little bit off. When the asterisk is too big, dogs are wild, fearful, and ungovernable; they view people not as members of the pack, nor even as rivals from another pack, but as aliens altogether. Aliens are either predators or prey, and this is not the basis of a good working relationship. Improperly socialized dogs never learn to extend dog social rules to people and usually remain forever fearful of humans.

On the other hand, puppies that are raised exclusively with people during their critical socialization period often end up treating people as *too* doglike. These are the dogs that become a special nuisance when they begin to try to relate sexually to humans, notably by mounting on their legs and thrusting gleefully away. Because some adult sexual motor patterns, mounting in particular, are a normal part of play in juvenile mammals, this can be another one of those creatively playful dog inventions that end up getting out of hand. As with other irritating canine attention-getting devices, it is often unintentionally reinforced by people who find it hard to ignore.

The failure of dogs to make too much of an exception for people in their doglike rules is the source of many other weird behaviors. The dog who would throw up in his owner's shoes, to be sure, had some other wires crossed somewhere, but he also had a hard time seeing his owner as something in any way undoglike. The reaction of dogs to mail carriers, UPS men, and other regular invaders of a dog's home territory is also at its root a behavior based on seeing people as doglike. Animal behavior therapists see a lot of dogs with this "problem," and some claim to find it rather puzzling. Nicholas Dodman, a veterinarian who specializes in behavioral problems, says that dogs who are excessively prone to attack visitors suffer from pathological, abnormal anxiety and fear, and he frequently prescribes the anti-anxiety and muscle-relaxing drug propranolol (which is also used in humans who suffer from heart conditions and high blood pressure or psychological conditions such as stage fright). Dodman says it doesn't make sense to consider this kind of aggressive behavior in dogs as a territorial behavior, since people are not dogs: "Robins will defend their territory to the death if necessary against other robins. But who ever heard of a robin defending its territory against assault by a lizard?" Perhaps, Dodman suggests, it is a form of "canine dyslexia" in which dogs get people and dogs confused.

But this is surely overwrought. We know that in countless ways dogs *do* relate to people using the innate repertoire they have for relating to other dogs. There is nothing "abnormal" about this at all; or at least it is no more abnormal than the entire story of domestication. Dogs come with an instinct to socialize and will readily bring that instinct to bear on the humans in their lives. Indeed, getting the asterisk attached to humans in the dog's mind is more a matter of training and reinforcement than it is of that fundamental instinct; it is a matter of tempering that instinct with lessons that usually have to be explicitly taught. So it is perfectly natural that dogs react to strange people coming onto their home territory in just the way that members of the wolf pack react to intrusions by strange wolves. Now, as studies in feral dogs have shown, the territorial instinct is greatly attenuated in dogs compared to wolves, and the territories of free-ranging dogs overlap considerably without apparent strife. But even among happy-go-lucky village dogs that wander freely about, there is a small core territory consisting of the dog's usual resting place that is defended tenaciously against intruders. This central point may be as little as a couple of hundred yards away from another dog's, but the dog does regard it as a home base and clearly shows a vestige of wolflike territoriality in his regard for it.

This territorial behavior can be amplified by fear and anxiety, some of it unwittingly reinforced by owners. Fear is certainly a signficant component in the seeming protectiveness of a dog toward his masters in the face of a territorial intruder; his is really the action of a coward seeking reassurance by sticking close to the dominant member of the pack (i.e., us) when encountering a fearful stimulus. This is another example of facilitated aggression: the dog feels emboldened by the demeanor of a more dominant member of the pack to display an aggressiveness he might otherwise not dare. When a dog runs close to his master in the face of an external intrusion, he usually acts exactly like a puppy that will dash outward on a quick foray, bark furiously at something, and then dash back to the safety and comfort of the nest and littermates. No one would suggest that puppy was "protecting" his littermates under this circumstance. Many owners deliberately or unwittingly reinforce such behavior, either by deliberately encouraging what they see as a useful guard dog behavior or, just as effectively, by unwittingly petting and trying to "reassure" the dog that "it's just the mailman." Dogs take that nice tone of voice as reinforcing praise for their barking, snarling, and leaping on the door.

When the intrusion comes every day at a regular time, dogs will learn to anticipate it, and this in turn can create an anticipatory anxiety that builds up more and more. (Precisely the same thing happens with dogs that are greeted too effusively by owners on their return. The dog's anticipation of such an overpowering stimulus creates more and more anxiety, which can reach the level of hyperactive and destructive behavior as the time of the owner's return approaches each day.) Dogs also are able to learn some interesting general rules—bark at men, bark at men in uniforms, bark at men who drive up in large delivery trucks, and so on. My old collie could recognize the sound of the UPS truck a quarter of a mile away and begin to wind herself up for the excitement. So Dodman is probably right about the more serious cases having a component of fear and anxiety, and breaking the cycle might be a valid reason to use drugs for a while. But at its root there is no mystery. Dogs are territorial animals, and dogs are built to react with alarm and hostility to intrusions of their territory.

The complex way people fit into the dog's social schema is also the source of often extremely serious social conflicts that occur in multi-dog households. In the typical scenario, the low dog on the totem pole is slightly picked on by the other dogs; he gets bones taken away from him, gets pushed out of the choice lying-down spots, is growled at when he comes too near one of the others, and is body-blocked or snapped at if he tries to come near a human who is paying attention to one of the more dominant dogs. Even without the confusing component of humans and their bizarre behavior, struggles for dominance status within a group of several dogs can take some time to sort out, and there is always a certain inherent instability given how much dogs are all natural social climbers. The aging and enfeeblement of an older once-dominant dog can provoke a challenge from a subordinate dog even if the two have gotten along fine for years. The introduction of a new adult dog to a group will frequently trigger a disruption of a settled hierarchy and can degenerate into a melee until things get straightened out. The challenges that occur can be quite violent. (They certainly are in wolves.) Yet what is so interesting about the classic syndrome in multi-dog households is that usually the dogs *have* worked things out for themselves; they usually get along fine, and almost never have violent fights, in the owner's absence. But in the presence of the owner serious and even violent fights occur in which one of the dogs may be seriously injured. The trouble almost always starts when the human attempts to impose democracy on the feudal dog social structure. The owner thoroughly messes things up by feeling naturally sorry for the low dog, and tries to even things out by reprimanding the dominant dogs for being bullies. The owner may give the subordinate dog back a toy that has been swiped from him, or may give him special privileges like lying down in favored places next to a person, or may simply try to be "fair" to all the dogs by giving them equal amounts of petting. The subordinate dog then learns a very simple lesson: when the owner is present, he can get away with things vis-à-vis the rest of the pack that he never could on his own. This, unsurprisingly, emboldens him to try. And that unsurprisingly provokes a strong reaction from the more dominant dogs, who take it as a direct challenge to their social status. It is all rather like encouraging the downtrodden peasants to revolt with vague promises of American aid, and then sending only a few cases of Spam and some radios so they can listen to Voice of America. In the face of such provocation, it would take a huge escalation of force to keep the top dog from attempting to quell the incipient revolution with his full arsenal of weaponry.

As in dominance struggles within wolf packs, these aggressive encounters in multi-dog households predominantly occur between animals of the same sex. There are separate male and female dominance hierarchies within wolf packs, and thus the very fact that most dog-on-dog attacks within a household are between dogs of the same sex offers pretty persuasive confirmation that these disputes are indeed about social status.

The only effective solution is, alas, to abandon notions of democratic values and equality. Trying to reform canine society is a losing proposition. Unfortunately that means propping up a dictatorship to keep the peace. The tactic is to maximize the stability of society by reinforcing the dominant position of the top dog and avoiding anything that might give the low-ranking dogs any ideas. Petting the top dog first when greeting the dogs, letting the top dog be the first of the bunch to go through doorways and receive treats or food, and tolerating without intervention a modicum of threatening gestures (fang baring, growling, and body-blocking) on the part of the dominant dogs toward the subordinate ones are all ways to stabilize the situation. As much as it goes against our sense of fair play, it is also effective to scold the subordinate dog rather than the dominant dog during a mild altercation between the two. (Though it is possible to overdo this, and one interesting bit of wolf-pack behavior is that an attack on a lower-ranking wolf by a higher-ranking wolf often triggers other members of the pack to join in the attack. This piling-on effect may be another example of "facilitated aggression"—an animal being emboldened by the actions or presence of a more dominant animal to go on the offensive in a way it wouldn't dare under other circumstances. So chastising the low-ranking dog too severely can actually trigger an attack.) But the general principle is that peace reigns when a low-ranking dog accepts his place and does not try to lay claim to a status that he cannot hold on his own.

This is a tough prescription for us to follow precisely because it goes against both our own deep-seated values of fairness and all of the ideas we've had hammered into us for years from psychologists about how we have to raise our own children to protect their tender sense of self-esteem. It is hard for us not to think that being in a socially subordinate position is bad; that along with inferior position comes oppression, downtroddenness, psychological torment, and general misery.

But in canine society a dog that knows his place and accepts it—whether high or low—is a happy dog. Psychological stress and suffering, not to mention outright violence, are in the dog world the result of upsets to the social order.

In the dog behavior-therapy literature these disputes between dogs of one household are usually referred to as manifestations of "sibling rivalry," but that is a terrible term, not just because it is so gratuitously anthropomorphic, but because it misses the key point of what is actually going on. It is not rivalry on the part of the dogs; it is rather incitement to riot on the part of the owner. The cure for sibling rivalry in humans is to reassure each child that he is receiving an equal amount of parental love and attention. The cure for the canine syndrome is to reassure each dog that he is *not* receiving equal amounts of attention.

ATTENTION-GETTING DEVICES

What makes human hypochondriacs so odd and disturbing is that they really do believe that they are suffering from an illness in spite of all evidence to the contrary. Canine hypochondriacs are in many ways far more innocent. They have simply learned that certain actions are rewarded, and behave accordingly. Given the inventive repertoire of behavior that dogs are capable of thanks to their playful propensities, and given how strong a drive social attention is for a dog, they are adept at forming such associations in their minds and sticking with them.

Dogs that have been genuinely sick and who get a lot of attention as a result are the prime candidates for the "sick pet syndrome." They can quickly discover that when sitting quietly or acting normally they are ignored, but if they suffer a sudden relapse of an alarming symptom, their owner immediately rushes over, pets them, makes concerned cooing sounds, and so on. Dogs that suffer gastric upheavals, as all dogs do, often get extra attention and sometimes special food. It doesn't take long for certain dogs to learn that bouts of vomiting and diarrhea are rewarded with hamburger and rice dinners, while behaving normally results in the same old dry dog food. Dogs have acquired such imaginary ailments as lameness, paralysis, muscle twitches, and runny noses, among others.

The surefire test for whether a dog is faking an illness is to leave the house and then sneak back and peek through a window to watch what the dog does when no one is around to provide the immediate reward of attention. As Benjamin Hart notes, many alarmed owners, concerned that their pets are suffering from some horrible disease, who refuse to believe that it could just be an act, quickly become converted when they see their lame or paralyzed dogs get up and prance around the house when they think no one is there. (Hart also observes that, because these kinds of behavioral problems can usually be cured with dramatic results, veterinarians can enjoy the satisfaction of making their clients think they are geniuses.) The solution, once it is clear that it is an act rather than a true illness, is simply to ignore the dog whenever he is performing his routine, and to pet him and give him extra attention and food treats whenever he is acting normally, or even just lying quietly. This exactly reverses the previous reinforcement schedule, under which the dog was rewarded for acting goofy and ignored for being normal.

It might seem that a dog that can put on an act only when it has an audience must have some ability to understand the mental state of its audience, a conclusion that seems at odds with the experimental evidence that dogs lack a "theory of mind" and an ability to imagine what others are thinking, perceiving, and feeling. But most likely the dogs in these cases have learned a fairly simple association. Dogs that seek attention seek that attention from a human, so the presence of a human is the stimulus for its learned behavior. This is no different from a dog that learns to jump up on a bag of dog food—it is the simple presence of an object associated with a reward that is the trigger for the behavior. A dog does not have to grasp the idea that another being is watching and interpreting his actions; all he has to learn is that taking such an action when a person is present results in a reward—and doing it when no one is present does not. It is interesting and significant that some "hypochondriac" dogs will still occasionally display their fake ailment even when no one is present. A dog that truly understood the idea that it was putting on an act for the purpose of influencing another being's perception of him ought never to make such a simpleminded mistake as acting with no audience present.

Dogs will produce many other extraordinary acts if they come to be associated with extra attention. Dogs have an innate propensity for performing certain stereotyped behaviors, such as snapping at and chasing things, so these often are the raw material they draw upon for attention-getting behaviors—snapping at imaginary flies, barking at shadows, chasing flashlight beams. But the very nature of play is that it involves mixing up innate behaviors in novel and odd ways, and dogs' lifelong propensity for play thus generates an almost infinite number of possible gimmicks for attracting attention. Some dogs will throw their heads about in odd ways, or walk backward, or emit strange howling sounds, or leap in and out of the dishwasher. (I have had dogs that do all of the above, though not all at the same time and not all in the same dog.)

The importance dogs attach to social contact and attention can outweigh even the importance they attach to food, and one not uncommon form of attention-getting behavior in dogs is a refusal to eat. Dogs that refuse to eat can usually be coaxed to do so by standing next to the dog's food bowl and feeding bits by hand, and some dogs find this great fun and so learn to refuse their food regularly. This can rapidly lead to an escalation of the stakes, and the things owners will put up with to get their dogs to eat are at times extraordinary. Some dogs invent all sorts of rituals that must be performed before they will deign to eat. There are in the scientific literature reports of dogs that, for example, regularly refused to eat until they had nipped their owners' ankles. There are also a number of reported cases of dogs with severe anorexia—they actually became emaciated—as a result of these attention-getting maneuvers.

A related, and probably more common, situation is dogs that learn to hold out for something better than ordinary dog food. They learn that if they refuse to eat, their owner will put bacon grease or meat scraps on their food, and this too can lead to a rapid upping of demands. The veterinarian Katherine Houpt reported having one patient, an Alaskan malamute, that had successfully trained his owner to feed him a bowl of ice cream and dog biscuits every day, supplemented by a variety of cooked-to-order servings of foods such as scrambled eggs and fresh beef. The dog would accept each such novelty for a few days, then refuse it, too, until some new dish was created for him.

Just as with all attention-getting behaviors, this one can be cured by ignoring the stunts and giving the dog nothing but dog food once a day, removing the dish promptly at the end of a fifteen-minute window of opportunity. Usually within several days the dog is completely cured. Some dogs are quite stubborn, but they generally will not starve to death if given no choice in the matter. Bob Murphey, the great Texas storyteller, once told of the old farmer who was complaining to a neighbor about how much it cost to feed his dog.

The neighbor said, "Well, you should do what I do. I feed my dog turnip greens."

"Turnip greens?" the farmer exclaimed. "My dog wouldn't eat turnip greens."

"Well, mine wouldn't either for the first two weeks."

That's the basic attitude required to handle manipulative dogs.

Reading the literature on all of the creative behavioral problems dogs develop can make one rather paranoid about raising a puppy at all, imagining that one false move or one bit of ill-timed attention will lead to a permanently warped dog. This is akin to the medical student syndrome, in which budding young doctors are convinced they are developing the symptoms of every lurid ailment they have just read about. The good news is that most of these potential ills in dogs are self-correcting, at least in dogs owned by people possessed of a minimal amount of self-respect and a refusal to be pushed around, taken advantage of, and have their minute-by-minute schedule set by a member of another species.

CHAPTER 8

Troubled Dogs, Troubled People

FAR AND AWAY the most frequent canine behavioral problem that drives dog owners to seek professional help is aggressiveness, and especially aggressiveness directed toward humans. Surveys estimate that as many as 5 million people in the United States are bitten by dogs each year, a million of them seriously enough to require medical attention, and a dozen seriously enough not to require medical attention because they are already dead as a result. More than half of bite victims are children. On a typical workday in the United States, ten mailmen are bitten.

The law has attempted to grapple with this interesting dimension of canine behavior by branding dogs with a record of biting as "dangerous" or "vicious," and generally declining to delve into the animal's state of mind. Aggressiveness is aggressiveness, courts have ruled, and it doesn't matter whether the dog's actions are a result of abnormal genetic propensity, normal canine instincts, permissive upbringing, moral turpitude, a tragic blow to the head in puppyhood, or a hormonal imbalance. Animal behavior therapists, on the other hand, naturally stress rehabilitation, since that is their bread and butter, much along the lines of human psychologists who have sought to transform issues of guilt and innocence into highly complex technical issues of behavioral medicine (issues that they, needless to say, are the only ones competent to decide). Animal behavior therapists have thus come up with myriad clinical distinctions among aggressive behaviors in dogs.

From a biological point of view, however, both the legal and the therapeutic views are unsatisfying; they do not really explain the very peculiar things that are going on in dogs these days. The extraordinarily high rate of dog attacks on people might simply imply that aggressiveness is a fundamental aspect of the canine character, that it was ever thus. Yet one peculiar thing, as I noted earlier, is that the typical stray or scavenger dog is not very aggressive toward people. By far most dog bites are inflicted by pet dogs, not strays. If anything, one would expect pet dogs to be less aggressive, as the dogs typically kept as pets have been subjected to hundreds or even thousands of years of deliberate, selective breeding that presumably would have weeded out the violent misfits. Pet dogs have also been generally well socialized to people, having been brought up within a human family.

Nevertheless, some anecdotal evidence suggests that the problem has actually been getting worse in recent years. The veterinary journals are full of articles on canine aggression. Also on the rise is the reported incidence of problems with destructive behavior by pet dogs that chew up furniture, carpeting, doors, and sundry other household goods and materials when left alone at home. If this seems peculiar, it is peculiar, and it points to a number of biological and human forces at work, with some very unintended consequences.

"DANGEROUS" BREEDS

The standard explanations for a rise in canine aggressiveness all contain a germ of plausibility, but all fall short of fully accounting for the phenomenon. The most obvious is that the notoriously aggressive breeds are driving the statistics, and these breeds have become more popular of late, at least within certain human subcultures. Cases of pit bulls or rottweilers attacking children receive a great deal of attention in the press, and these reports have led a number of municipalities to enact legislation banning specific breeds as inherently dangerous. There is little doubt that certain breeds are often trained to behave viciously for their role as watchdog, macho status symbol, or drug dealer's accoutrement. Statistics on dog-bite fatalities that occurred in the United States over a fifteen-year period identified pit bulls and rottweilers as the perpetrators in about half the cases for which the breed of the dog was known. But high on the list, too, were huskies and malamutes; St. Bernards, Great Danes, and Akitas also made an appearance. The breed breakdown of dogs that haven't actually killed anyone but have been dragged into veterinary behavior clinics by desperate owners seeking help for aggressive attacks on humans is even more diverse. An Australian clinic reported that the dogs most frequently brought in for aggressive behavior were bull terrier (16 percent), German shepherd and crosses (15 percent), cattle dog breeds (blue heeler and crosses, 9 percent) terriers (9 percent), Labrador retriever (8 percent), poodle (6 percent), cocker spaniel (6 percent), and rottweiler (5 percent). Of 110 dogs brought to Cornell University's behavioral clinic that were eventually euthanized because their aggressive behavior was incurable, the predominant breeds were English springer spaniel (13 percent), beagle

(5 percent), Labrador (5 percent), and cairn terrier, Old English sheepdog, cocker spaniel, and miniature poodle (4 percent each).

Obviously these statistics are skewed by many factors. Poodles, cocker spaniels, Labradors, and terriers are among the most popular breeds, so they will naturally be overrepresented in any sample, even if they suffer no greater incidence of aggression than any other breed. Another inherent bias has to do with expectations: the proprietor of a junkyard who buys a pit bull may expect and want it to behave aggressively, and thus will not view such behavior as a "problem" to be cured, whereas the same behavior in a small-breed dog bought as a family pet would send the owners rushing for the nearest dog shrink. Surveys that ask dog owners about the problems they have with their dogs are equally unreliable for just this reason of reporting bias. One veterinarian who tried to conduct such a survey of his clients found that perceptions of problems varied enormously among owners of different breeds. (One poodle owner did not check any of the possible complaints listed on the form and wrote, "None, except he craps all over the house.") Still, this survey of 2,249 dogs did at least correct for the differing popularity of different breeds, as it included responses from owners who said they did *not* have problems with their dogs; that made it possible to calculate what percentage of owners of a given breed reported aggressiveness or biting. Topping the list were dachshund owners, 14 percent of whom reported their dogs to be aggressive, followed by 13 percent of Great Dane owners, 11 percent of Lhasa apso owners, 9 percent of German shepherd owners, and 8 percent of St. Bernard and malamute owners. The dogs with the highest percentage of owners complaining of biting were Sydney silky (15 percent of owners); schnauzer and German shepherd (13 percent); cocker spaniel, Lhasa apso, and Shetland sheepdog (11 percent); cockapoo (9 percent); and Dalmatian (8 percent). Mixed breeds checked in at about 6 percent in both the aggressiveness and biting categories, well down the rankings.

All of this data suggests that while pit bulls and other notoriously aggressive dogs are the cause of a significant number of reported attacks on people, they fall far short of accounting for all of the bad dogs out there. The appearance of such seemingly innocuous breeds as springer and cocker spaniels, Labradors, beagles, and dachshunds high up on the lists of problem dogs suggests that this cannot simply be a result of deliberate encouragement of aggressive behavior, either through breeding or training. Some 15 million dogs are relinquished to animal shelters and euthanized each year in the United States; this constitutes about a quarter of the entire owned dog population, and most of these dogs are abandoned because of some intractable behavioral problem, most commonly aggression. These owners certainly did not get what they were looking for in a dog.

Three popular explanations are offered for this more general persistence, and possibly rise, of canine aggression. All imply very different things about who is to blame for aggression by dogs—whether the dog's victim, the dog, or the dog's owner bears the greatest responsibility—and all imply very different ways to deal with the problem. Perhaps it is no surprise that all parallel with uncanny similarity the debates over what causes antisocial behavior and crime and mental illness in human society.

Explanation number one is that aggression is just an irreducible part of the canine character. This is the "we're all beasts" school of thought. In practice, it often is the "blame the victim" or the "she was asking for it" school, because people who advance this notion are always talking about "appropriate" and "inappropriate" aggression on the part of the dog and asking whether the dog was "provoked" or not by his victims. In this view, dogs are all basically wild animals (or wild animals domesticated by man specifically for their "protective" traits), and while some breeds are wilder than others, all dogs are potentially aggressive, just as all dogs have fur. This view seems to appeal ideologically to groups such as the Humane Society of the United States, which like to cast all human–animal conflicts as the fault of humans failing to comprehend or respect animals, who are simply being their irrepressible selves. The adherents of this school have thus launched a number of high-profile education efforts (National Dog Bite Prevention Week) in which responsibility for avoiding dog bites is placed squarely on the shoulders of would-be bitees. Their advice is exactly the sort meted out in the pamphlets you get from rangers at Yellowstone National Park on how to avoid getting eaten by a grizzly bear or stampeded by a bison. Children are told to "be a tree" or "act like a log" if approached by a dog. The idea, explains one proponent of this approach, is to assume "a neutral, nonthreatening posture that minimizes the antagonism of dogs." To "be a tree," one stands "with the feet together and the fists folded under the neck with arms and elbows against the chest. This is a good posture to assume when approached by any dog that could be a biter or aggressor. Also, doing this is harmless when the dog is friendly." Harmless, yes, except that one looks like an idiot perhaps.

(A subset of this school of thought is the "stresses of modern society" branch, which attributes crime to the pressure cooker of modern and increasingly urban life: all dogs are potential criminals, but some just get pushed over the edge by the stressful and unnatural environment they are forced to live in.)

Second is the "bad genes" theory: through modern breeding practices, inbreeding, and dog shows that have emphasized all the wrong traits, aggression has been inadvertently selected for and is thus showing up in an increasing percentage of individual dogs of various breeds. In this view aggression is *not* a fundamental part of the dog psyche at all but rather an abnormal behavior, though one that is nonetheless genetic in origin. This school of thought appeals greatly to those who see the American Kennel Club as the root of all evil, as well as those who like to let individual owners off the hook. It removes responsibility from the owner for his dog's misdeeds and blames some large faceless force under the control of a sinister organization motivated by greed. It also "medicalizes" the problem, and is thus very much in keeping with the therapeutic spirit of our times, which sees alcoholism, drug addiction, indolence, compulsive gambling, and sexual promiscuity as diseases rather than moral failings.

Third is the "Dr. Laura" theory: bad behavior in dogs is, too, a human moral failing. This is the traditional view of dog obedience trainers, who insist that there no bad dogs, only bad owners. It is also, naturally, the favored view of dog breeders, who like to deflect any blame for problem dogs onto their purchasers and away from any suggestion that there might be a hereditary trait at work. In this view, dogs that bite people or show aggression have been treated permissively and indulgently by their too-soft owners. They have been allowed to have their way and to ignore and disrespect their masters. The dogs' behavior is nothing that a little personal accountability and moral backbone would not cure. This is obviously a self-serving stance for obedience trainers and breeders to take, but they can point as evidence to many well-behaved dogs among even the supposed problem breeds. Defenders of even pit bulls insist that, if properly trained, the animals make wonderful and perfectly reliable pets. It is all a matter of proper education and the setting of firm limits.

There is a germ of truth to all three of these popular theories, but none really gets at the underlying issue of what causes aggression. That is fundamentally a biological question; and to address it requires an approach from a very different angle.

MANY WAYS TO BE ANGRY

For practical reasons, canine behavioral therapists (many of them veterinarians who have found this to be a terrific new business) have tended to duck the issue of what causes aggression altogether, taking refuge in the studiously nonjudgmental language of "disease" and "treatment" or "therapy" and leaving it at that. This is a wise strategy, for it avoids pointing the finger of blame at anyone—owner, dog, victim, or even society at large. Aggression is portrayed as a definitely abnormal behavior, but one that is no one's fault at all.

Of course, professional medical "intervention" is absolutely necessary to effect the cure. As Karen Overall, a veterinary behavioral therapist at the University of Pennsylvania, solemnly warns,

> Obedience training, puppy kindergarten, and individual training all have their roles. . . . [but] once a problem develops, such measures are an *inappropriate* substitute for intervention from a behavioral specialist. Most dogs with behavioral problems are *not* just misbehaving, they are *not normal*, and to treat them as normal, but misbehaving, ani-

mals and expect normal responses to ever-intensifying corrections is dangerous to the pet and client alike.

Another like-minded behavioral specialist, Roger Mugford, explains that part of the role of the therapist is explicitly to relieve the "undue sense of guilt" that owners have: "There is a widespread belief that many of the behavioral problems presented by dogs arise from mistakes by their owners, . . . The implication that dogs' problems are the fault of their owners is still widely held amongst dog trainers and some veterinarians." This, he insists, is untrue; worse, it is counterproductive to the therapeutic approach he advocates. Mugford also proudly writes that dogs come to his clinic with only a lead and collar and leave "festooned"—his word—with gadgets, toys, audiotapes, diets, behavioral protocols, massage devices, halters, and extendable leads, which conjures up an interesting picture.

The language that veterinary behavioral therapists use to describe their patients' problems is well calculated to reinforce this neutral disease model of canine misconduct. Giving a syndrome a name carries with it the unstated implication that it is an objective phenomenon with an objective cause, and the canine behavioral therapy business is lousy with names for canine behavioral syndromes. This is a standard bit of medical artifice, of course. In medicine we are so accustomed to treating the names of things as if they were an actual explanation of things that plastering a name onto something is a convenient way of shutting patients up. If the doctor says we have Haldanish-Gzorenplatz syndrome, that's usually good enough for us. And so there has been a great incentive within the canine behavioral therapy business to make fine distinctions between different dog misbehaviors that can then be diagnosed and treated. Some veterinarians who have published learned articles on the subject list more than a dozen separate different types of canine aggression. These include competitive aggression, protective aggression, fear aggression, pain-induced aggression, territorial aggression, interdog aggression, sexual aggression, maternal aggression, redirected aggression, play aggression, learned aggression, food-related aggression, possessive aggression, dominance aggression, irritable aggression, predatory aggression, and idiopathic aggression. (*Idiopathic* is a particularly valuable word in this connection, for although it sounds scientific and precise, it means "of no known cause.") Other authors break down aggression according to whom the aggression is directed at: owners, strangers, familiar dogs, strange dogs.

It is certainly true enough that dogs exhibit aggression under many different circumstances; it is also true enough that effective treatment can vary depending on the things that trigger aggression in a particular dog. But these clinical distinctions between different "types" of aggression are just that—clinical distinctions that may or may not reflect underlying biological differences or causes.

The great advantage of this schema is that every conceivable canine misbehavior involving the baring of teeth or a growl has attached to it a medical diagnosis requiring "intervention" by a qualified "behavioral specialist." The very great disadvantage is that this approach tells us nothing about underlying biological causes. That is, it says nothing about prevention. Nor does it explain why some dogs and not others develop such problems.

From a biological point of view, it is certainly suspect to break down aggression into so many separate categories. "Food-related aggression" is defined as growling when a person or another dog approaches the dog's food. "Possessive aggression" is defined as growling when a person or another dog approaches a toy. This is rather like breaking down anger in humans into "trying to find a parking place anger," "reading something stupid in the newspaper anger," "getting a telephone call offering a time-share vacation condominium in West Virginia during dinner anger," and "listening to vulgar teenage conversation anger." If you were trying to establish whether an angry person was angry because he was a normal person who had been provoked beyond normal bounds, or whether he was a sick individual with a true mental aberration, or whether he had never as a child been taught to keep his temper under control, or whether he was from a family of short-fused type A types, then categorizing anger by such categories would be useless.

The biologically more interesting question is whether different kinds of aggressiveness are handled by different channels in the brain, or involve different hormones or neurotransmitters. That sexually mature males are disproportionately represented among dogs that exhibit many of the supposedly distinct forms of aggression that the therapy crowd has defined—dominance, territorial, competitive, interdog, protective, possessive—strongly suggests that a common mechanism, closely related to the male hormone testosterone, is at work. When male dogs are castrated, the incidence of these same forms of aggression is often reduced, further evidence that these are really all the same thing: castrated dogs often show a marked reduction in their aggression toward other dogs and humans in many contexts, including defending territory, asserting social dominance, and fighting over access to food or other desirable objects. Likewise, female puppies treated after birth and in the uterus with testosterone were found to be more successful at competing for a bone with littermates than were normal females. It is probably safe to say that all forms of aggression shown toward members of the social group have the same biological point of origin. It is also safe to say that such social aggression is part of the basic behavioral tool kit of the dog. It makes as much sense to speak of a dog "with territorial aggression," as if that were a disease, as it makes sense to speak of a dog "with a tail." That is not to say of course that dogs' tails do not vary from one to another. Some dogs have really big tails. There is evidence (at least in other mammalian species, principally from experiments in mice) that social aggressiveness is both a genetic and a quantitative trait; it is possible to produce strains of animals that consistently show one particular level of social aggression toward their fellows. In other words, much of the aggressive behavior commonly seen in dogs is probably *not* pathological; it is a natural part of the makeup of the dog, but it can vary dramatically from individual to individual on a continuous scale that is under genetic control.

Two other forms of aggressiveness, however, do not show the same sort of relationship between sexes or to sex hormones, and thus are probably controlled through very different biological mechanisms. Fear biting is the defensive reaction of a cornered animal, and in dogs it is unaffected by castration at all. Predatory behavior is also fundamentally different from intraspecies aggression, and also is unaffected by castration and shows no male–female differences. In a sense it is not really aggression at all—it is just about getting something to eat, and a dog or wolf that is stalking and biting prey does not experience the same flow of hormones or nervous system impulses as does a dog that is snarling at a fellow dog or chasing off the mailman. Breeding studies in mice have confirmed that social aggression and predatory behavior are controlled by different genes altogether: it is possible to produce socially belligerent mice that are unmotivated hunters, and vice versa.

MORAL FAILINGS

That individual dogs vary in their innate quota of social aggressiveness does not in itself answer the question of what causes aggression in some household dogs to reach problem proportions. It could be that people simply do not handle this natural tendency of the dog properly; it could be that breeding has deliberately or inadvertently selected for a more socially aggressive population as a whole; or it could be that some dogs suffer from truly pathological disorders that reflect an inherited flaw in the neural and chemical pathways that handle aggression.

Although practitioners of judgment-neutral therapy have an ideological and economic interest in maintaining that their clients are not to blame for their dogs' behavioral problems, solid scientific evidence from several studies shows that in a significant portion of cases the owner's personality really is the problem. In fact, some studies suggest that owners of problem dogs are definitely more likely to be neurotic or anxiety-ridden than owners of normal dogs, and were so before the dog entered the picture.

The behavioral therapists are of course touchy about this. Roger Mugford, doing his version of the lawyer's "my client is a respectable businessman" routine ("my clients are NOT wackos"), has stated that an "ad hoc evaluation" of one hundred dog owners who came to his clinic determined that 84 percent were perfectly normal human beings. The ad hoc evaluation apparently consisted of Mugford deciding whether they looked like wackos to him. Perhaps more solid is his observation that 41 percent of his clients owned a second dog that had no problems and that 85 percent had previously owned problem-free dogs.

Other behavioral therapists insist that clients who come to them have generally "done all the right things." Yet their own published case reports often suggest otherwise. In a typical case, owners have for months or years tolerated their dog growling when he is disturbed while eating or resting on the floor in his favorite spot; they have responded with petting and attention and food treats whenever the dog has demanded them; they have allowed the dog to sleep in their bedroom and to precede them through doors and down stairs. Typically the dog keeps upping the ante, and finally, when the dog starts biting people, the owner is at last driven to seek professional help. By that point the owner has already lost hundreds or thousands of dominance encounters with his dog, and the dog has a pretty clear idea of who is the alpha member of the pack.

There is in fact no contradiction between Mugford's data about other nonproblem dogs in the same household and the idea that the owners are still a major part of the problem. Dogs obviously do vary in their innate tendency toward social dominance and aggression. An owner might have gotten away with being a nincompoop with a naturally subordinate and compliant dog, but when faced with a dog that exhibits even a bit more of a dominant tendency—though still well within the normal range of normal dog behavior—the owner's passivity and wimpiness creates a monster.

Dogs, again, come on a sliding scale of innate tendency toward dominance, and owners come on a sliding scale of human personality types, and so there is no one type of dog or one type of owner that is responsible for all problem dogs. But there is certainly much anecdotal evidence to support the view that aggressively dominant dogs are often the product of lax and loving owners. The "yuppie puppy" syndrome is a well-characterized subset of this phenomenon: a dog is left to his own devices much of the day, then doted on by his loving, childless owners. Miscommunication adds to the problem. Many owners of problem dogs don't realize that a dog that jumps up and puts his paws or head on your shoulder is not hugging you with an affectionate embrace; he is asserting his dominance, and owners who do take it as a sign of affection have just lost a dominance encounter. They often come to think that a dog growling to defend his food dish is just doing what dogs do. Many people have a picture of truly aggressive dogs as junkyard specimens snarling and foaming at the mouth and ready to kill anyone at any time, and so do not understand why their often affectionate and even good-natured and well-behaved pet will begin biting, sometimes seemingly without warning. But dominant dogs are perfectly content to be with, and get along with, the rest of the members of the pack, as long as they get their own way. Many dominant dogs are extremely demanding of attention and will come up and nose their owners to be petted; the owners are mystified why a dog that so obviously "likes" them should start growling and biting at odd times. In fact, these odd times are odd to humans but not at all to dogs. It usually turns out that the attack that drives the owners to a clinic for help has been set off when the dog reacts to what in dog terms is a dominance challenge from a (now firmly established in that role) subordinate—approaching the dog who is lying in what he imagines is the preferred spot in the home territory (under a table or in the bedroom); reaching over the dog, for example, to clip on a leash; trying to hug the dog or pet him in a way that seems to the dog like a dominant gesture; or even looking at the dog, which can seem like a dominance-challenging stare. Such dogs will frequently behave perfectly nicely to strangers, especially strangers such as veterinarians and obedience trainers who know how to act nonchalantly confident around dogs—and who haven't already spent months or years establishing themselves in the dog's mind as the scum of the earth.

Two empirical studies on the correlation between owner personality and aggressive behavior back up these anecdotal impressions. An intensive study of a thousand English cocker spaniel owners was carried out by two researchers, Anthony Podberscek and James Serpell, to try to find out why a surprisingly high proportion of dogs of this breed displayed aggressive behavior. Owners were asked about the circumstances that would trigger aggression and also general data about age, sex, and neuter status of the dog. A follow-up survey then asked owners of the most aggressive 25 percent and least aggressive 25 percent to fill out a questionnaire about their household—what type of house they lived in, the sex of the dog's owner, the number of children in the house. They were also asked, rather circumspectly one might suspect, if they would answer a "personality questionnaire" that assessed sixteen different factors of human personality ("cool, aloof" vs. "warm, outgoing"; "concrete-thinking" vs. "abstract thinking"; "self-assured" vs. "self-blaming"; and so on). The two groups of cocker spaniel owners did not differ significantly in any of the demographic variables, nor in the age or sex of the dog. They *did* differ markedly on four of the sixteen personality factors. Owners of the high-aggression dogs were much more likely to score high on tenseness ("tense, frustrated, overwrought, has high drive"), emotionally instability ("emotionally less stable, affected by feelings, easily annoyed"), shyness ("shy, threat-sensitive, timid, hesitant, intimidated"), and lack of self-discipline ("undisciplined, self-conflict, lax, careless of social rules").

A second study, conducted by Valerie O'Farrell, asked fifty owners about behavior problems (Had their dog ever growled or bitten? Does the dog pester people for attention?), their own feelings toward their dog (How upset would they be if something happened to their dog? Do they like their dog to be loving and dependent? Do they feed their dog tidbits?), and then asked them to fill out the Eysenck Personality Inventory, which has a good record in fingering neurotics.

O'Farrell found two clusters of problem dogs, one associated with emotionally attached owners, the other with neurotic owners. O'Farrell drew a distinction between people who are attached to their dogs and people who are emotionally involved with their dogs. It is possible, for example, to be attached—in the sense of liking to be with one's dog and being devastated if anything happened to him—while also being more intellectual as opposed to emotional about one's attachment. Such "intellectual" owners take pride in their dog being intelligent, independent, and obedient, and this group tends not to have the most problems. But people who are both attached and emotionally involved—who want their dogs to love them and depend upon them exclusively—are highly correlated with problems of dominance aggression. As O'Farrell explains,

> An owner who is emotionally attached to his dog is more likely to behave as if it is a friend and equal rather than as if it is a subordinate; therefore he will be likely to respond

> to the dog's initiatives and requests. If it barks to go out he will open the door; if it brings a ball to him, he will play with it and so on. If the dog is predisposed to dominance by virtue of genetic or hormonal factors, it is likely to interpret this acquiescent behavior of the owner as confirmation of its dominant status.

Dogs of neurotic owners, on the other hand, had a higher proportion of a variety of behavioral problems—including biting, but also destructiveness and inappropriate sexual behavior. Podberscek and Serpell believe that this is much the same phenomenon that they found: anxiety-ridden and shy owners (whether actually neurotic or not), they argue, are the kind of owners who are incapable of asserting themselves, and the dogs take advantage of the fact.

O'Farrell offers a somewhat more complex explanation for the link she found between human neuroses and this second group of problem dogs: many of the objectionable things these dogs of neurotic owners do are not so much expressions of canine dominance as they are "displacement activities," which reflect overall anxiety and excitement. It is not that the dogs directly learn to be anxious or fearful from their owners' anxieties and fears—it is not a contagion, as is sometimes suggested. Rather, anxious and neurotic people tend to be more easily upset by their dogs' displays of instinctive behaviors, especially things having to do with sex, elimination, messiness, and dependency, and so these owners react more strongly to such canine behaviors in a way that induces "excitement and conflict" in the dog. Inconsistent punishment adds to the dog's state of conflict. A dog that is worked up will often find an outlet for its excitement by exercising its instinctive motor patterns on any convenient object: tail chasing, digging and chewing and scratching at things, barking at imaginary objects, biting at anything handy.

HIGH ANXIETY

Destructiveness is second only to dominance aggression in the problems canine behavioral therapists see most often, and while there are no solid statistics, practitioners such as Katherine Houpt say that cases have definitely been on the rise over the last couple of decades. It is one of the less treatable conditions, as well. By no means all destructive dogs are the product of neurotic owners, but there is a good case that nearly all destructive dogs are the product of their owner's personality or way of life in one way or another.

Some destructive dogs are just plain bored. Dogs need a certain amount of social interaction, running, chewing, digging, and other doglike things each day, and if they do not get the chance to exercise these basic instincts in a natural way they will create ways to exercise them in an unnatural way. Dogs that are left alone for long hours by working couples or students may just not have enough to do: Houpt had one interesting case of a beagle owned by a veterinary student who left the dog alone for ten or more hours a day. The dog was an obedience champion and behaved well in the owner's presence. But when left alone, the dog would chew up anything left on the floor, usually books and shoes that belonged to the owner's roommate—who, unsurprisingly, finally moved out.

Some destructive dogs are genuinely hyperactive. That is, they have a truly abnormal condition. There is some biochemical evidence that such animals may have below-normal levels of the brain chemicals known as endorphins, which are natural opiate compounds produced in the brain itself. These animals, especially under stressful conditions, engage in self-stimulation activities such as chewing and running, which tend to stimulate the release of endorphins; a vicious circle is then established in which self-stimulating activities are automatically rewarded, and the animals become endorphin junkies, doing whatever it takes to get their fix. In truly pathological cases dogs may engage in self-mutilation, such as repetitive biting of their flanks, to achieve this end. This is a natural grooming motor pattern gone haywire, which is typical of all the destructive things that destructive dogs do.

On the other hand, most dogs are by their natures impressively well adapted to just lying around. In a natural setting herbivores such as horses will spend half of their time in a twenty-four-hour day grazing and a further 10 percent walking or running. Feral dogs and wolves, by contrast, spend at least half their day sleeping or resting; a study of sled dogs housed outdoors found they spent 80 percent of a twenty-four-hour day resting. So dogs arguably do not need very much stimulation to satisfy their daily quota. O'Farrell's finding that neurotic and anxious owners tend to inflict their anxieties on their dogs certainly seems to explain some of the wild and destructive things dogs will do in their owner's absence—such as tearing newspapers into shreds or eating window frames. But there is also a certain type of not-necessarily-neurotic owner who is extremely good at creating highly anxious dogs. When destructive dogs are filmed in their owner's absence, it often turns out that the dogs do not seem bored or concerned most of the time they are alone, and do not engage in any destructive behavior until just before the time their owner usually returns home each day. These are typically dogs owned by people who engage in boisterous and highly stimulating greetings of their dogs, smothering them with petting and hugs and racing to let the dogs out to play. The dogs simply learn to anticipate this and get themselves more and more worked up as the great moment approaches each day. Other dogs of highly emotional owners may simply become so attached to one person that they cannot tolerate being left alone. These dogs that suffer from what is inevitably termed "separation anxiety" will sometimes engage in incredibly self-destructive actions in their frantic attempts to escape the confines of solitary confinement, tearing through window screens or even launching themselves through glass windows.

Because destructive behavior can have a number of different causes, it can be difficult to cure. Sometimes providing more exercise is enough; sometimes conditioning the dog to chew acceptable objects like dog toys works; sometimes providing another dog or a cat for companionship (or even, Houpt reports, a turtle) does the trick; sometimes desensitizing the dog to the owner's departure and return by having the owner ignore the dog for several minutes each time helps. In general, though, the success rate is not great once the pattern is established.

Anxieties such as fear of thunderstorms, gunshots, and fireworks are more complex. O'Farrell's study found no evidence that abnormal fears on the part of owners were transmitted to their dogs. The dogs of neurotic owners did not exhibit any particular increase in fearful behavior compared to those of normal owners. Dogs, like many animals, start with an instinctive fear of loud noises. The ones who turn these fears into phobias are sometimes dogs who have had one truly fearful experience, such as being in a house struck by lightning. But most have not had any such traumatic event in their past;

rather they have simply found that being scared pays. They may begin by whining at thunder. When the owner responds by comforting and "reassuring" the dog with petting and a soft tone of voice, the dog starts to escalate his fearful response to trembling or other more dramatic acts. Dogs that learn to become afraid of thunder may then start to show the same fears to rain, then to cloudy days, then even to changes in barometric pressure. The best prevention is to simply ignore the dog when it exhibits signs of fear toward noises. The only cure once this problem pattern is established is a prolonged course of desensitization in which a recording of thunder is played starting at a very low volume and gradually increased, with the dog praised and rewarded at each stage when it reacts without fear to the sound. (People who have used this technique emphasize that it is important to first run a test to make sure the dog views the recording as the real thing—that is, it is necessary to play the recording at a high volume and see if the dog reacts the way he does to an actual thunderstorm.) Hunting dogs that are afraid of gunshots have been successfully treated in a similar fashion, by firing a starter pistol that is first muffled inside a series of nested cardboard boxes, and then removing one box at a time every couple of days to make the sound gradually louder. But multiple training sessions a day are required, and the success rate is not terribly great once fearful behaviors are well established. Hunting dogs are best habituated to gunshots from puppyhood, when it is easier to establish good lifetime habits. Similarly, some trainers even suggest playing recordings of thunderstorms to puppies that are growing up out of the usual thunderstorm season.

TOUGH LOVE

It also can be hard to shake dominance aggression displayed toward an owner once the pattern is well set. As studies of wolf social dynamics underscore, once a member of the pack has been pegged in a spot in the social standings, it can take a rather serious fight to change the order.

The canine therapy types thus have a point that by the time a problem such as excessively dominant behavior becomes well established, the standard advice of obedience trainers simply to assert oneself may be too late. In principle it is quite an easy matter for a person to establish dominance when the first challenges arise, by meeting a growl or snap with an unmistakable and swift physical reply in the dog's own language—lifting the dog by the scruff, staring at him, or whapping him on the nose. Lifting up a puppy a few times a day and looking right in his eyes until he turns away, or standing astride a dog that's too heavy to lift; always making a dog obey a command such as sit or lie down before he gets petted or fed or goes through a doorway—in short, not letting oneself be pushed around—is usually enough to prevent the problem from ever arising.

But once a dog has decided that he's on top of the heap, even the meekest attempts at asserting oneself can provoke a serious attack. And it is probably too much anyway to ask a congenitally nonassertive person to undergo a personality transformation: someone who is capable of the direct approach would not have got himself into the mess in the first place.

On the other hand, a great many of the touchy-feely therapeutic types sanctimoniously declare that physical punishment is *never* "appropriate"; or that "aggressiveness only creates aggressiveness." This is patently absurd in the case of social animals like dogs, who from infancy learn to communicate and respond to aggressiveness in the form of biting. And the demonstrable fact is that dogs that are given one swift whack the first time they try to assert themselves in a menacing manner will often never try it again. Dogs respond to aggressiveness from someone they perceive as dominant not by becoming more aggressive, nor by becoming fearful, but rather by immediately and lavishly demonstrating their submissiveness.

On the other other hand, the owner who confronts a dog physically had better be prepared to win. Responding with force and then backing off if the dog responds in kind leaves things far worse than they were before the confrontation. As Benjamin Hart observes in studiously clinical language (amusing because we know exactly what he is *really* thinking about such people), "There are many dog owners who are physically or emotionally unable or unwilling to meet a dog's aggressive episodes with the kind of force that is necessary to win, or who feel they must treat their dogs the same way they treat their children. The indirect approach is recommended for such circumstances."

The "indirect approach" is more psychological warfare than a direct assault. The usual scheme is to have the owners withdraw all affection, attention, and normal feeding. They also are told to steer clear of situations that have provoked an aggressive response in the past. The dog is then made to work for everything. Before the dog is given any attention, he is called over, made to sit or lie down, and only then petted and praised. He is also given small portions of his normal food throughout the day, only after he has obeyed a command.

This is repeated frequently throughout the day so that "the dog is constantly reminded of its subordinate position," Hart writes. If the dog comes up and nudges a person to get attention, or brings a ball to be thrown, he is just ignored. The idea is that if an owner is incapable of becoming Clint Eastwood overnight, he can at least stop acting like Woody Allen. Sometimes a dog's aggressiveness is displayed only to one member of the family, and in such cases the prescribed treatment is to have everyone in the family ignore the dog completely except for the one whose status needs to be raised in the dog's eyes. The dog is forced to confront the reality that he is completely dependent on that one person for all food and attention. If forced to behave in a subordinate fashion—and the very act of sitting, or better yet lying down, is a subordinate gesture in the canine communication scheme, separate and apart from the fact that the dog is forced to be subordinate by obeying a command from a person—the readjustment of the social hierarchy can take place very quickly. Owners can then begin to up the pressure a bit, taking away the dog's food bowl halfway through a meal and not giving it back until the dog again obeys a command to sit or lie down; making the dog move from a favorite spot; and generally acting like a bully.

Most dogs respond well to this treatment. Follow-up studies at Cornell found that at least two-thirds, and perhaps as many as 85 percent, of dogs brought in for dominance-related aggression improved as a result of such treatment. That such relatively high success rates are achieved by a fairly simple bit of behavior-modification training is a very strong argument against viewing most cases of social aggressiveness as some sort of pathology or organic disease. Again, while dogs vary in their inherited will to dominate, it seems clear based on the outcome of treatment that even many of the hard cases could have been prevented if owners had really done the right things to begin with.

SPRINGER RAGE

Still, if the number of hard cases is on the rise, then it is not a complete answer to simply point the finger at lax owners. If car makers began selling lots of cars capable of going 200 miles per hour, the number of accidents would surely increase—regardless of the indisputable fact that drivers ought to be sure they have the skill to handle such a muscle car before hopping into one. There is no hard data to show that a dominant tendency is more prevalent among the current generation of dogs than in the past, and indeed it would be extremely hard to develop such evidence when dominant behavior is the product of such a complex combination of inherited tendency and environment. But anecdotal reports of aggressiveness in breeds like cocker spaniels and springer spaniels does suggest that there may indeed be an underlying genetic trend toward increasing aggressiveness in these populations as a whole.

Again, it is not provable, but there is at least suggestive evidence that some of the anti–American Kennel Club conspiracy theorists may have a point here. The standards set for breeds emphasize fine points of physical conformation and coat color; they also describe the breed's behavior, at least in general terms, but often in highly suspect and anthropomorphic terms—it would be an interesting exercise to count how many breed standards contain words like *regal* or *aloof*. But dog shows do not award prizes to Miss Congeniality. The judging in reality is based almost entirely on looks, with a shot of highly subjective favoritism toward dogs whose body posture and demeanor happens to be precisely that of a dominant, assertive, and bullying dog—head and tail up, standing erect. ("Proud," some breed standard would no doubt say.) Moreover, many dog breeders do not actually live under the same roof with their champion dogs, who are out back in the kennel, and so don't have to put up with their obnoxious behavior all the time. That dogs are being selected so heavily on the basis of minor points of physical appearance with little regard to behavior means that if an unfavorable behavioral trait happens by chance to appear within one breeding line, it will tend to stay there. So higher levels of aggressiveness could just be the chance product of restricting breeding to a relatively small number of dogs who are bred only to others within a relatively small and closed population that defines a single breed. Because dogs that win shows—"champions"—are much sought after as the sires and dams of the next generation of puppies, a few bad genes in the wrong places can spread like wildfire throughout a population. Champions have a hugely disproportionate impact on the entire breed, especially in less popular breeds with small numbers of founders. Add to this that breeders may actually be positively selecting *for* dominant dogs, since those dogs with the "regal" bearing are the ones that bring home the ribbons, and you have the ingredients for a deteriorating situation. Again, one does not have to assume a pathology or abnormality at work here: dogs vary in their innate tendency toward asserting dominance, and it may be that we are simply selecting a greater fraction of dogs at the high end of the normal range—and that is more than some dog owners can handle.

A few of the aggressive streaks that have been observed lately in certain breeds, however, seem to be more violent and abnormal than run-of-the-mill dominance-related aggression, and may be the result of a more pathological genetic flaw than just a cranking up of the general social aggressiveness rheostat. "Springer rage" has been a much talked about phenomenon, and owners of St. Bernards, Bernese mountain dogs, German shepherds, Great Pyrenees, English cocker spaniels (particular those from certain coat-color lines—red and golden predominantly), and several other breeds have also reported incidents in which their otherwise friendly and well-behaved dogs attack without warning or provocation. The dogs are sometimes said to get an almost glazed look in their eyes, as if they no longer recognize the person they are going after.

A certain caution is warranted in interpreting these reports, as what might seem to be "no warning" or "no provocation" to a human might not be such to a dog, however, and it is quite possible that some of these so-called rage or idiopathic aggressive attacks are really just the work of dominant dogs who have imagined some infringement of their status, such as a false step or a wayward glance. That does appear to be the case with English cocker spaniels; the Podberscek and Serpell survey of behavior problems with the breed found that most so-called rage attacks were really just expressions of dominance aggression.

But that caveat aside, some of these attacks clearly are the work of a canine psycho. A few studies have found abnormal brain wave patterns suggestive of epilepsy or other seizure disorders in dogs that exhibit rage attacks, and some dogs have been treated with apparent success using anticonvulsant or other psychoactive drugs. But the samples have been small, and it is hard to draw any hard and fast conclusions. Moreover, many of these dogs show no physical abnormalities in the brain at all. Still, whatever the precise cause, there is enough evidence to establish that the phenomenon is definitely inherited. Such streaks of idiopathic aggression are pretty clear instances of bad genes getting locked into a breeding population by chance and then spreading rapidly. When idiopathic aggression began showing up in Bernese mountain dogs in Holland, a survey of pedigrees was able to trace the appearance of the syndrome to two sires imported into the country. A conscientious program of screening and selective breeding has since mostly weeded out the problem in this breed. Short of eliminating problem dogs, though, the treatment options are not good. Given the unpredictability and danger of such attacks, especially in large breeds, the treatment of choice is generally euthanasia, which is rather a costly price to pay for insisting on owning the offspring of a champion dog.

The other sorts of aggressive dogs that clearly have some wires crossed are the ones that direct predatory behavior toward people. This a particularly spooky syndrome, since dogs that treat people as prey sneak up and stalk silently and then spring into the attack without warning. The way ancestral predatory motor patterns have been chopped up and reassembled in dogs leads to sometimes painful but essentially never truly dangerous predatory biting and nipping in terriers, corgis, cattle dogs, and Border collies; they just can't seem to help themselves when they see a small child or a heel move quickly by and chomp down on it. More dangerous, at least to human infants, are dogs with a more complete, intact predatory drive. Like wolves and wolf hybrids raised in human households, they will sometimes attack human infants whose uncoordinated movements and high-pitched cries trigger an almost automatic response of the sort that predators exhibit toward wounded prey. But these same dogs are unlikely to attack older children or adults, whose movements are not so preylike.

More serious still are dogs that show predatory aggression toward humans as a result of deliberate breeding for this trait. Breeds bred for dog fighting, such as pit bulls, have been purposely selected to attack their opponents in a fight silently and without the usual outward signs of antagonism that are a normal part of social aggression. That selective force probably tapped directly into predatory aggression. In keeping with the mixed-up behavioral nature of dogdom, this instinctive behavior has been wrenched from its original purposeful context and reinserted somewhere else in the ever-plastic dog psyche. A dog that behaves in a predatory fashion toward other dogs will behave in a like fashion toward humans, too, to the extent he views humans as his social equals. And this may indeed explain the efficient and otherwise inexplicable savagery of attacks on humans by pit bulls and other traditional fighting breeds. Whereas socially aggressive dogs just want to inflict a good scare and show who's boss, these dogs really are aiming to kill. The best advice I ever received for how to react if a predatorily aggressive dog like a pit bull goes after you is just to ram your whole arm down his throat and hope he chokes to death: better that he gets your arm than your throat.

CHAPTER 9

Brave New Dogs

Breeders aren't opposed to making dogs that are good for something, it is just that that is not their job. Their job is to preserve a breed's original purity and bring the breed up to a visual standard. Given the nature of dogs this is very hard, and takes intense concentration. Besides, pure breeders, like pure scientists, would lose face with their peers if they attempted something useful.

—Raymond Coppinger, *Fishing Dogs*

THE NOTORIOUS fixation of dog breeders on looks and purity have, for many decades now, been the subject of strident denunciation, leavened only by rare bits of parody like Ray Coppinger's quoted above. Animal rightsniks rail against the production, for the satisfaction of human vanity, of "deformities" such as short legs in basset hounds and wrinkled skin in shar-peis. Admirers of the working qualities of traditional working breeds like Border collies rail against the takeover of these breeds by purebred breeders and the inevitable adoption of kennel club standards for the breed based on looks. Border collie enthusiasts actually sued the American Kennel Club in an unsuccessful attempt to prevent the breed from being added to the list of 150 or so AKC-recognized breeds, fearing that the end result will be a bunch of furry, pretty, black-and-white dogs incapable of herding sheep. And even many less politically driven people, in this day when everyone has absorbed some vague notion that biodiversity is good, have learned to make vague disapproving noises about inbreeding.

The critics and parodists have a good case. But the responsible subpopulation of breeders have a good case, too. There is no doubt that most purebred dogs are very inbred indeed. The chances that two members of a human family will show a genetic difference at any given gene on the genome are 71 percent, according to one study. Among crossbred dogs it is 57 percent; among purebred dogs, 22 percent; and among some breeds of highly inbred dogs it is 4 percent. And there is no doubt that some dog breeders are obsessed—there is no other word—with cultivating fanciful forms or arbitrary ideals of appearance, all other consequences be damned. The sheepdog handler and writer Donald McCaig reported that one breeder at the Westminster Kennel Club show explained to him that breeding is like "painting with genetics." There is also no doubt that the incidence of many genetic disorders is definitely on the rise in purebred dogs and is causing real problems. But it is also true that the standard criticisms leveled against inbreeding are not always well informed from the point of view of modern genetics. Curing the problems that inbreeding has engendered in purebred dogs will require more subtlety than either most breeders or most of their more vocal critics have so far displayed.

SEND IN THE CLONES

Inbreeding is basically cloning the old-fashioned way. All selective breeding is based on the obvious principle that you want to breed from individuals who have the traits you want, and cull the ones that don't. The natural variation that exists in any population is the raw material that both the natural selection of evolution and the artificial selection of humans draw upon. But the very same genetic mechanisms that ensure that variation exists in the first place—that multiple offspring of even the same two parents will receive a different combination of their parents' genes—works against the breeder's goal of perpetuating with reliability and consistency the desirable traits of any one individual.

The biggest monkey wrench in the works is that every gene in an individual's cells exists in duplicate. Genes are part of long strands of DNA that form chromosomes, and chromosomes come in matched pairs, one inherited from each parent. When variant forms of a gene occur in a population, as is very often the case, offspring may inherit one variant from one parent and another variant from the other. It is also often the case that one variant (or allele, in the terminology of genetics) is "dominant" over the other. For example, one gene in dogs determines whether the skin and coat can produce black pigment. This "B" gene comes in two alleles, B and b. If both chromosomes contain the b allele, the dog cannot produce black pigment at all and will be chocolate, liver, tan, or red colored. A dog that carries the B allele on both chromosomes can produce black pigment. But so can a dog with a B allele on one chromosome and a b on the other. Such animals have inherited a B from one parent and a b from the other. But the effect of the B allele—which directs the black pigment to be manufactured by the cellular machinery of the body—overrides the effect of the b allele on the other: B is dominant over b, b is recessive to B.

The major practical consequence of all this for breeders is that breeding from a black dog does not guarantee that all of its offspring will be black. That is because while a Bb dog will look as perfectly black as any other black dog, it has a 50 percent chance of passing on the b allele to the next generation.

Most of the time, of course, breeders don't have a clue what genes control what traits. It may be several genes that control one trait. But, whatever the case, they may have one dog with some exceptional traits that they like, and would like to preserve them in the population. Breeding that dog to a close relative—a parent, or offspring, or sibling—increases the odds that the next generation will inherit whatever genes are responsible for those desirable traits. If, for example, a breeder wanted to generate nonblack dogs from a population that was nearly all black, then a black close relative of a rare liver-colored bb dog would be more likely than the average black dog to be a silent carrier of the b gene—that is, to be Bb rather than BB. Crossing a bb dog with a Bb dog would then yield a 50 percent chance of producing the desired nonblack (bb) offspring. Crossing a bb dog with a BB dog, on the other hand, would yield zero chance of producing that desired result.

Such inbreeding is thus a way to rapidly generate a higher percentage of offspring that exhibit the good traits of one parent. (Inbreeding is sometimes called "linebreeding" in its less incestuous forms, but the insistent distinction that is sometimes made between these two forms of breeding is, from a genetics standpoint, fundamentally meaningless.) Inbreeding has another very important consequence. Inbred animals are much more likely to end up with the same allele on both chromosomes. That is, crossing close relatives will increase the chances that their offspring will be all BB or bb. Such a state is known as homozygosity, and it is probably the most important point about inbreeding. Inbreeding is a way to double up the desired genes of an exceptional animal. And an animal that is homozygous for a certain trait breeds true to type: what you see is what you really get. There are no silent or hidden traits being carried and concealed by dominance at that particular gene site. A black dog that is BB as opposed to Bb can pass on nothing but B alleles. Thus inbreeding is a way to produce *consistent* results in breeding.

Inbreeding is a basic tool of all modern agricultural breeding programs. Inbred lines of corn and rice launched the green revolution; inbred lines of dairy cattle achieved huge gains in average milk production. Inbreeding is a way to get a desired trait into a line very quickly and to make it appear consistently thereafter.

The price, however, is that inbreeding does not discriminate between good traits and bad traits. It duplicates the good genes from a founding sire or dam; it also duplicates the bad genes. Alleles that cause defects, even fatal defects, generally get away with persisting at a low level in any population over time if they are recessive. A dominant allele that causes a fatal defect will get quickly weeded out because any animal that carries even a single copy of that allele will drop dead. But a recessive disease can be silently carried. Only an animal that has two copies of the recessive allele—that is, only an animal homozygous for that allele—will actually exhibit the disease. The problem with inbred animals is that inbreeding increases homozygosity at *all* gene sites, and it increases homozygosity for recessive alleles just as it does for dominant alleles. Thus hidden recessive traits that may not have caused much trouble in the past are now brought together far more frequently. They become all the more of a problem if the disease is one that does not appear until late in life, such as cancer or some degenerative nerve disorders or progressive eye diseases.

The genetic diseases that have been popping up in purebred dogs of late are unquestionably a result of this unmasking of once-latent problems. They are many, varied, and often very weird. Scottish terriers suffer from "Scottie cramp," a nervous disorder in which the muscles of the back and legs go rigid, particularly when the dog is overexcited or engages in strenuous exercise. From an analysis of pedigrees it appears to be caused by a simple recessive trait. Epilepsy has been showing up in many breeds, notably poodles. Flat-coated retrievers have been suffering from an epidemic of tumors. Deafness runs in Dalmatians and Australian cattle dogs. Collies, Norwegian elkhounds, cocker spaniels, Irish setters, and several other breeds are afflicted with retinal degeneration that leads to blindness. Boxers have a well-documented susceptibility to a defect that leads to congestive heart failure. Manchester terriers and poodles suffer from von Willebrand's disease, a hemophiliac disorder caused by a defect in blood-clotting factors. It is all rather like reading an account of the royal families of Europe after everyone had spent a few hundred years marrying their first cousins.

DRAINING THE GENE POOL

Less dramatically, but more insidiously, inbreeding leads to what is known as inbreeding depression. This is the accumulation of homozygous recessive alleles that have a cumulative, deleterious effect. These may not be anything so gory or dramatic as seizures or hemophilia; rather they are often small, additive traits that affect growth, vigor, and reproduction. In crossbred animals, these recessive traits may be masked by dominant alleles. But after several generations of inbreeding, the homozygosity in the genes that control these traits begins to take its toll. An inbreeding experiment in one research colony of beagles demonstrated a marked increase in the death rate of puppies born as inbreeding increased. About a quarter of puppies born to unrelated parents died. As the degree of inbreeding approached the point at which 50 percent of the genes for variable traits could be expected to be homozygous, the death rate increased to about a third of all puppies born; at homozygosities of up to 67 percent, half the puppies died; and at a maximum of 78.5 percent, three-quarters died.

All animals carry some deleterious recessive alleles, and some of these will be homozygous and thus expressed. But two unrelated individuals are unlikely to carry the same deleterious alleles at the same genes. Thus when two unrelated parents interbreed, the deleterious recessive alleles from one parent are likely to be canceled out by a dominant gene from the other parent. This is what lies behind the phenomenon of hybrid vigor: offspring of two inbred but unrelated parents are highly heterozygous—that is, they have many genes of the kind Bb, where B is a dominant allele that covers up the effect of a deleterious recessive allele b. Many traits, such as growth rate, are controlled by multiple genes whose total effect is additive. A medium-size parent may carry "big dog" alleles at gene locations A and B but not at C. Another medium-size parent may have "big dog" alleles at genes A and C but not B.

Crossing those two could produce offspring with "big dog" alleles at all three sites, resulting in offspring that are bigger than either parent.

So there is a fundamental tension in any breeding program between uniformity and diversity. Uniformity is obviously desirable, because it means offspring with predictable characteristics. But diversity is an inherent source of vigor and a protection against the unmasking of highly deleterious traits carried by recessive alleles. In the livestock business, the tension between these two goals is typically resolved by maintaining breeding stock in purebred lines with specific desirable breed characteristics, but then crossing purebred animals of two different breeds to produce the offspring that are actually raised for production. Thus a beef cattle farmer might cross a purebred Angus bull with purebred Hereford cows to produce the calves he raises for market. The other typical solution in the livestock business is to maintain large populations of what are called "grade" animals—outbred animals with the general characteristics of a pure breed but which benefit from the regular injection of genes from other breeds.

It is certainly possible for dog breeders to eschew the more extreme and deliberate forms of inbreeding, and especially in breeds like Labradors with a very large number of registered dogs, there is a lot of material to choose from. Unrelated dogs, even if similar in appearance, may have a lot of different genes. Crossing two parents who are each homozygous at different genes produces a first generation (the F_1 generation) that is highly heterozygous. Crossing the members of this F_1 generation yields an F_2 generation that contains the full mix-and-match reassortment of these alleles. Thus outbreeding can lead to the rapid expression of a great deal of latent diversity. (The F_2 descendants of two unrelated medium-size dogs,

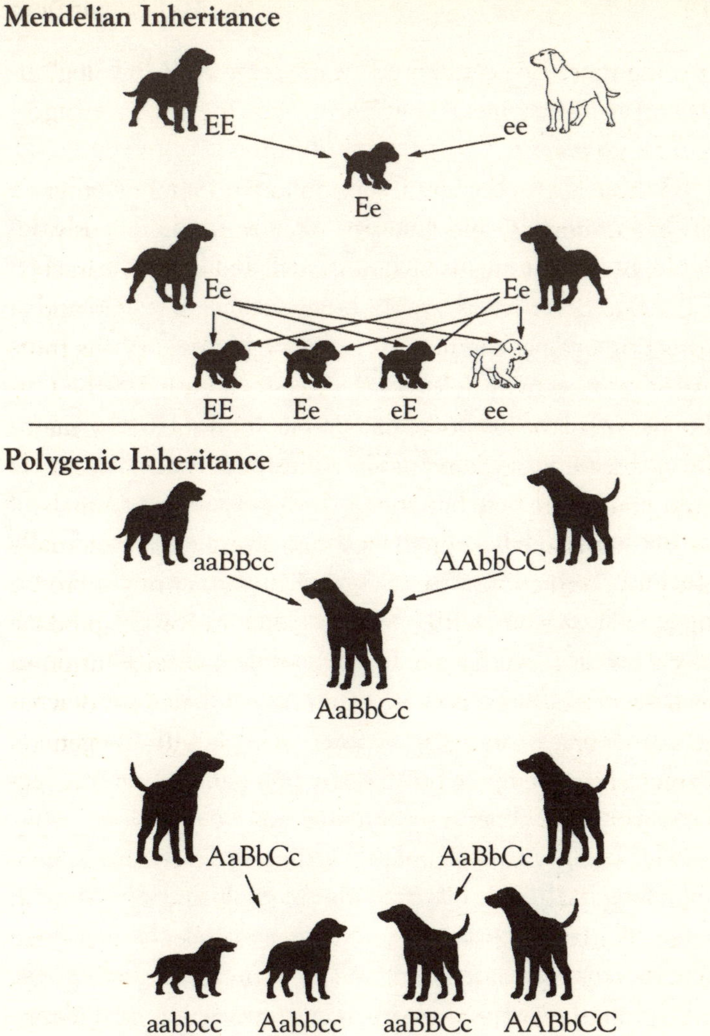

Simple single-gene Mendelian traits, such as many coat-color patterns, are either-or, with a dominant allele (capital letters) overriding the effect of a recessive allele (lowercase letters). Multi-gene traits, such as body size, are often additive and show a far more complex inheritance pattern—the second-generation offspring of a cross between two inbred parents may exhibit the full range of possible forms.

for example, might well come in a full range of heights from very short to very tall.)

The problem is that such outbreeding is not even an option within many breeds of dogs: the total population is simply so small that all members of the group are already interrelated. The phenomenon of splitting breeds into more and more separate and further isolated subbreeds has accelerated the problem. Even a few hundred years ago there was a great deal of gene flow between dogs of separate "breeds" but similar type. But dog breeding registries ended that; following the purity for purity's sake model, they insist that a dog may be registered in the breed only if both its parents were registered in that breed. That is the *only* thing they insist upon. There continues to be a certain amount of surreptitious crossbreeding among registered dogs: registries such as the AKC simply take a breeder's word that the sire and dam of a litter of puppies are what the breeder says they are, and so a breeder has little difficulty injecting some genes from another breed into his lines if he so desires. But at the same time there has been fragmentation of breeds into smaller and smaller closed populations. Even within populations that are still considered a single breed, there is often an almost exclusive separation in breeding lines according to some superficial characteristics such as coat color or type. Collies with rough and smooth coats, long-haired and short-haired and wirehaired dachshunds, solid-colored and broken-colored English cocker spaniels, all have quite distinct breeding lines. Within the solid-colored population of English cocker spaniels there is a further segregation into red/golden and black bloodlines.

The effective size and diversity of the breeding population is further reduced by two other forces that have afflicted many breeds. Many breeds have been passed through a genetic "bottleneck" in their recent past. Some breeds almost vanished at one point or another, victims of the ever-changing fads and fancies in the dog world, to be revived at a later date by a few die-hard enthusiasts. Many of the large breeds of European dogs were driven to near extinction as a result of the chaos, dislocation, and food shortages during World War II and were subsequently revived after the war. As a result, the modern population of these breeds are often all descendants of a very few founding sires. The Portuguese water dog, for example, which was revived in the 1930s and 1940s, is based on a founding population of thirty dogs. But of those thirty only about five have contributed to any major extent to the modern population; those five popular founders in fact are responsible for about 80 percent of the current gene pool of the breed.

A similar "popular sire" effect afflicts even some breeds with large populations. A dog that wins a champion ribbon at a major show will be in great demand to sire litters of puppies left and right. And every time that happens, the genetic diversity of the next generation is dramatically narrowed. In a closed breeding population, such practices are a one-way process, driving diversity ever downward. There is simply no way to bring that lost diversity back into a closed gene pool. The point is that as the effective size and diversity of the breeding population is reduced, breeders are inbreeding whether they want to or not, and whether they know it or not.

BRAINS VS. LOOKS

Just as the many well-characterized genetic diseases caused by recessive alleles may be brought out during deliberate inbreeding, so other undesirable recessive traits can get locked in just by chance in any small, closed population. The rise of behavioral problems such as "rage" in English cocker spaniels may well be a case in point. The study of this phenomenon found that solid-colored English cocker spaniels were far more likely to exhibit this aggressive behavior than were those with broken-colored coats; the red/golden spaniels were on average more aggressive than the black ones. A slightly convoluted theory has been ginned up advancing some underlying biochemical mechanism linking behavior to coat color, but a more plausible explanation is simply that these different color variants have quite distinct breeding lines. By chance, any inbred line will expose certain underlying recessive traits, and because inbreeding tends to duplicate genes good and bad, that now-exposed trait will be faithfully passed on to subsequent generations as long as the line remains closed.

Simply from a mathematical view, it is very hard to dispute that in the single-minded pursuit of a fairly narrow set of mostly visual criteria, many dog breeders have tipped way too far toward uniformity on the uniformity–diversity continuum. There is no inherent reason one cannot breed for looks and healthiness or looks and good temperament simultaneously. But it requires striking a better balance between inbreeding and outbreeding than has been pursued by many to date.

Of course humans generally respond to incentives, and the circular logic of the dog show and dog-breeding business has for a century now favored precisely what has been happening. Looks are the easiest thing to change about a dog. They are the easiest thing to distinguish from one dog to another. People want dogs that win dogs shows because they win dog shows. There is a self-sealing circularity about it all, in which breed clubs establish highly arbitrary criteria for distinguishing a winning dog from a nonwinning dog (my Bernese mountain dog, thank God, has a few white hairs on the tip of his tail; if he did not, he would be a distinctly inferior specimen, according to the dog show judges), and then the same people who set the criteria breed the dogs to meet these criteria so they can sell more dogs that meet these criteria to people who want to meet the criteria. The development of breed standards in the late nineteenth century was an explicit attempt to give dog show judges a basis for awarding places. It was an implicit attempt to create dog fancy as a sort of connoisseurship in which extremely fine points bore great significance to those in the know. There is of course a certain phoniness to any sort of connoisseurship, whether it is wine tasting or the cultivated admiration of fine painting, but the highly arbitrary nature of dog breed standards—and their tendency to change every few years—carried with it the frank implication that this was phonier, or at least more arbitrary, than most. Popular breeds like the collie were particularly prone to the tendency on the part of fanciers to "fabricate subtle points of distinction between animals and artificial models to measure them against," the historian Harriet Ritvo has written. In the 1890s, for example, came the craze for long, pointed noses, which had not been a characteristic of the breed before.

From a scientific point of view, inbreeding is merely one tool, to be used to achieve a desired end: it is not an end in itself. But the establishment of closed breeding populations and registries of breeds by their very nature sets inbreeding up as something to be cultivated for its own sake. It is, as far as modern genetics is concerned, a slight absurdity. That some breed groups are now seeking to develop genetic probes to tell whether an animal is truly purebred only coopts the tools of modern genetics in support of a Victorian notion of genetics. Vizsla breeders are one such group; they want to make sure no one has interbred their Vizsla with a pointer and tried to pass off the offspring as the real McCoy. But of course there is no such thing as a "Vizsla gene." There will be some random bits of DNA that will just happen to be associated with any closed breeding population simply by virtue of the fact that it is closed. So it is possible to find a marker statistically associated with the closed population of Vizslas. But that marker is not what genetically *makes* a Vizsla a Vizsla, and indeed if someone were determined about it, they could probably produce a dog that has such a marker without having much in common with a Vizsla at all. It might look like a cross between a St. Bernard and an Irish water spaniel, but if you select for it, you'll get it.

This points up a larger problem in genetic selection. It is easy to select for looks because looks are, well, looks—they are there for anyone to see. Also, many physical traits are well correlated with specific genes. Thus by choosing to breed from dogs that have certain desirable physical traits, we are actually choosing dogs with specific genes that really do directly influence those traits: a good physical trait really means that a good gene is behind it. But selecting based on outward appearance is still only an approximation; there is no perfect, one-to-one correspondence between what geneticists call the animal's phenotype—the outward appearance—and the genotype, or the actual genes it carries.

Selecting animals that have good behavioral genes is especially hard because any given behavior is almost certainly the result of many genes interacting with one another, and with the environment in which the animal is raised. We can try to breed only from animals that are well behaved, but that does not guarantee well-behaved offspring the way that breeding two inbred black-coated Labradors ensures black-coated progeny. We don't really know what the genes are that underlie behavior, and indeed behavior as we are likely to define it is not going to map onto those underlying genes very precisely. There is no gene for "cooperation" or "house trainability" or even herding ability.

One way that livestock breeders deal with the practical uncertainty that this rough fit between traits and genes engenders is by a unit of measure known as heritability. Any given trait is going to be influenced in part by genes and in part by environment. As a practical matter, a breeder would like to know how much he can influence a trait of interest by selecting as breeding animals individuals that have this trait in abundance. Heritability is a purely empirical measure of this. A trait with a heritability of 1.0 means that differences in offspring are accounted for completely by differences in parentage. A trait with a heritability of 0 means that parentage makes no difference at all; even identical twins will exhibit the full range of variability in this trait seen within the population.

This is, again, a totally ad hoc device, but it has been put to extremely good use among breeders of cattle, sheep, pigs, and other animals that are measured against some extrinsic and objective standards, things like growth rate, size at maturity, milk production, meat quality, aggressiveness under confinement—precisely the sorts of rational, objective criteria that play almost no part in traditional purebred dog breeding. Only a limited number of studies of heritability have been carried out in dogs. Heritability of pointing ability in various bird dog breeds varied from .10 to .25 in one of the few studies that have been done; nose ability varied from .19 to .35. The highest heritability of bird dog behavior was searching and tracking in German shorthaired pointers, which was about .5.

Heritability of various body measurements in German shepherds has been found to vary from .32 to .81. Using such data can tell breeders what traits they should pay attention to in selecting sires and dams and which they can ignore. Basically, a low heritability for a genetically determined trait means that the variation within the population is small, so little room is left for improvement on that score. That is extremely valuable information for a breeder to know, for it means that inbreeding or even crossing the best with best unrelated animals is not going to be of any further use in improving or maintaining that trait of interest.

There again is no inherent reason breeders cannot aim for pretty dogs that are also good-natured and healthy. But they first of all have to want to accomplish those goals. They also have to keep in mind that inbreeding in pursuit of *any* selection criteria, while a perfectly valid tool to fix in place the manifest virtues of an animal in a breeding line, equally fixes in place the hidden flaws of that same animal. Dog breeders could usefully take a page from modern breeders of purebred cattle and swine and other animals that are judged more by the bottom line of performance than by the circular dictates of fashion. These breeders have embraced the benefits of combining inbreeding to hone desired traits with outbreeding to cancel out the inevitable defects inherent in any one inbred line of purebred stock. Intelligent crossbreeding between breeds would be an even more efficient means of achieving this much-needed balance, but as long as the closed breeding books of registries like AKC hold sway, that is a lost cause. Interestingly, though, there is a small but growing and increasingly lucrative market in certain hybrid dogs, something that didn't exist even a few years ago when the price of mutts was basically zero. Crosses such as cocker spaniel/poodles are beginning to find a loyal following, and the prices that breeders can charge rival those of some purebred dogs. This is surely a healthy development, and one that parallels the wisdom that commercial livestock breeders recognized years ago.

HIP DYSPLASIA

Working against any effort to breed for behavior, health, and hybrid vigor are not only the traditional incentives of the dog world but also the fact that when multiple genes influence a single trait, progress can be slow and frustrating. In trying to eliminate a disease or behavior that is of complex origin, we are only remotely grappling with the underlying genes. Even a very physical syndrome such as hip dysplasia is not a direct product of a single gene. A strategy of breeding only from dogs without hip dysplasia is a crude, sledgehammer approach. It is a bit like my trying to sort out the books about sheep on my bookshelf but being permitted to do the final sorting only on the basis of the color of the binding. If I first pull enough books out and look at their title pages, I might find that sheep books are more often red than blue and so on that basis put all the red books in one pile and throw out the blue books, but it isn't a very accurate procedure. The real aim would be to change the rules so I could read the titles directly—that is, for hip dysplasia, figure out which specific anatomical traits contribute to the clinical disease and then tease out the genetics that determines each of these separate traits.

Hip dysplasia is perhaps the most publicized genetic defect that has afflicted purebred dogs, but a great deal of misunderstanding about it persists despite all of the ink that has been spilled on the subject. The basic syndrome can be described as a misfit between the ball and the socket of the hip joint. If the socket is too shallow, more like a saucer than a cup, the ball will not be held tightly in place and will be able to wobble loose and dislocate. Also, if the shape of the ball and the shape of socket do not match, or if the ball is too big for the socket, the bone surfaces of the joint will grind against one another and gradually wear away, resulting in arthritis and a progressively worsening fit. Large breeds such at St. Bernards, Bernese mountain dogs, and German shepherds are notoriously susceptible. At worst the defect can be literally crippling.

The inheritance of the trait is complex enough, influenced by multiple genes, that progeny of animals with mediocre hips can have excellent hips, and vice versa, and this complexity still encourages some breeders to believe that breeding has nothing to do with it. That of course is precisely what they wish to believe, for it lets them nicely off the hook for the crippled misfits they produce and sell. There was great excitement a couple of decades ago when one bit of not very well substantiated research seemed to suggest that hip dysplasia was all really just the result of poor nutrition—a vitamin C deficiency, or scurvy. Even now many breeders of large breeds of dogs insist that nutrition plays a determining role, and blame cases of hip dysplasia in the puppies they sell on too rapid weight gain. They thus advise their purchasers to take the dogs off puppy chow at an early age, as young as three months, and feed the dogs a lower-protein diet from that point on.

Although it is true that overweight animals with hip dysplasia do suffer worse symptoms, obesity does not cause hip dysplasia: the underlying disease is purely genetic in origin. And indeed one could argue that the best way to rapidly eliminate a genetically caused disease is to expose animals to environmental conditions that maximally express those genetic predispositions, rather than trying to conceal or counteract them. Indeed, by restricting the diet of large dogs, breeders may be covering up underlying genetic problems in their line and allowing the problem to get progressively worse. (By analogy, there is little doubt that the incidence of myopia in humans has been on a definite rise since the invention of glasses. In the good old days, nearsighted humans walked off cliffs or got run over by speeding chariots and didn't survive to pass on their defective genes to the next generation.)

Since the 1960s a number of organized programs have been established to reduce hip dysplasia in afflicted breeds by X-raying adults before breeding. The X rays are submitted to a registry that evaluates them and issues a certification rating how good or bad a dog's hips are. These schemes have produced some definite improvements, at least among the stock of breeders who are willing to go to this trouble. Because many genes are apparently involved, hip dysplasia is very much a percentage game, however, not an all-or-nothing proposition. X rays submitted for grading to the Orthopedic Foundation for Animals, one of the major registries in the United States, have shown a marked trend in many breeds toward reduction of the problem. Bernese mountain dogs, for example, went from 33 percent dysplastic in 1980 to 16 percent in 1995, while the percentage of this breed with "excellent" hips went from 3 to 9 percent. There is of course a certain selection bias in such data, for only breeders motivated to do something about the problem participate, and even they may not bother to submit X rays for dogs that have obviously bad hips. But the increasing percentage of dogs with excellent ratings is some indication that genuine improvement in the breed is probably taking place. More persuasive data comes from the Swedish Army's breeding program for German shepherds, in which selection was able to reduce the incidence of dysplasia in the breeding colony from 46 percent to 28 percent.

But this is still groping in the dark, and substantial progress may only come when the genes responsible for the various anatomical components that contribute to hip dysplasia are identified and their action understood. Studies have shown that the tendency toward a shallow and loose socket may be inherited separately from the tendency toward an ill-fitting ball and socket. Greyhounds, which have an extremely low rate of hip dysplasia thanks to rigorous selection over the years for dogs that can run well, were crossed with highly dysplastic Labradors. The resulting F_1 generation consisted of animals that had loose joints similar to those of their Labrador parents but did not develop arthritis or other manifestations of the disease. Apparently the dogs inherited from their greyhound parents a dominant, "protective" gene that endows a good structure of the bone and cartilage that makes for a good fit even if the joint is potentially loose. But even this is one step removed from the real genetic level of analysis. Up until now the effort to reduce hip dysplasia has been based on trying to find measurable features in X rays that hopefully correspond to underlying genes, so that when one is selecting for dogs with these good measurable features, one is really choosing dogs with the desired genes that they will reliably pass on to their offspring. The only way to be sure of that, though, is to find the genes themselves. It may even turn out that separate clusters of genes control the ball and the socket independently, which would be a truly maddening complication, for it would mean that breeding dogs with good hips to other dogs with good hips is no guarantee of producing good progeny at all in itself: the offspring could inherit a large socket from one parent and a small ball from the other, for example.

FIXING THE PROBLEM

Several genes responsible for specific recessive diseases in dogs have been identified and isolated, and genetic tests are available for several of these. The Irish Setter Club of America funded research to develop a DNA probe that can detect the presence of the allele responsible for retinal degeneration and now requires all breeding animals to be screened with a blood test for this gene.

Having prizewinning dogs drop dead or suffer from terrible degenerative illnesses is perhaps beginning to make an impression on many dog enthusiasts, and there is clearly a new interest at least in some dog-breeding circles to do something about the epidemic of inbred defects. This effort has also received a well-timed boost from basic research: the completion of a linkage map to the dog genome has been a milestone in the effort to pin down genes that control these defects, as well as desirable traits. The linkage map takes advantage of the handy fact that interspersed throughout the genome at specific locations are bits of nonfunctional DNA. These are not genes that direct the cell's machinery to do anything at all; they are just random bits of accumulated genetic debris. And precisely because they are nonfunctional, these sequences have been subjected to little selective pressure over the eons, so mutations have tended to grow and flourish in these regions of "junk" DNA. They thus tend to be highly variable within a population: they are "polymorphic," and at any given region of junk DNA, individuals may carry one of many possible polymorphisms. That gives these junk DNA sequences the highly useful function of acting as "markers" to help locate real genes of interest. When a mutation in a functional gene occurs, it may originate in a single individual and then spread through the population over time. But because fairly large chunks of chromosomes tend to be inherited in a piece from a parent, any member of a subsequent generation that carries this mutant allele will also carry the particular polymorphism that its parents had in a nearby junk region of the chromosome. The polymorphism thus acts as a marker for that mutant allele.

Of course not every individual who has that polymorphism will have the mutant allele. But every individual with the mutation will have that polymorphism. So the standard method for putting a linkage map to work is to cross individuals who have the disease with ones that don't, then in the F_2 generation see if all individuals with the disease consistently share some marker with the original diseased breeding population. If such a consistent marker shows up, then the gene responsible for the disease must be not too far away from the location of that marker on the genome. Standard statistical calculations establish how many individuals are needed to pin down such a correlation. Elaine Ostrander and her coworkers published a framework linkage map in 1997, and more details are being filled in.

Purebred dogs may have a higher-than-normal incidence of genetic diseases, but they also are a geneticist's dream come true. Litter sizes are large, which makes for excellent statistical power in these linkage analyses. The high degree of inbreeding means that experimental crosses between dogs of different breeds are very likely to produce the necessary discriminatory power, as dogs of different breeds are likely to share relatively fewer numbers of polymorphisms at each marker site. That means it is statistically more certain which parent supplied any given polymorphism in an F_2 animal. And because pedigrees are meticulously recorded by breeders, many studies can be done retrospectively; researchers do not need to have any animals in the lab at all, but can just ask breeders to send in blood samples and pedigrees. A major project launched by geneticist Gordon Lark at the University of Utah on Portuguese water dogs is using this methodology; a pilot study involving about 150 dogs from whom blood samples and X rays were obtained was able to pin down one highly statistically significant genetic marker linked to parameters for overall skull dimensions. (Lark devoted most of his career to soybean genetics. Then his Portuguese water dog Georgie died of a genetically linked cancer peculiar to the breed. A breeder of the dogs gave him a new puppy for free, explaining, "I am giving you this $1,500 dog so you will feel guilty and work on dog genetics." It apparently did the trick. The breeder later told him it would be the most expensive dog he would ever own. Lark's "Georgie Project" has been funded in part from the proceeds of a lucrative commercial license of his soybean research.)

When an actual gene and its allele responsible for a defect is discovered, and genetic probes are developed to screen for its presence, a new danger arises, however. A genetic probe offers the great benefit of being able to detect animals that are silent carriers; that is, animals that do not show any signs of disease but who possess a single copy of the deleterious recessive allele. Yet the most obvious, and also just about the worst, way to deal with a genetic disease is to eliminate all carriers from the breeding population as a whole. That would almost surely eliminate one disease at the cost of greatly increasing the incidence of another, for all it would do is dramatically narrow the breeding population still further and increase the degree of inbreeding—and thus the extent of homozygosity at other gene sites. One might cull all dogs with any hip dysplasia and be left with a population of dogs with great hips that are dropping dead left and right from cancer.

The defter and far better tactic is simply to avoid mating carriers with other carriers (such matings carry a 1 in 4 chance of producing offspring homozygous for the recessive allele, and thus suffering from the actual disease). But the whole point of having a test is that if it is employed conscientiously to eliminate such carrier × carrier matings, then one need no longer fear suffering the continued presence of the recessive allele in the gene pool. The price of keeping the breeding population diverse may require suffering the presence of alleles for physical traits that do not always precisely meet the enshrined breed standards. Genetic tests can make that price affordable by neutralizing the painful consequences of these alleles' presence—which, at least in the case of recessive diseases, are realized only when two carriers are crossed.

With the help of such tools, it should be perfectly possible to satisfy the desires of dog breeders to maintain distinctive breeds while preserving genetic diversity within each breed, and avoiding the more serious consequences of historical inbreeding and narrow founding populations, at the same time. In endangered zoo populations of rare species, zookeepers go to great lengths to ensure that subsequent generations of the species as a whole—considered as a worldwide population—will reflect the total range of existing genetic diversity within the species. Any time one progenitor's contribution is lost out of the family tree, that bit of diversity is gone forever. So zookeepers are continually swapping breeding animals or, in the case of species that can successfully be bred through artificial insemination, frozen semen.

Individual dog breeders do not have the same incentive to act in concert; the short-term rewards still go to those who can offer puppies sired by a champion dog. There are no immediate rewards for offering puppies that embody the cause of keeping the breed as a whole healthy and vigorous and diverse. In the long run, however, there is hope even on that score, for the fact is that in the long run the breeder who only wants the flashy name is going to have a flashy name and a lot of puppies with bad genes. The increased availability of genetic tests will make that obvious even to the uninformed consumer who is all too typical of puppy purchasers these days. Genetic probes to detect carriers of cystinuria in Newfoundland dogs, von Willebrand's disease in poodles and Manchester terriers, and copper toxicosis in Bedlington terriers are but the first of many more to come. Many breed clubs are requiring, or providing strong incentives for, the use of such tests as they become available.

The sheer diversity of modern dog breeds, and the worldwide gene flow that went on among all dogs until a hundred years ago or so—a blink of an eye in evolutionary terms—imply that we still have ample genetic reserves that can be drawn on to undo any damage done in the last century. Taken as a whole, the genetic diversity of the dog remains as great as that of its wild ancestors.

Those who are incurably cynical about the motives and interests of purebred breeders can take some reassurance, too, from the consoling fact that mutts, owned and unowned, will always be with us. Despite the efforts of neoeugenicists to stamp them out, mutts constitute a vibrant reservoir of canine genetic diversity. There are millions of free-ranging dogs throughout the world that live alongside humans, though without being owned by anybody. Mutts tend to be healthy dogs because of hybrid vigor. They also tend to be good dogs. They also, in a very real sense, embody the evolutionary heritage of the True Dog. The True Dog is that animal that evolved with us, that adapted to and exploited our society, and that did so on terms largely dictated by himself. Defiant of human fashion and whim, selected only in accordance with the ancient evolutionary dictate that demands nothing more than an ability to get along with rather gullible humans, they are really what dogs are about. If worst comes to worst, perhaps they will set us straight, just as their ancestors so ably did, at least for 99,900 of the last 100,000 years.

AND FINALLY, A WORD OF SOLACE

For those who love dogs in the here and now, as I do, warts, fleas, genes, and all, there is also solace and wonder to be had in some other insights that dog science has given to us. A lot of the trouble with dogs these days, after all, has ultimately to do with the unrealistic expectations we have about them. It is not just that we are disappointed when dogs don't act as we imagine they should; our unrealistic expectations actually induce many of the odd and troubling behavioral problems that dogs are plagued with in contemporary human society. This is an ill that, at least in principle, is far more easily corrected than are defective genes, or inbred populations, or abnormal hormone levels. All it takes is a healthy respect for what dogs really are. True love is a matter of understanding and acceptance, after all—not of trying to remake reality in conformity to a preconceived romantic ideal. We are happier when we see dogs for what they are, and dogs are happier, too.

To recognize that dogs view the world and its social order so differently from us is not to deny them their due; it is to appreciate the diversity and wonder of life on earth. There are undoubtedly many feats of intellect and subtleties of feeling that are beyond canine capacity and ken. Yet I have always thought it odd that people seem to think they are paying a compliment to the members of another species by trying to make them out to be human. Again, dogs do not particularly appreciate or understand the compliment. To be forced into playing the role of degenerate human instead of fully realized dog is not what a dog would choose. Dogs don't even really like the role of full and equal human. They want to be dogs. Luckily, being a dog means happily subordinating oneself to a social order and a social leader, a role that they are happy to see us fill. Dogs are dogs; humans are humans; and the remarkable and ennobling thing is that the twain can meet, and communicate, and enrich one another's lives in spite of their very different minds and very different ways of conceiving of the world.

The enrichment to us is visceral and cerebral—the joy of touching and feeling the mind of another so different, the awe, even, of contemplating the sublime forces of evolution that have fashioned such a wondrous array of life on earth. Dogs are a constant reminder that we are just one species among many, and that our automatic and daily assumptions about the set nature of society and the rules of the world are the height of parochialism for all that evolution cares about it. Knowing something about the rules that govern canine society, appreciating how dogs see and perceive their world and make sense of the interconnections therein, understanding their motives and emotions—these are what the scientific studies I have discussed can do for us, and as I have said, this is good for us and good for dogs. It is rather a pathetic kind of love that seeks a mirror image of ourselves in the object of our affections; it is also a shallow and ultimately a fruitless and sterile love. Man and dog have much in common, and had we not, we would never have pitched up together in the same ecological niche thousands of years ago, would never have made common cause, would never have penetrated the wall of mutual incomprehension that keeps most minds ever apart. But within that common destiny that evolution fashioned for us it is our differences, too, that made the tie between our species possible, and interesting in the long run: "As lines so Loves oblique may well/Themselves in every angle meet." Let's face it: If dogs truly were human, they would be jerks. As dogs, they are wonderful.

ACKNOWLEDGMENTS

Jay Neitz and Phyl Summerfelt produced the ingenious photographs showing how colors look through a dog's eyes.

Gregory Acland, Gustavo Aguirre, Raymond Coppinger, Nicholas Dodman, Katherine Houpt, Gordon Lark, Euan Macphail, Norton Milgram, Eugene Morton, Jay Neitz, Elaine Ostrander, and Robert Wayne were generous with their time in answering my many questions.

The staff of the National Library of Medicine went out of their way to help and made my hours spent there profitable and pleasant.

Lew Lord reminded me about the turnip-green joke.

SOURCES

1. The Irredeemable Weirdness of the Dog: An Introduction

Beck, Alan M. *The Ecology of Stray Dogs: A Study of Free-Ranging Urban Animals*. Baltimore, Md.: York Press, 1973.

———. "The Public Health Implications of Urban Dogs." *American Journal of Public Health* 65 (1975): 1315–18.

Brown, Donna. "Cultural Attitudes Towards Pets." *Veterinary Clinics of North America: Small Animal Practice* 15 (1985): 311–17.

Budiansky, Stephen. *The Covenant of the Wild: Why Animals Chose Domestication*. New York: Morrow, 1992; New Haven: Yale University Press, 1999.

Hart, Benjamin L., and Lynette A. Hart. *Canine and Feline Behavioral Therapy*. Philadelphia: Lea & Febiger, 1985.

Houpt, Katherine A., Sue Utter Honig, and Ilana R. Reisner. "Breaking the Human–Companion Animal Bond." *Journal of the American Veterinary Medical Association* 208 (1996): 1653–59.

Juarbe-Díaz, Soraya V. "Assessment and Treatment of Excessive Barking in the Domestic Dog." *Veterinary Clinics of North America: Small Animal Practice* 27 (1997): 515–32.

Overall, Karen L. *Clinical Behavioral Medicine for Small Animals*. St. Louis, Mo.: Mosby, 1997.

2. Proto-Dog

Arons, Cynthia D., and William J. Shoemaker. "The Distribution of Catecholamines and ß-endorphin in the Brains of Three Behaviorally Distinct Breeds of Dogs and Their F_1 Hybrids." *Brain Research* 594 (1992): 31–39.

Brisbin, I. Lehr, and Thomas S. Risch. "Primitive Dogs, Their Ecology and Behavior: Unique Opportunities to Study the Early Development of the Human-Canine Bond." *Journal of the American Veterinary Medical Association* 210 (1997): 1122–26.

Clutton-Brock, Juliet. "Origins of the Dog: Domestication and Early History." In *The Domestic Dog: Its Evolution, Behaviour, and Interactions with People*, edited by James Serpell. Cambridge: Cambridge University Press, 1995.

Coppinger, Raymond, and Lorna Coppinger. "Differences in the Behavior of Dog Breeds." In *Genetics and the Behavior of Domestic Animals*, edited by Temple Grandin, San Diego, Calif.: Academic Press, 1998.

Coppinger, R., and R. Schneider. "The Evolution of Working Dog Behavior." In *The Domestic Dog: Its Evolution, Behaviour, and Interactions with People*, edited by James Serpell. Cambridge: Cambridge University Press, 1995.

Macdonald, D. W., and G. M. Carr. "Variation in Dog Society." In *The Domestic Dog: Its Evolution, Behaviour, and Interactions with People*, edited by James Serpell. Cambridge: Cambridge University Press, 1995.

Morey, Darcy F. "The Early Evolution of the Domestic Dog." *American Scientist* 82 (1994): 336–47.

Ostrander, Elaine A., and Edward Giniger. "Semper Fidelis: What Man's Best Friend Can Teach Us about Human Biology and Disease." *American Journal of Human Genetics* 61 (1997): 475–80.

Polsky, Richard H. "Wolf Hybrids: Are They Suitable as Pets?" *Veterinary Medicine*, December 1995, 1122–24.

Rindos, David. *The Origins of Agriculture*. Orlando, Fla.: Academic Press, 1984.

Ritvo, Harriet. *The Animal Estate: The English and Other Creatures in the Victorian Age*. Cambridge: Harvard University Press, 1987.

Tsuda, Kaoru, et al. "Extensive Interbreeding Occurred among Multiple Matriarchal Ancestors during the Domestication of Dogs." *Genes and Genetic Systems* 72 (1997): 229–38.

Vilà, C., J. E. Maldonado, and R. K. Wayne. "Phylogenetic Relationships, Evolution, and Genetic Diversity of the Domestic Dog." *Journal of Heredity* 90 (1999): 71–77.

Vilà, Carles, et al. "Multiple and Ancient Origins of the Domestic Dog." *Science* 276 (1997): 1687–89.

Wayne, Robert K. "Limb Morphology of Domestic and Wild Canids: The Influence of Development on Morphological Change." *Journal of Morphology* 187 (1986): 301–19.

———. "Developmental Constraints on Limb Growth in Domestic and Some Wild Canids." *Journal of Zoology* 210A (1986): 381–99.

———. "Cranial Morphology of Domestic and Wild Canids: The Influence of Development on Morphological Change." *Evolution* 40 (1986): 243–61.

———. "Molecular Evolution of the Dog Family." *Trends in Genetics* 9 (1993): 218–24.

Wayne, Robert K., and Elaine A. Ostrander. "Origin, Genetic Diversity, and Genomic Structure of the Domestic Dog." *BioEssays* 21 (1999): 247–57.

Wright, John C. "Canine Aggression toward People: Bite Scenarios and Prevention." *Veterinary Clinics of North America: Small Animal Practice* 21 (1991): 299–313.

Young, Margaret Sery. "The Evolution of Domestic Pets and Companion Animals." *Veterinary Clinics of North America: Small Animal Practice* 15 (1985): 297–309.

Zimen, Erik. *The Wolf: A Species in Danger*. Translated from the German. New York: Delacorte Press, 1981.

3. Social Etiquette, Doggie Style

Asa, Cheryl S., et al. "The Influence of Social and Endocrine Factors on Urine-Marking by Captive Wolves *(Canis lupus)*." *Hormones and Behavior* 24 (1990): 497–509.

Askew, Henry R. "Understanding Dog Behavior." Chap. 7 in *Treatment of Behavior Problems in Dogs and Cats*. Oxford: Blackwell Science, 1996.

Beach, Frank A. "Coital Behavior in Dogs III: Effects of Early Isolation on Mating in Males." *Behavior* 30 (1968): 218–38.

Beach, Frank A., Michael G. Buehler, and Ian F. Dunbar. "Competitive Behavior in Male, Female, and Pseudohermaphroditic Female Dogs." *Journal of Comparative and Physiological Psychology* 96 (1982): 855–74.

Bradshaw, John W. S., and Stephen M. Wickens. "Social Behaviour of the Domestic Dog." *Tijdschrift voor Diergeneeskunde* 117, suppl. 1 (1992): 50S–51S.

Breazile, James E. "Neurologic and Behavioral Development in the Puppy." *Veterinary Clinics of North America* 8 (1978): 31–45.

Doty, Richard L., and Ian Dunbar. "Attraction of Beagles to Conspecific Urine, Vaginal and Anal Sac Secretion Odors." *Physiology and Behavior* 12 (1974): 825–33.

Freedman, D. G., J. A. King, and O. Elliot. "Critical Period in the Social Development of Dogs." *Science* 133 (1961): 1016–17.

Godec, C. J., and A. S. Cass. "Psychosocial Aspects of Micturition." *Urology* 17 (1981): 332–34.

Hart, Benjamin L. *The Behavior of Domestic Animals*. New York: Freeman, 1985.

Houpt, Katherine A. "Companion Animal Behavior: A Review of Dog and Cat Behavior in the Field, the Laboratory and the Clinic." *Cornell Veterinarian* 75 (1985): 248–61.

———. *Domestic Animal Behavior for Veterinarians and Animal Scientists*. 3d ed. Ames: Iowa State University Press, 1998.

Lund, J. D., and K. S. Vestergaard. "Development of Social Behavior in Four Litters of Dogs *(Canis familiaris)*." *Acta Veterinaria Scandinavica* 39 (1998): 183–93.

Mech, L. David. *The Wolf: The Ecology and Behavior of an Endangered Species*. 1970. Reprint. Minneapolis: University of Minnesota Press, 1981.

Peters, Roger P., and L. David Mech. "Scent-Marking in Wolves." *American Scientist* 63 (1975): 628–37.

Phillips, D. P., et al. "Food-Caching in Timber Wolves, and the Question of Rules of Action Syntax." *Behavioural Brain Research* 38 (1990): 1–6.

Scott, John Paul, and John L. Fuller. *Genetics and the Social Behavior of the Dog*. Chicago: University of Chicago Press, 1965.

Serpell, James, and J. A. Jagoe. "Early Experience and the Development of Behaviour." In *The Domestic Dog: Its Evolution, Behaviour, and Interactions with People*, edited by James Serpell. Cambridge: Cambridge University Press, 1995.

Shafik, Ahmed. "Olfactory Micturition Reflex." *Biological Signals* 3 (1994): 307–11.

Vollmer, Peter J. "Do Mischievous Dogs Reveal Their 'Guilt'?" *Veterinary Medicine/Small Animal Clinician*, June 1977, 1002–5.

———. "Canine Socialization—Part 1." *Veterinary Medicine/Small Animal Clinician*, February 1980, 207–10.

———. "Canine Socialization—Part 2." *Veterinary Medicine/Small Animal Clinician*, March 1980, 411–12.

Wilson, Erik. "The Social Interaction Between Mother and Offspring During Weaning in German Shepherd Dogs: Individual Differences between Mothers and Their Effects on Offspring." *Applied Animal Behaviour Science* 13 (1984): 101–12.

Wright, John C. "The Development of Social Structure During the Primary Socialization Period in German Shepherds." *Developmental Psychobiology* 13 (1980): 17–24.

Zimen, Erik. *The Wolf: A Species in Danger*. Translated from the German. New York: Delacorte Press, 1981.

4. Canine Kabuki

Baru, A. V. "Discrimination of Synthesized Vowels [a] and [i] with Varying Parameters (Fundamental Frequency, Intensity, Duration and Number of Formants) in Dog." In *Auditory Analysis and Perception of Speech*, edited by G. Fant and M. A. A. Tatham. London: Academic Press, 1975.

Coppinger, Raymond, and Mark Feinstein. "'Hark! Hark! The Dogs Do Bark . . . and Bark and Bark." *Smithsonian*, January 1991, 119–29.

Doty, Richard, and Ian Dunbar. "Attraction of Beagles to Conspecific Urine, Vaginal and Anal Sac Secretion Odors." *Physiology and Behavior* 12 (1974): 825–33.

Goldman, J. A., D. P. Phillips, and J. C. Fentress. "An Acoustic Basis for Maternal Recognition in Timber Wolves (*Canis lupus*)?" *Journal of the Acoustical Society of America* 97 (1995): 1970–73.

Goodwin, M., K. M. Gooding, and F. Regnier. "Sex Pheromone in the Dog." *Science* 203 (1979): 559–61.

Krebs, J. R., and R. Dawkins. "Animal Signals: Mind Reading and Manipulation." In *Behavioural Ecology: An Evolutionary Approach*, edited by J. R. Krebs and N. B. Davies. Sunderland, Mass.: Sinauer Associates, 1984.

Morton, Eugene S., and Jake Page. *Animal Talk*. New York: Random House, 1992.

Owings, Donald H., and Eugene S. Morton. *Animal Vocal Communication: A New Approach*. Cambridge: Cambridge University Press, 1998.

Riede, Tobias, and Tecumseh Fitch. "Vocal Tract Length and Acoustics of Vocalization in the Domestic Dog (*Canis familiaris*)." *Journal of Experimental Biology* 202 (1999): 2859–67.

Scott, J. P. "Genetic Variation and the Evolution of Communication." In *Communicative Behavior and Evolution*, edited by Martin E. Hahn and Edward C. Simmel. New York: Academic Press, 1976.

Shalter, M. D., J. C. Fentress, and G. W. Young. "Determinants of Response of Wolf Pups to Auditory Signals." *Behaviour* 60 (1977): 98–114.

Simpson, Barbara Sherman. "Canine Communication." *Veterinary Clinics of North America: Small Animal Practice* 27 (1997): 445–64.

Zimen, Erik. *The Wolf: A Species in Danger.* Translated from the German. New York: Delacorte Press, 1981.

5. Two Colors, a Million Smells

Ashmead, Daniel H., Rachel K. Clifton, and Ellen P. Reese. "Development of Auditory Localization in Dogs: Single Source and Precedence Effect Sounds." *Developmental Psychobiology* 19 (1986): 91–103.

Davis, Richard G. "Olfactory Psychophysical Parameters in Man, Rat, Dog, and Pigeon." *Journal of Comparative and Physiological Psychology* 85 (1973): 221–32.

Engen, T., ed. "The Biology of Olfaction." *Experientia* 42 (1986): 211–328.

Heffner, Rickye S., and Henry E. Heffner. "Hearing in Large Mammals." *Journal of Comparative Psychology* 106 (1992): 107–113.

Hepper, Peter G. "The Discrimination of Human Odor by the Dog." *Perception* 17 (1988): 549–54.

Kalmykova, I. V. "Localization of Dichotically Presented Sounds in Dogs." *Neuroscience and Behavioral Physiology* 11 (1981): 268–72.

Miller, Paul E., and Christopher J. Murphy. "Vision in Dogs." *Journal of the American Veterinary Medical Association* 207 (1995): 1623–34.

Murphy, Christopher J., et al. "Effect of Optical Defocus on Visual Acuity in Dogs." *American Journal of Veterinary Research* 58 (1997): 414–18.

Murphy, Christopher J., Karla Zadnik, and Mark J. Mannis. "Myopia and Refractive Error in Dogs." *Investigative Ophthalmology and Visual Science* 33 (1992): 2459–63.

Myers, Lawrence J., and Ross Pugh. "Thresholds of the Dog for Detection of Inhaled Eugenol and Benzaldehyde Determined by Electroencephalographic and Behavioral Olfactometry." *American Journal of Veterinary Research* 46 (1985): 2409–11.

Neitz, Jay, Timothy Geist, and Gerald H. Jacobs. "Color Vision in the Dog." *Visual Neuroscience* 3 (1989): 119–25.

Passe, D. H., and J. C. Walker. "Odor Psychophysics in Vertebrates." *Neuroscience and Biobehavioral Reviews* 9 (1985): 431–67.

Sato, Masanori, et al. "Olfactory Evoked Potentials: Experimental and Clinical Studies." *Journal of Neurosurgery* 85 (1996): 1122–26.

Schoon, G. A. A., and J. C. De Bruin. "The Ability of Dogs to Recognize and Cross-Match Human Odors." *Forensic Science International* 69 (1994): 111–18.

Steen, B., et al. "Olfaction in Bird Dogs During Hunting." *Acta Physiologica Scandinavica* 157 (1996): 115–19.

These, Aud, Johan B. Steen, and Kjell B. Døving. "Behaviour of Dogs During Olfactory Tracking." *Journal of Experimental Biology* 180 (1993): 247–51.

Tonosaki, Keiichi, and Don Tucker. "Responsiveness of the Olfactory Receptor Cells in Dog to Some Odors." *Comparative Biochemistry and Physiology* 81A (1985): 7–13.

6. If They're So Smart, How Come They Aren't Rich?

Budiansky, Stephen. *If a Lion Could Talk*. New York: Free Press, 1998.

Chapuis, Nicole. "Detour and Shortcut Abilities in Several Species of Mammals." In *Cognitive Processes and Spatial Orientation in Animal and Man*, edited by Paul Ellen and Catherine Thinus-Blanc. Dordrecht: Martinus Nijhoff, 1987.

Chapuis, Nicole, and Christian Varlet. "Short Cuts by Dogs in Natural Surroundings." *Quarterly Journal of Experimental Psychology* 39B (1987): 49–64.

Coren, Stanley. *The Intelligence of Dogs: Canine Consciousness and Capabilities*. New York: Free Press, 1994.

Cummings, Brian J., et al. "The Canine as an Animal Model of Human Aging and Dementia." *Neurobiology of Aging* 17 (1996): 259–68.

Davenport, J. A., and L. D. Davenport. "Time-Dependent Decisions in Dogs *(Canis familiaris)*." *Journal of Comparative Psychology* 107 (1993): 169–73.

Grandin, Temple, and Mark J. Deesing. "Behavioral Genetics and Animal Science." In *Genetics and the Behavior of Domestic Animals*, edited by Temple Grandin. San Diego, Calif.: Academic Press, 1998.

Hart, Benjamin L., and Lynetta A. Hart. *Canine and Feline Behavioral Therapy*. Philadelphia: Lea and Febiger, 1985.

———. *The Perfect Puppy*. New York: Freeman, 1988.

Head, E., et al. "Spatial Learning and Memory as a Function of Age in the Dog." *Behavioral Neuroscience* 109 (1995): 851–58.

———. "Visual-Discrimination Learning Ability and ß-amyloid Accumulation in the Dog." *Neurobiology of Aging* 19 (1998): 415–25.

McNaughton, Bruce. "Cognitive Cartography." *Nature* 381 (1996): 368–69.

Macphail, Euan. *The Evolution of Consciousness*. Oxford: Oxford University Press, 1998.

Milgram, Norton W., et al. "Cognitive Functions and Aging in the Dog: Acquisition of Nonspatial Visual Tasks." *Behavioral Neuroscience* 108 (1994): 57–68.

———. "Landmark Discrimination Learning in the Dog." *Learning and Memory* 6 (1999): 54–61.

Mills, Daniel S. "Using Learning Theory in Animal Behavior Therapy Practice." *Veterinary Clinics of North America: Small Animal Practice* 27 (1997): 617–35.

Russell, Michael J., et al. "Age-Specific Onset of ß-amyloid in Beagle Brains." *Neurobiology of Aging* 17 (1996): 269–73.

Scott, J. P., Jane H. Shepard, and Jack Werboff. "Inhibitory Training of Dogs: Effect of Age at Training in Basenjis and Shetland Sheepdogs." *Journal of Psychology* 66 (1967): 237–52.

Vauclair, Jacques. *Animal Cognition*. Cambridge: Harvard University Press, 1996.

Vollmer, Peter J. "Do Mischievous Dogs Reveal Their 'Guilt'?" *Veterinary Medicine/Small Animal Clinician*, June 1977, 1002–5.

Weiskrantz, L. "Categorization, Cleverness and Consciousness." *Philosophical Transactions of the Royal Society, London* 308B (1985): 3–19.

Wiseman, Richard, Matthew Smith, and Julie Milton. "Can Animals Detect When Their Owners Are Returning Home? An Experimental Test of the 'Psychic Pet' Phenomenon." *British Journal of Psychology* 89 (1998): 453–62.

7. Odd, but (Mostly) Normal Behavior

Beerda, Bonne, et al. "Chronic Stress in Dogs Subjected to Social and Spatial Restriction, I: Behavioral Responses." *Physiology and Behavior* 66 (1999): 233–42.

Campbell, William E. "The Effects of Social Environment on Canine Behavior." *Modern Veterinary Practice*, February 1986, 113–15.

Dodman, Nicholas. *The Dog Who Loved Too Much*. New York: Bantam Books, 1996.

Hart, Benjamin L., and Lynette A. Hart. *Canine and Feline Behavioral Therapy*. Philadelphia: Lea and Febiger, 1985.

Horwitz, Debra. "Canine Social Aggression." *Canine Practice* 21 (1996): 5–8.

Houpt, Katherine A. "Ingestive Behavior Problems of Dogs and Cats." *Veterinary Clinics of North America: Small Animal Practice* 12 (1982): 683–92.

———. "Sexual Behavior Problems in Dogs and Cats." *Veterinary Clinics of North America: Small Animal Practice* 27 (1997): 601–15.

———. *Domestic Animal Behavior for Veterinarians and Animal Scientists*. 3d ed. Ames: Iowa State University Press, 1998.

Houpt, Katherine A., and Harold F. Hintz. "Obesity in Dogs." *Canine Practice* 5 (1978): 54–58.

Houpt, Katherine A., Sue Utter Honig, and Ilana R. Reisner. "Breaking the Human–Companion Animal Bond." *Journal of the American Veterinary Medical Association* 208 (1996): 1653–59.

Juarbe-Díaz, Soraya V. "Social Dynamics and Behavior Problems in Multiple-Dog Households." *Veterinary Clinics of North America: Small Animal Practice* 27 (1997): 497–514.

———. "Assessment and Treatment of Excessive Barking in the Domestic Dog." *Veterinary Clinics of North America: Small Animal Practice* 27 (1997): 515–32.

Sherman, Cynthia Kagarise, et al. "Characteristics, Treatment, and Outcome of 99 Cases of Aggression Between Dogs." *Applied Animal Behaviour Science* 47 (1996): 91–108.

Voith, Victoria L. "Play: A Form of Hyperactivity and Aggression." *Modern Veterinary Practice*, July 1980, 631–32.

8. Troubled Dogs, Troubled People

Beach, Frank A., Michael G. Buehler, and Ian F. Dunbar. "Competitive Behavior in Male, Female, and Pseudohermaphroditic Female Dogs." *Journal of Comparative and Physiological Psychology* 96 (1982): 855–74.

Blackshaw, Judith K. "An Overview of Types of Aggressive Behaviour in Dogs and Methods of Treatment." *Applied Animal Behaviour Science* 30 (1991): 351–61.

Campbell, William E. "Which Dog Breeds Develop What Behavior Problems?" *Modern Veterinary Practice*, March 1974, 229–32.

Centers for Disease Control and Prevention. "Dog Bite Related Fatalities." *Morbidity and Mortality Weekly Report* 46 (1997): 463–66.

Cornwell, J. Michael. "Dog Bite Prevention: Responsible Pet Ownership and Animal Safety." *Journal of the American Veterinary Medical Association* 210 (1997): 1147–48.

Dodman, Nicholas H., Robin Moon, and Martin Zelin. "Influence of Owner Personality on Expression and Treatment Outcome of Dominance Aggression in Dogs." *Journal of the American Veterinary Medical Association* 209 (1996): 1107–9.

Ebert, Patricia D. "Selection for Aggression in a Natural Population." In *Aggressive Behavior: Genetic and Neural Approaches*, edited by Edward C. Simmel, Martin E. Hahn, and James K. Walters. Hillsdale, N.J.: Lawrence Erlbaum Associates, 1983.

Grognet, Jeff, and Tony Parker. "Further Diagnosis and Treatment of Canine Dominance Aggression." *Canadian Veterinary Journal* 33 (1992): 409–10.

Hart, Benjamin L. "Effects of Neutering and Spaying on the Behavior of Dogs and Cats." *Journal of the American Veterinary Medical Association* 198 (1991): 1204–5.

Hart, Benjamin L., and Lynette A. Hart. "Selecting, Raising, and Caring for Dogs to Avoid Problem Aggression." *Journal of the American Veterinary Medical Association* 210 (1997): 1129–34.

Hattaway, Dan. "Dogs and Insurance." *Journal of the American Veterinary Medical Association* 210 (1997): 1143–44.

Houpt, Katherine A. "Disruption of the Human–Companion Animal Bond: Aggressive Behavior in Dogs." In *New Perspectives on Our Lives with Companion Animals*, edited by A. H. Katcher and A. M. Beck. Philadelphia: University of Pennsylvania Press, 1983.

Hunthausen, Wayne. "Effects of Aggressive Behavior on Canine Welfare." *Journal of the American Veterinary Medical Association* 210 (1997): 1134–36.

Mugford, Roger A. "Canine Behavioural Therapy." In *The Domestic Dog: Its Evolution, Behaviour, and Interactions with Peo-*

ple, edited by James Serpell. Cambridge: Cambridge University Press, 1995.

Neilson, Jacqueline C., Robert A. Eckstein, and Benjamin L. Hart. "Effects of Castration on Problem Behaviors in Male Dogs with Reference to Age and Duration of Behavior." *Journal of the American Veterinary Medical Association* 211 (1997): 180–82.

O'Farrell, Valerie. "Owner Attitudes and Dog Behaviour Problems." *Journal of Small Animal Practice* 28 (1987): 1037–45.

———. "Effects of Owner Personality and Attitudes on Dog Behaviour." In *The Domestic Dog: Its Evolution, Behaviour, and Interactions with People*, edited by James Serpell. Cambridge: Cambridge University Press, 1995.

Overall, Karen L. *Clinical Behavioral Medicine for Small Animals*. St. Louis, Mo.: Mosby, 1997.

Podberscek, Anthony L., and James A. Serpell. "The English Cocker Spaniel: Preliminary Findings on Aggressive Behaviour." *Applied Animal Behaviour Science* 47 (1996): 75–89.

———. "Aggressive Behaviour in English Cocker Spaniels and the Personality of Their Owners." *Veterinary Record* 141 (1997): 73–76.

Reisner, Ilana R., Hollis N. Erb, and Katherine A. Houpt. "Risk Factors for Behavior-Related Euthanasia among Dominant-Aggressive Dogs: 110 Cases (1989–1992)." *Journal of the American Veterinary Medical Association* 205 (1994): 855–63.

Salmeri, Katharine R., et al. "Gonadectomy in Immature Dogs: Effects on Skeletal, Physical, and Behavioral Development." *Journal of the American Veterinary Medical Association* 198 (1991): 1193–1203.

Uchida, Yoshiko, et al. "Characterization and Treatment of 20 Canine Dominance Aggression Cases." *Journal of Veterinary Medical Science* 59 (1997): 397–99.

Van der Velden, N. A., et al. "An Abnormal Behavioural Trait in Bernese Mountain Dogs (Berner sennenhund): A Preliminary Report." *Tijdschrift voor Diergeneeskunde* 101 (1976): 403–7.

Voith, Victoria L., and Peter L. Borchelt. "Diagnosis and Treatment of Dominance Aggression in Dogs." *Veterinary Clinics of North America: Small Animal Practice* 12 (1982): 655–63.

Waelchli, Jessica L., and Donald D. Draper. "Canine Dominance Aggression." *Iowa State University Veterinarian*, spring 1997, 76–82.

Wright, John C. "Canine Aggression Toward People: Bite Scenarios and Prevention." *Veterinary Clinics of North America: Small Animal Practice* 21 (1991): 299–313.

9. Brave New Dogs

Aguirre, Gustavo D., and Gregory M. Acland. "Variation in Retinal Degeneration Phenotype Inherited at the prcd Locus." *Experimental Eye Research* 46 (1988): 663–87.

Canine Health Foundation. *Mapping the Future of Canine Health: 1997 Annual Report*. Aurora, Ohio: American Kennel Club, 1997.

Cattell, Raymond B., and Bruce Korth. "The Isolation of Temperament Dimension in Dogs." *Behavioral Biology* 9 (1973): 15–30.

Coppinger, Raymond. *Fishing Dogs*. Berkeley, Calif.: Ten Speed Press, 1996.

Francisco, L. V., et al. "A Class of Highly Polymorphic Tetranucleotide Repeats for Canine Genetic Mapping." *Mammalian Genome* 7 (1996): 359–62.

Fuller, John L., and Martin E. Hahn. "Issues in the Genetics of Social Behavior." *Behavior Genetics* 6 (1976): 391–406.

Langston, A. A., et al. "Toward a Framework Linkage Map of the Canine Genome." *Journal of Heredity* 90 (1999): 7–13.

Mellersh, Cathryn S., and Elaine A. Ostrander. "The Canine Genome." *Advances in Veterinary Medicine* 40 (1997): 191–216.

Mellersh, Cathryn S., et al. "A Linkage Map of the Canine Genome." *Genomics* 40 (1997): 326–36.

Ritvo, Harriet. *The Animal Estate: The English and Other Creatures in the Victorian Age*. Cambridge: Harvard University Press, 1987.

Schmutz, S. M., and J. K. Schmutz. "Heritability Estimates of Behaviors Associated with Hunting in Dogs." *Journal of Heredity* 89 (1998): 233–37.

Stur, I. "Genetic Aspects of Temperament and Behaviour in Dogs." *Journal of Small Animal Practice* 28 (1987): 957–64.

Todhunter, R. J., et al. "An Outcrossed Canine Pedigree for Linkage Analysis of Hip Dysplasia." *Journal of Heredity* 90 (1999): 83–92.

Wang, X., et al. "Analysis of Randomly Amplified Polymorphic DNA (RAPD) for Identifying Genetic Markers Associated with Canine Hip Dysplasia." *Journal of Heredity* 90 (1999): 99–103.

Willis, Malcolm B. "Breeding Dogs for Desirable Traits." *Journal of Small Animal Practice* 28 (1987): 965–83.

———. *Genetics of the Dog*. New York: Howell, 1989.

Zajc, Irena, Cathryn S. Mellersh, and Jeff Sampson. "Variability of Canine Microsatellites Within and Between Different Dog Breeds." *Mammalian Genome* 8 (1997): 182–85.

INDEX